WRITING RESEARCH PAPERS

A Guide
to the Process
Second Edition

WRITING RESEARCH PAPERS

A Guide to the Process

Second Edition

STEPHEN WEIDENBORNER

DOMENICK CARUSO

St. Martin's Press   New York

Acknowledgments

"Davis, Jefferson" reprinted with permission of the *Encyclopedia Americana*, Copyright 1983, Grolier Inc.

"Goldman, Emma," reprinted by permission of the publishers from *Notable American Women, 1607–1950: A Biographical Dictionary*, Vol. II, G–O, edited by Edward T. James et al., Cambridge, MA: The Belknap Press of Harvard University Press, Copyright © 1971 by the President and Fellows of Harvard College.

Excerpts from *The Readers' Guide to Periodical Literature*, Copyright © 1977, 1978 by the H. W. Wilson Company. Material reproduced by permission of the publisher.

Excerpt from *The New York Times Index* for 1977 © 1977 by The New York Times Company. Reprinted by permission.

Helmut A. Abt, paragraph from "The Companions of Sunlike Stars." Reprinted with permission from *Scientific American*, April 1977.

Malcolm W. Browne, "Arguing the Existence of ESP." © 1980 by The New York Times Company. Reprinted by permission.

Roger D. McGrath, "The Myth of Frontier Violence," based on chapter 13 of his book, *Gunfighters, Highwaymen, and Vigilantes: Violence on the Frontier* (University of California Press, 1984). Reprinted by permission of the author. The material appearing on pp. 114–116 was excerpted from a lecture given November 1984 at California State University, Long Beach.

Annalyn Swan, "The End of Eden," from *Newsweek* (February 18, 1985). Copyright 1985 by Newsweek, Inc. All Rights Reserved. Reprinted by Permission.

"Cassatt, Mary" reprinted with permission from *The New Columbia Encyclopedia*. Copyright © 1975 by The Columbia University Press.

Emily Dickinson, "Poem 1475," reprinted by permission of the publishers and the Trustees of Amherst College from *The Poems of Emily Dickinson*, edited by Thomas H. Johnson, Cambridge, MA: The Belknap Press of Harvard University Press, Copyright 1951, © 1955, 1979, 1983 by the President and Fellows of Harvard College.

Emily Dickinson, "Poem 406." Copyright 1929 by Martha Dickinson Bianchi. Copyright © 1957 by Mary L. Hampson.

Preface

The library research paper can be a freshman English student's most exciting and liberating assignment. It is also, of course, the most demanding. Ideally, the student chooses a research topic that is both significant and workable, conceives a realistic plan for executing the project, and compiles a broad yet selective list of available sources. The student then extracts information and ideas from these sources through critical reading and composes a confident and enlightening essay.

That's asking a great deal, of course, and we have found that students need considerable help at every stage. Yet many books on the research paper—even those intended, like ours, specifically for freshmen—seem to presuppose readers who are already comfortable with the techniques of planning, writing, and revising and whose main requirement is advice on matters of form. In our book, although we treat formal matters fully, our main concern is to explain the *process* of producing a research paper, with particular attention to the steps that give students the most trouble.

The first such steps involve planning. Every experienced researcher knows that the success or failure of a research project often depends on the first choice made: that of a topic. The risk of a mistake is especially great when the researcher is a beginner, with only a sketchy knowledge of the field in which he or she is working. Consequently, in this second edition of *Writing Research Papers: A Guide to the Process*—as in the first—

we start with suggestions and problem-solving examples that show students how to inform themselves well enough to choose practical, worthwhile topics. We also demonstrate how a tentative thesis, or hypothesis, can be a powerful tool for evaluating the potential usefulness of sources and for guiding the actual research. The earlier the student can determine what she or he is looking for, the more focused and efficient the process becomes; and even if the hypothesis or topic is subsequently changed, the benefits from these preliminary steps are not entirely lost.

Getting from a stack of note cards to a rough draft is another especially troublesome stage in the process, and we continue to devote two chapters to it. Chapter 6 has been revised to provide more clear-cut directions for moving from hypothesis to thesis; as before, however, the discussion of assimilating research notes emphasizes composing an introductory paragraph and developing a preliminary outline. Chapter 7 is a guide to drafting and revision, including detailed advice about revising paragraphs, sentences, and word choice, supplemented in this new edition with excerpts from consecutive versions of a sample student paper.

Finally, chapter 8 presents a fully revised and updated discussion of documenting sources, beginning with a thorough explanation of when documentation is required. The bulk of this chapter now offers a complete description of the new MLA style of parenthetical notation, incorporating a wide range of sample notes and Works Cited entries as well as detailed guidelines for inserting references effectively. We also illustrate the traditional footnote/endnote system, provide expanded treatment of the author/year format of the American Psychological Association, and show students which among the various styles of documentation to use for specific disciplines across the college curriculum.

As in the first edition, chapters 2 through 8—the core of the book—include questions to help students review the concepts introduced and exercises to give students practice in applying those concepts. And we still illustrate each step in the process by following the work of several student writers as they progress through the stages of choosing topics, formulating (and reformulating) hypotheses, gathering and evaluating sources, reading the sources and taking notes, organizing and writing their drafts, and preparing their final manuscripts. However, along with the two papers—one literary, one historical—that we traced throughout the first edition, we have added a third, new paper dealing with a scientific topic. Reproduced in full in chapter 9, these three papers exemplify the three primary modes of documentation: the new MLA system, the traditional system, and the APA system of footnoting.

In addition to the changes already described, we have tried in various ways to improve on the first edition of *Writing Research Papers*. Most notably, we have augmented our list of basic reference sources in chapter 2 with eight new categories, including computer science, film, math, and women's studies. Chapter 3 now includes a section on computers in the library, particularly on-line catalogs of holdings. In chapter 4 we have given more detailed advice about the need to evaluate the reliability of sources. And our discussion of outlining in chapter 6 now provides examples of informal as well as formal outline techniques.

In making these and other revisions, we have benefited greatly from the thoughtful, constructive advice we received from composition instructors across the country. In particular, we wish to thank Carl W. Brucker (Jamestown College), Claire van Breemen Downes (St. Cloud State University), James W. English (University of Illinois—Chicago), Jan Geesaman (College of DuPage), Sandra Hanson (LaGuardia Community College—City University of New York), James Hathaway (University of Texas—San Antonio), Robert W. Hill (Clemson University), Michael S. Kearns (Ohio Wesleyan University), Hazel Koskenlinna (University of Wisconsin—Stevens Point), Lyle W. Morgan (Pittsburg State University), and Raymond William Stedman (Bucks County Community College). We also want to express our appreciation to the editorial staff at St. Martin's Press, particularly to Mark Gallaher, whose understanding of our basic concept made his editorial advice especially valuable, and to Emily Berleth, who conscientiously carried this book through many complicated editorial situations.

Stephen Weidenborner
Domenick Caruso

8 DOCUMENTING YOUR SOURCES   150

9 PREPARING THE FINAL MANUSCRIPT   188

Index   257

1

An Introduction to the Process

As you think about writing a research paper, you may wonder how this assignment differs from other kinds of papers you have written. The fundamental difference is that most of the information that goes into a research paper comes from materials found in a library. Research papers do not grow out of your personal experiences and opinions to the same extent that other compositions do.

Sometimes virtually all the information and ideas will have been drawn from books, magazines, newspapers, and even non-print sources. In these cases, your work will consist mainly of finding the information and organizing it into a coherent report. More often, however, you will be encouraged to make judgments about the information you discover in the sources. For example, if you had chosen to investigate the controversy over the effect of acid rain on forests and lakes, you would be expected to evaluate (as an intelligent citizen, not as an expert, of course) the arguments put forth by both sides. You might conclude that the environmentalists have made the better arguments, or you might believe the experts working for the smokestack industries have given good reasons for doubting the accuracy of their opponents' charges. Or you might feel there is little to choose between the two positions, but that would also amount to a judgment on your part.

Producing a good research paper is no easy task. But completing this work has its rewards, not only in the beneficial effect a good paper will have on your course average, but also in the satisfaction you will get from having met this formidable challenge. Furthermore, as you increase your knowledge of a topic and begin making judgments as to which sources are most believable, you rapidly become an "expert" on the topic—someone who knows the subject well and whose opinions other people will listen to.

Before you examine the research process step by step, it is important to cut through the numerous details and discover the basic kinds of work you must be ready to perform. The research process boils down to three essential operations—searching, reading, and writing.

- **Searching**—You must search harder than most people realize for a good topic; rarely can you find a topic merely by thinking about the matter. Then, you must learn how to find information within a library, going far beyond the card catalog.

- **Reading**—This operation involves more than understanding the materials you are reading; you must learn how to recognize what information is likely to be truly useful to your research goals.

- **Writing**—Since you will be dealing with a great many ideas and pieces of information, most of which will have come from your sources, the ability to organize intelligently may count as much if not more than a fine writing style. But that does not mean that style doesn't count, as you well know.

All three of these operations demand constant exercise of good judgment as well as competence in dealing with language. And neatness counts! Not just from the instructor's point of view, but from your own, for carelessness can prove very costly when you are working with large amounts of information.

Mastering these skills and developing your judgment will take time and experience; so you should plan to spend several weeks, more likely a month, completing your first research assignment.

Some Essential Definitions

By now, you should be ready to look at an outline of the full research process. Before we do that, however, it is necessary to present some basic definitions. Be careful to note the specific ways these terms are used here, for they are often tossed around much more loosely in daily conversation. You will need to understand their precise meaning if you are to benefit fully from the discussions that follow.

- **Subject**—an area of interest that can be narrowed down to a suitable topic; subjects are either too broad or too loosely defined to serve as topics for research papers.

Too broad: adolescent behavior; Italy's political troubles; Shakespeare's tragedies; prehistoric animals. Entire books have been written on these subjects.

Too loosely defined: acid rain; cancer cures; computer assisted education; illegal immigration. What would you be looking for in your readings? What questions would you be answering?

- **Topic**—a reasonably narrow, clearly defined area of interest that could be thoroughly investigated within the limits set for a given research assignment. Here are some topics that might work quite well for a paper of seven to ten pages.

  1. the effect of parental attitudes on teenage alcoholism
  2. the effects of terrorism on the social policies of the Italian government over the last ten years
  3. the relationship between young women and their fathers in several Shakespearian tragedies
  4. the role of humans in the extinction of large prehistoric mammals
  5. acid rain's effect on the recent deterioration of forests and lakes in the Northeast
  6. the role of emotions in the cure of certain cancers
  7. the effectiveness of computer programs in the remediation of writing problems
  8. the effect of illegal immigration on unemployment in the Southwest.

- **Thesis**—a general statement that announces the major conclusions you reached through a thoughtful analysis of all your sources. This statement appears at the beginning of your paper; the main body will then explain, illustrate, argue for, or in some sense "prove" the thesis.

- **Hypothesis**—your prediction, made sometime before reading the sources, as to what your research will reveal about the topic; that is, what answers you expect to find for the major questions raised by the topic. As you will see, this "educated guess" helps you to find exactly the information you need, as quickly and efficiently as possible, by keeping your attention focused on a limited number of specific aspects of the topic.

A More Detailed Look at the Research Process

Now that you have these definitions clearly in mind, we can examine the process more closely.

PHASE ONE: SEARCHING FOR A TOPIC AND FOR SOURCES

STEP ONE: preliminary research

Choose an interesting subject, if the choice is left to you. Then read up on that subject in your textbook, encyclopedias, and other general reference works, looking for a topic that can be easily covered within the assigned limits for your paper. This background reading will help you form a hypothesis that will guide the rest of your research.

STEP TWO: finding sources

In the library, search for any and all sources that seem likely to provide information relevant to your hypothesis. (Broaden the topic if you cannot find enough potential sources; limit the topic further if you find far too many.) Then skim through the sources, weeding out those that turn out to be irrelevant. Finally, check to see if your hypothesis still sounds reasonable. Be ready to revise the hypothesis to conform to whatever information the skimming reveals.

PHASE TWO: READING SOURCES AND REACHING CONCLUSIONS

STEP THREE: reading and taking notes

Only after you feel that you have a reasonable hypothesis and a sufficient number of sources should you begin reading the sources closely and taking detailed notes. Be sure to take notes on all information that has a direct bearing on your hypothesis.

STEP FOUR: arriving at the thesis

Analyze the information contained in your notes to determine whether your hypothesis was correct. If it was, it becomes your thesis. If the hypothesis was not fully supported by the evidence you gathered, write a thesis statement that reflects the full picture discovered through your research. Here is the point at which your judgment plays its most important role.

PHASE THREE: WRITING THE PAPER

STEP FIVE: preparing to write

Sketch out a full introductory paragraph that includes a precise statement of your thesis. Then arrange your notes into a sensible order that can serve as an outline for the paper. Write that outline.

STEP SIX: writing the paper

Write the paper in three drafts: (1) a rough version, concentrating on the flow of thought; (2) a first revision, reorganizing the paper, if necessary, and improving the style; (3) a second revision, eliminating all mechanical errors.

PHASE FOUR: ADDING NOTES AND PREPARING THE FINAL DRAFT

STEP SEVEN: noting the sources

Prepare the list of Works Cited (bibliography), showing all the sources that contributed information to the paper. Also insert parenthetical notes (or note numbers) that identify each source as it is used in the paper.

STEP EIGHT: preparing the final draft

Type the final draft (manuscript), following the format in this book or whatever format your instructor recommends. Make at least one copy for yourself to insure against accidental loss. Submit the original to the instructor.

A glance at this outline might lead you to believe that a research paper can be produced by following a simple, step-by-step prescription— moving from subject to topic to hypothesis to thesis. In actual practice, however, you must be ready at every step to revise your earlier decisions in light of the additional information you are continually discovering. This advice applies in particular to the hypothesis, which is, after all, only an educated guess as to what your research might disclose.

Much of the discussion so far has been rather abstract. To get a good idea of what an actual research paper consists of, read a couple of the sample student papers in chapter 9. Note how each writer states, in the first or second paragraph, the thesis that he/she intends to ''prove.'' As you go through the main body of a paper, think about the way the writer presents the ideas and information that led to that thesis. Finally, notice the parenthetical (or numbered) notes that indicate where the various pieces of information were found. After you finish looking over the sample papers, return to chapter 2, where we begin discussing each step of the process in detail.

2
Laying the Groundwork

At the heart of a successful research paper lies a clearly defined *thesis*, which states in a sentence or two the major conclusions reached after a thorough investigation of a topic. The main purpose of the paper itself is to explain, illustrate, argue for, or in some sense ''prove'' that thesis. The proof, or defense, of the thesis consists of evidence gathered from a fair number of sources, expressing various points of view toward the topic. The task of finding such sources can be very difficult if you have nothing more than a topic as a guide. That is why we recommend that you proceed one step further and form a hypothesis, or prediction of your eventual thesis. A hypothesis, if it is carefully worded, can greatly reduce the problems of searching for sources and extracting from them the most useful information.

An effective hypothesis focuses your attention on the essential questions that the research is intended to answer, and thereby helps you to select the most valuable sources from the large number of possibilities you are likely to come across. And when reading a particular source, you need a sharply defined objective to keep you from taking too many notes. A good hypothesis provides you with such guidance.

The more you know about your topic, the easier it is to form a good hypothesis. In many courses, however, you will be required to deal with relatively unfamiliar topics. At such times, it will be important to have an orderly procedure for coming up with an effective hypothesis. This chapter describes several ways to accomplish this first crucial objective in the research process.

Choosing a Subject

Step One of the research assignment consists of deciding just what question the research will answer—what problem will be worthwhile exploring. Your first thoughts, however, are likely to be very general, only indicating the direction of your immediate interests. "I want to write about the trouble in the Middle East." "I want to know more about dinosaurs." "I am interested in some problems faced by the Catholic Church today." "I might as well write about my favorite subject, the Civil War." You don't yet know what to say about the subject, or even whether it will lead to a satisfactory topic, but you are moving in the right direction. The question now becomes, "How do I know the subject is any good?"

First of all, you must like the subject well enough to spend a good many days and nights working on it. More important, however, the subject must lead to a good topic—one that raises some questions which have not been answered to the satisfaction of all the authorities in the field. Such uncertainty among the experts gives you the opportunity to examine the different points of view and arrive at those conclusions which will become your paper's thesis. We have found that the best subjects are those that suggest a good many interesting topics to choose from, for then, if the first one you pick does not work out well, you have several alternatives ready at hand.

One last point about the subject: Start thinking about it as soon as you know a research paper is required. Don't wait for the instructor to push you into action.

Finding a Topic

Never choose a topic hastily. Many students make the mistake of picking the first attractive topic that comes along, then rushing to the library, getting a stack of books off the shelves, and taking piles of notes, all before they have defined a problem to be solved. After days or even weeks of work, they suddenly realize that they have no control over the project, no clear sense of direction, and worst of all, no time to go back and begin again.

A good topic raises questions that have no simple answers. When there is no single, accepted answer, the experts (your sources) will disagree to some extent, which is just what you want. This means you should avoid topics that can be fully covered by reading just one, or two, brief sources. For example, the question "Why is the sky blue?" has been answered to everyone's satisfaction. Any general science book or encyclopedia contains the explanation. And all such "sources" say much the same thing, although they may use different examples as well as different words to express the idea. In order to complete your research, you would need just one of these sources, for they all present you with the same idea. There would be no challenge in such a project. The same holds true for many seemingly more complex questions, such as "How does vitamin C help the body fight disease?"; "Why did the popes leave Rome for southern France in the 1300s?"; or even "Why did Guiteau shoot President Garfield?" (Perhaps no one really knows, but historians—the experts—agree on one view of the event.)

As you are searching for a topic, then, remember that research should take you beyond mere reporting, beyond just finding information. Be prepared to demonstrate your ability to evaluate the information and ideas that you discover, to arrive at a clear, well-thought-through, conclusion, which gives the reader something to think about. Therefore, in your quest for a topic, look for significant points on which the experts disagree.

Such disagreements tend to fall into two categories:

1. highly controversial issues, such as *the value of a new, expensive weapon; the causes of alcoholism; the long-range benefits of a particular vitamin, such as C or E.*

2. less well-known questions, such as *the leadership qualities of Jefferson Davis; Emily Dickinson's reasons for not publishing her poems; the possibility of extending the human life span.*

Warning: you should probably avoid topics in which the controversy derives solely from opinion. For example, these questions would *not* lead to the kind of research you are expected to perform. "Is football too violent?" "Was Ali the greatest boxer ever?" "Should public schools be allowed to mandate that pupils pray?" "Should selling marijuana be legalized?" "Should abortion be banned?" We are not saying that these issues are not important. Some of them may be more important to more people than any topic you will write about. But such questions can only be resolved by each individual in light of his/her personal values.

Similarly, you must beware of topics involving the paranormal (UFOs and ESP, for example) because almost all the "sources" consist of personal accounts of occult phenomena or weird sightings. This is not to say that good topics cannot be found in these subjects; however, you must take great care to avoid simply reporting mere opinion and unusual tales. The subject *UFOs* could lead to a reasonable topic such as *the Air Force's response to reports of UFO sightings.* (Questions: Are they hiding something? out of fear of public panic? or to keep new weapons secret?) And the subject *ESP* could lead to the topic *scientific techniques for investigating ESP*. (Question: Have scientists found any reason to consider parapsychology a valid field of study?)

Some excellent topics do not concern issues as such; they pose the general question, "What is being done in this area?" Your research in such a case does not move toward a judgment as to who is right. Instead, the research consists of assembling information from various sources in order to present your readers with a composite picture. This kind of topic almost always deals with very current events, such as the use of genetic engineering to detect and cure disease, or the use of computers in banking or education. When the topic is so current, you are unlikely to find a single source that describes all the work being done, much less all the possibilities currently being investigated. Therefore, you will need to locate a fairly large number of articles in magazines and journals if you are to cover the topic thoroughly.

BACKGROUND READING, OR PRELIMINARY RESEARCH

Once you believe you have a good topic, take time to do some background reading in the subject area. Background reading consists of looking up your subject or topic in general reference works—encyclopedias, biographical dictionaries, or books that survey wide areas such as the Middle Ages, Eastern religions, American Indians, English literature, and the history of psychology. Textbooks may also serve as general references if they cover broad areas such as business administration, vertebrate biology, and United States history 1900–74.

For example, if your subject were *astronomy* and your idea for a topic *the beginning of the Universe*, you could (1) look up "the Universe" in the *Encyclopedia Americana* or an encyclopedia of science; (2) read the section on astronomy in an atlas such as *Earth and Man*. And, (3) if writing the paper for a science course, you could read ahead, or reread, the section on astronomy in your textbook.

Unfortunately, you will sometimes be required to work with a subject about which you are not very well informed. In that case, you can start your search for a topic by reading one or more background studies in the assigned subject area. If you begin your search in a textbook, do not stop there. Go to the reference room of the library and look up other background sources which might offer different points of view. (A list of such reference materials can be found at the end of this chapter. And you can always ask the reference librarian for others if you need them.)

The purpose behind preliminary research, or background reading, is twofold. First, you want to feel certain that you have chosen the best available topic. Other possibilities may appear during your background reading, and one of them might be even better than your first one. One of the students whose papers appear in chapter 9 found his topic in the *Encyclopedia Americana*, as we shall see on pages 11–19. Second, even if your original idea for a topic was a fine one, you will benefit from refreshing your knowledge of the subject, thereby giving yourself a better handle on the many new facts and ideas your research will uncover.

Do not read entire books during preliminary research. For instance, if your subject is *Martin Luther King, Jr.*, do not begin by reading a full-length biography. Since you have not yet settled on a topic, most of the book will not be directly relevant to whatever topic you eventually select. Even if you have a definite topic in mind, such as *King's relationship with militant Black leaders*, you should first review King's career as a civil rights activist in an encyclopedia or a biographical dictionary, where you would find a concise account of the major events of his life.

When reading background studies, take notes you can refer to later if you need to revise your topic and/or hypothesis. In taking these notes, avoid recording detailed factual information. Concentrate instead on major ideas and possible topics. You want to prevent the general outlines of the subject area from becoming lost in a flood of facts.

BRAINSTORMING

Another useful approach to finding the best topic is an exercise called "brainstorming." If you are already fairly familiar with your subject area, a little brainstorming may turn up a number of good possibilities for research. Brainstorming consists of wide-open, no-holds-barred thinking about some subject, in which your mind is free to produce any and all ideas that come along. Since you are looking for a problem to investigate, these ideas will probably come to you as questions. Note: Do not reject any idea during the brainstorming session. Record every thought, large or small, either in shorthand notes or, better yet, on a tape recorder. The important point is to collect every idea, even if it sounds irrelevant or silly or otherwise useless. Stop after about fifteen minutes (a little longer if writing rather than taping) and review your notes. Check off the ideas that seem best. Then put all the notes aside overnight and review them again in a fresh light the next day.

Let's look at what one student's mind produced when unleashed on what was for her a fairly familiar subject, dinosaurs.

What exactly was a dinosaur? How do we know what it was, aside from the bones? When did people first find dinosaur bones? Where did they live? What did they eat? Did any other creatures prey on them? What caused dinosaurs to die out? How long were they around? Did they evolve from earlier life forms?

from sharks? from little lizards? Are crocodiles really modern dinosaurs? Are there any other dinosaurs around now, possibly in some unexplored jungle or on a deserted island? Someone said birds evolved from dinosaurs—are they right? Were humans alive at the same time as dinosaurs? Did they kill dinosaurs for food? What caused the extinction of dinosaurs? Did they just become too big? But what about the smaller ones? Did they run out of food? If so, how could that happen? Did they become unfit for survival? How? Were other creatures smarter than they were? How could we know how smart they were? Their brains were probably larger than ours. How do we know about these long-gone beasts? Or don't we know? Is it all guesswork? Do we find each skeleton all in one spot, or do we assemble possible skeletons from a mixed heap of bones? How come no animals are that big today (except whales)? Why are today's lizards and other reptiles no larger than alligators?

Obviously, this student had to know something about this subject or she couldn't have produced so much specific material. Notice that she returned to some points and that some ideas lead to dead ends. (For example, "Were humans alive then?" leads nowhere because dinosaurs became extinct 65 million years ago, and primitive humans did not appear until 5 million years ago.)

Did you sense several themes recurring throughout the notes?

Why did dinosaurs become extinct? Topic: *cause of extinction.*

What exactly was (or is) a dinosaur? Topic: *their place in evolution.*

How do we *know* what we say we know? Topic: *the basis of our knowledge of prehistoric creatures.*

Any of the three topics would do just fine, for these questions have no simple, uncontroversial answers.

THREE STUDENTS FIND THEIR TOPICS

We asked the writers of the papers in chapter 9 to describe how they went about getting started. Their approaches were not identical, to be sure, but all three understood what kind of topic to look for. The student who wrote the paper on Jefferson Davis found his topic during background reading, whereas the one who wrote on Emily Dickinson first came upon her topic in her textbook.

George Pitman had been fascinated by the Civil War since junior high and had recently read an interesting magazine article about Jefferson Davis, the only president of the Confederate States of America. He realized that *Jefferson Davis* was far too broad to be considered a topic; therefore, he trimmed that down to *Davis's public life*. George's instructor pointed out that although this topic excluded many parts of Davis's life—

his childhood, his family life, and his years in private business—it was still too broad. After all, Davis had served in a significant capacity in the Mexican War and as a United States senator before assuming the presidency of the Confederacy. To cover so much material within just seven to ten pages would create a very superficial report, one that could probably be extracted from an encyclopedia. And that task would not qualify as "research," as the term is defined in this book.

But that was only one reason for rejecting the topic *Davis's public life*. It was also a poor choice because it suggested no questions for investigation. The instructor advised George to find a topic that raised some controversial question concerning Davis, about which the experts, in this case, Civil War historians, disagreed. He suggested doing some background reading, starting with the entries for "Civil War" and "Jefferson Davis" in the *Encyclopedia Americana*.

Here then, is the "Jefferson Davis" entry, reproduced in its entirety. Notice that several fairly narrow areas that might lead to good topics are suggested by the headings within the article: Service as Senator— Secretary of War—President of the Confederacy—Fighting the Civil War. George's keen interest in the war itself led him to focus on the last two sections. What particularly caught his attention were the mixed judgments of Davis as president; therefore, he decided to work on the topic *Davis's performance as president of the Confederacy*.

Marginal comments illustrate the way this student analyzed the information in terms of a topic for research and indicate the points at which he wrote notes.

Student notes a possible topic in Davis's being "personally blamed" for the South's failure but later admired for his "devotion to the Southern cause."

DAVIS, Jefferson (1808–1889), American political leader, who was president of the Confederate States of America during the four years of its existence (1861–1865). A senator and for a time secretary of war (1853–1857) in the United States government but a spokesman for the South, he reluctantly abandoned the Union during the secessionist movement. As president of the Confederacy, he led the South in the Civil War and was personally blamed for its failures. After the Confederate defeat, however, he was widely admired in the South for his unrelenting devotion to the Southern cause.

Student notes the possibility of comparing or contrasting Davis and Lincoln but suspects that this topic might be too big. Student wonders if this topic could be narrowed to a specific point of comparison or

Over six feet tall, strong-jawed and hollow-cheeked, his body worn thin by work, worry, and disease, Davis was blind in one eye, had an acutely sensitive nervous system, and suffered from neuralgia. In contrast to Abraham Lincoln, he was graceful and highly educated, but, though he pushed himself unmercifully, he could not approach Lincoln's simplicity, sincere eloquence, humanity, and insight into fundamental problems. Criticism stung Davis deeply, and lacking Lincoln's singleness of purpose, he was unable to dismiss detractors and concentrate on his goals.

<table>
<tr><td>

contrast. He notes
Davis's sensitivity to
criticism as a possible
area for research.

Student finds this
general biographical
information too
noncontroversial for a
research topic, but he
notes Davis's early
interest in military
affairs.

Student notes Davis's
attitudes toward
Blacks and slavery as a
possible area for
research.

Student reads about
Davis's early political
career but finds no
topics of interest to
him.

</td><td>

Early Life. Davis was born in Christian (now Todd) county, Ky., on June 3, 1808, the youngest of 10 children of Samuel and Jane Cook Davis, who were respectively of Welsh and Scotch-Irish heritage. A few years after his birth the family settled in the new but prosperous cotton region of Wilkinson county, Miss.

Because the frontier schools were inadequate, young Jefferson studied for a few years at a Dominican school in Kentucky and then returned home and attended nearby private academies. At the age of 13 he entered Transylvania College in Kentucky, and he had completed his junior year there when his already prominent oldest brother, Joseph, secured his appointment to West Point in 1824. Jefferson's record at the Military Academy was not distinguished; he was graduated 23d in a class of 33, and his drinking in a public tavern and other escapades brought more than the average number of demerits. However, he developed an abiding interest in military affairs, philosophy, and history.

After graduation in 1828, Davis served as a lieutenant on the northwestern frontier. There he met and fell in love with Sarah Knox, daughter of his commander, Col. Zachary Taylor. But Jefferson's attentions to an Indian girl at a dance and his opposition to Taylor's policies angered the colonel, and the marriage was delayed. The Black Hawk War (1832) gave Davis some military experience, but in 1835, having secured Taylor's reluctant consent, he resigned his commission to marry Sarah Knox. The young couple settled on a 1,000-acre (400-hectare) cotton plantation in the Mississippi delta given them by Joseph, but less than three months after the wedding Sarah Knox was dead of malaria.

Davis found release in developing the plantation, which was known as Brierfield. A beneficent master to his own slaves, he always saw slavery in its most ideal light, holding himself accountable both for the well-being of his slaves and for their training in responsibility. Yet he believed that God created Negroes inferior to whites, and that neither education nor environment could counteract the divine intent. Rather than seeing the conflict between Christianity and human bondage, Davis found justification in the Old Testament for slavery. The profits from Brierfield and the relative contentment of his slaves supported his convictions.

Political Beginnings. By 1843, Davis' reputation as a scholar together with the tradition of planter participation in politics, won him a last-minute Democratic nomination for the Mississippi legislature. His brief but intensive campaign gained an impressive, though not victorious, vote in a strong Whig county. He broke with his party's stand on repudiation of the Union Bank bonds, but political enemies later repeatedly and falsely accused him of being a repudiator. Campaigning for James Polk in

</td></tr>
</table>

1844 and advocating territorial expansion, he canvassed the state and proved himself a popular orator. The following year Davis married Varina Howell, a member of the local Mississippi aristocracy. He received the Democratic nomination for the House of Representatives and won election by advocating sound currency, a low tariff, and territorial expansion. In Congress he joined forces on the question of expansion with Southerners who urged moderation and compromise rather than war with Britain. But his stay in the House was short, for he resigned in 1846 to command the Mississippi Rifles in the Mexican War.

Student notes Davis's "personal bravery" in battle and wonders if this information connects with Davis's early interest in military affairs.

At the Battle of Monterrey, Colonel Davis won respect for his personal bravery; at Buena Vista, he demonstrated both courage and ability, but was wounded and returned home. Now a hero, his political career was advanced.

Service as Senator. In 1847, Davis was appointed by the governor of Mississippi to a vacancy in the U.S. Senate, and the next year the state legislature elected him for the remainder of the unexpired term. As a member of the Committee on Military Affairs he supported expansion and enlarging the army. Already the young Mississippi senator foresaw a transcontinental railroad and a Panama railway to promote commerce and secure Pacific coast defenses.

Student notes Davis's change from nationalist to sectionalist.

Student notes Davis's concept of the sovereignty of states under the Constitution as a possible topic.

Yet, little by little, Davis became more a sectionalist and less a nationalist. The Wilmot Proviso and the Compromise of 1850 (qq.v.) turned his energies toward the defense of slavery. He envisioned no relief in Calhoun's discredited doctrine of nullification, but held that the Union was composed of sovereign independent states, voluntarily confederated and free to resume their sovereignty. Thus secession was not revolution but a legal remedy. Davis favored preservation of the Union, if the Constitution remained "in the form and with the meaning it had when it left the hands of its authors." The federal government should respect the right of property in slaves; any interference with it was unconstitutional and a threat to state sovereignty. Davis voiced his convictions well and was an excellent debater, but in his constitutional theories he closed his eyes to custom and practice that had already brought a changed interpretation of the Constitution to a majority of Americans. He opposed the Compromise of 1850, contending that a strict fugitive slave law could not be enforced in face of adverse public opinion, that the states alone could exclude slavery from the territories, and that the Missouri Compromise line should be extended to the Pacific.

Student reads this background information but since it

After passage of the Compromise of 1850, Davis signed a vigorous protest and, notwithstanding his recent election to a six-year term in the Senate, resigned (1851)

adds little to his
understanding of
Davis, he takes no
notes.

Student notes Davis's
return to national
rather than sectional
interests. Student also
adds a note about
Davis as secretary of
war to his previous
ones on Davis's
interest in military
affairs. This topic,
however, still does not
seem to go beyond an
accumulation of facts,
so the student doubts
it will be a good topic.

Student adds to
previous note on
Davis's attitude toward
slavery.

Student takes more
notes on Davis's belief
in the sovereignty of
states but realizes that
these notes are much
like his previous ones
on the point. Student
suspects that further

to accept the Democratic nomination for governor of
Mississippi. He waged a strong campaign, but lost to
Henry S. Foote. Discredited and dismayed, Davis returned to his plantation until his interest in Franklin
Pierce's presidential candidacy brought him back to politics. After his election, Pierce urged Davis to accept a
cabinet position.

Secretary of War. Davis reached the apex of his national career as secretary of war. In his direction of the
War Department he was more a nationalist than a sectionalist. He revised military regulations, replaced wood
gun carriages with iron, adopted a better system of in-
fantry tactics, provided rifles, pistols, and the Minié ball,
used large-grain powder, and created the medical service.
The Military Academy was enlarged, four regiments
were added to the army, and coastal and frontier defenses
were strengthened. These reforms, plus increased pay,
endeared Davis to the military, but he failed in the attempt to make merit rather than seniority the basis for
promotion. His introduction of camels for transportation
in the West was interesting but ineffectual.

As secretary he had charge of enlarging the Capitol
building and constructing a viaduct that provided a better
water system for Washington. Undoubtedly his greatest
contribution was the survey of routes for western rail-
ways and the resulting detailed reports, which not only
laid the basis for future railroads but also emphasized the
importance of the great West. Though a strict construc-
tionist, Davis advocated federal land grants and bonds to
encourage railroad construction, on the ground that
transcontinental routes were necessary for national defense and thus within the war powers of the president.
Davis favored the Southern route to the West and was
instrumental in securing the Gadsden Purchase from
Mexico. He favored the acquisition of Cuba and territorial rights in Nicaragua.

Return to the Senate. On the expiration of his term as
secretary in 1857, Davis was elected to the Senate. He
returned to that body as the recognized spokesman of the
South, proclaiming slavery an economic and moral good
and openly supporting its extension. At the same time he
evidenced a sincere love of the Union and an unwilling-
ness to see it broken by radical Northern or Southern
action.

Representing the Southern wing of the Democratic
party, on Feb. 2, 1860, Davis introduced resolutions that
became the platform of most Southern men. In them he
reiterated his position that the federal Constitution was
adopted by free and independent sovereign states and
protested that Negro slavery was recognized as legitimate
and that attacks on it were manifest breaches of good
faith. He further declared that neither Congress nor a

research in this area
may uncover only
repetitious material.

Student takes notes on
Davis as a "cooperative
secessionist" and
considers how this
relates to his other
notes on Davis's
choices between
sectional and national
interests.

Student notes Davis's
relationships with other
Confederate leaders as
a possible topic.

territorial legislature could impair the right of a citizen to move freely with his property in the territories and that therefore it was the duty of Congress to provide adequate protection for slave property. This doctrine of congressional protection of slavery in territories was accepted as the minority platform at the Charleston Democratic Convention; upon adoption of the majority report supported by Stephen A. Douglas, eight Southern states left the convention.

Davis eventually favored John C. Breckinridge in the presidential campaign of 1860, and after the election of Abraham Lincoln, he was no more than a cooperative secessionist. He held that the Southern states should meet to determine a new policy and repeatedly warned that there could be no peaceful secession. Davis served on the Senate Committee of Thirteen and favored the Crittenden Compromise (q.v.), but, seeing no prospects for effective compromise, he voted against it. On Jan 5, 1861, he joined other Southern senators in urging each state to secede as soon as possible and to provide the means of organizing a Southern Confederacy. Yet even at this late date he realized the danger in leaving the Union and saw advantage to the South in keeping Southern senators and representatives in Congress.

After Mississippi seceded, Davis resigned and returned home, where he accepted the rank of major general and the command of his state's military forces before he was informed of his selection by the Provisional Congress as president of the Confederacy. Reluctantly he left for Montgomery, Ala., and the impossible task ahead, for he would have preferred an army command.

President of the Confederacy. Davis took office as president of the Confederacy on Feb. 18, 1861. He selected his cabinet with due regard to geography, personality, political connection, and ability. In Judah P. Benjamin, first attorney general, then secretary of war, and finally secretary of state; Stephen R. Mallory, secretary of the navy; and John H. Reagan, postmaster general, he found men of outstanding ability who remained with him throughout the Confederacy. Christopher G. Memminger and George A. Trenholm as secretaries of the treasury directed the department well—considering the financial deficiencies of the South. Eleven other men served in the cabinet, and most of them resigned because of personal ambition or congressional opposition.

Though confident that law and right were on his side, President Davis was equally convinced that the major force was on the other. Behind him he had little more than 9 million people, including slaves, and woefully inadequate industrial facilities in contrast to the North's population of 22 million, extensive industry, and almost unlimited possibilities for men and matériel. The South did, however, have certain advantages, including a citizenry accustomed to outdoor life and trained in the use of firearms, excellent military officers, a defensive position, and slaves who remained loyal and economically productive.

Davis pressed military preparation, but planned no overt act to give the North cause for war. Though anxious to avoid a test of strength, the course of events forced him to consent to the bombardment of Fort Sumter, S.C. (April 12–13, 1861), which gave Lincoln the opportunity to accuse the South of aggression.

Fighting the Civil War. Davis and his cabinet used Southern resources well. Approximately 900,000 men volunteered or were conscripted for the army: ordnance and munition works were constructed so rapidly that no Southern army really suffered a lack of these supplies; a poor transportation system was improved: and scrap iron and captured steam engines were converted into a modern navy, whose ironclad ships and torpedoes lessened the effectiveness of the Northern blockade, thereby enabling the South to obtain essential supplies by blockade runners from abroad. Confederate cruisers roamed the seas, effectively destroying the Union's carrying trade.

Excess cotton and the failure of England and France to demand it at the possible cost of war created a problem, because the blockade limited cotton's expected value as a source of exchange and made it impossible for the debtor South to finance an extended war. Yet cotton became the medium of exchange for matériel secured by blockade-running.

Southern opposition to heavy taxation, together with an inability to buy bonds, forced the financing of war with fiat money. The resulting depreciation of the currency created a morale problem and made necessary taxation in kind and impressment of commodities at fixed prices.

In foreign affairs Davis and Benjamin pushed every conceivable advantage, but for many reasons, including its critical need of Northern wheat, Britain refused recognition, and France feared to act alone.

From first to last, severe criticism fell on Davis. His accusers blamed him for the inadequacies of the South, charged him with being a dictator, condemned him for interfering with military commanders, criticized his appointments, and demanded an offensive rather than a defensive military policy.

With few exceptions, including his blind faith in Braxton Bragg and the removal of Joseph E. Johnston, Davis selected his officers intelligently; and the army of Robert E. Lee, which he visited and with which he interfered most often, had more successes than any other. Perhaps his greatest mistake lay in overemphasis on the defense of Richmond, Va., and failure to recognize the importance of the West. He probed the relative merits of East and West in 1863 and eventually supported Lee's planned

---

Student notes a possible topic dealing with Davis's success as president of the Confederacy.

Student notes for possible research the problems Davis faced as president.

Student notes criticisms of Davis's leadership and recalls his earlier note about Davis being blamed and then admired. Student notes the judgments about Davis's leadership as well as controversial decisions made by Davis.

Student takes notes on the problems Davis confronted as president and starts thinking that a paper evaluating Davis's performance as president might prove interesting.

Student takes notes on Davis's influence after the Civil War.

After the student finishes the article, he reviews the possible topics he has noted about Davis—his interest in military affairs, his attitude toward slavery, his change from nationalist to sectionalist, his concept of the sovereignty of states, his relationships with other Confederate leaders, and his influence after the Civil War. Student decides that Davis's

invasion rather than the reinforcement of Vicksburg, Miss.

The degree of congressional opposition was indicated by Davis' 39 veto messages, and, although the Congress could not override these vetoes, by 1865 the President had lost the confidence of Congress and the public. Opposition of Georgia's and North Carolina's governors, widespread desertions, and capture of the last port of entry, forced approval of arming Negroes. But before this became reality, the Confederacy fell.

In Defeat. On April 3, 1865, Davis and his cabinet fled Richmond (stopping briefly in Danville, Va., and Greensboro, N.C.) and at Charlotte, N.C., operated as a government for the last time. Davis sped through South Carolina and into Georgia. Ostensibly headed for the trans-Mississippi region and continued resistance, he actually loitered in Georgia awaiting capture, knowing that the Confederacy was at an end.

On May 10 he was taken at Irwinville, Ga. Accused of treason and of participation in planning the assassination of Lincoln, he was imprisoned at Fortress Monroe, Va. For a time he wore leg shackles and this, with other harsh treatment, restored his popularity in the South and made him, second to Lee, a symbol of the Confederacy. Though twice indicted, he was never brought to trial, and in two years (on May 13, 1867) he was released. That only Capt. Henry Wirz, commandant of Andersonville prison, was executed as a result of so long and bloody a war is remarkable in the annals of history.

The Remaining Years. For the rest of his long life, Davis was a defender and apologist of the South. Failure of several business ventures left him in straitened financial circumstances, which the gift of the Beauvoir plantation at Biloxi, Miss., partially eased. There he collected material for his *The Rise and Fall of the Confederate Government* (1881) and wrote an excellent exposition of the Southern point of view and a justification of secession. Yet, much of his writing was special pleading rather than history and was disappointing in its meager revelations of intimate associations during the war years. Davis accepted few of the numerous invitations for speeches; but, whenever he spoke, he stressed the right of secession, the justice of the Confederate cause, and on occasion disparaged the federal government. Acrimonious controversies with former Confederates such as Gen. Joseph E. Johnston and Northerners such as Gen. William T. Sherman clouded his declining years, but in 1886 he received triumphal ovations after appearances in Montgomery, Ala., Atlanta, Ga., and Savannah, Ga.

Although he remained the sharp-tongued defender of the Confederacy, Davis apparently had mellowed by his 80th year. He never requested or received a pardon, yet performance as president is his most promising topic since it combines his original interest in the Civil War period with a clear issue about Davis.

stated in a speech at Mississippi City, Miss.: "The past is dead; let it bury its dead, its hopes, and its aspirations; before you lies the future—a future full of golden promise, a future of expanding national glory, before which all the world shall stand amazed." In November 1889, while visiting Brierfield, he became ill and returned as far as New Orleans, La., where he died on December 6.

See also CIVIL WAR; CONFEDERATE STATES OF AMERICA.

REMBERT W. PATRICK
Author of "Jefferson Davis and His Cabinet"

The student now turns to the "Civil War" entry in search of additional information about this topic after noting for the future the other sources of information listed here. (This list will give the student a head start when he begins searching for sources.)

Bibliography

Davis, Jefferson, *The Rise and Fall of the Confederate Government*, 2 vols. (New York 1881).

Davis, Varina H., *Jefferson Davis, Ex-President of the Confederate States of America: A Memoir*, 2 vols. (New York 1890).

Dodd, William E., *Life of Jefferson Davis* (Philadelphia 1907; repr. New York 1965).

McElroy, Robert McN. *Jefferson Davis, the Real and the Unreal*, 2 vols. (New York 1937).

Patrick, Rembert W., *Jefferson Davis and His Cabinet* (Baton Rouge, La., 1944).

Strode, Hudson, *Jefferson Davis*, 3 vols. (New York 1955–1964).

Strode, Hudson, ed., *Jefferson Davis: Private Letters, 1823–1899* (New York 1966).

Vandiver, Frank E., *Jefferson Davis and the Confederate State* (New York 1964).

Finding a topic consumed less time in Susanna Andrews's case. While taking a course in American literature, she had been excited by Emily Dickinson's rather mystical poetry. While thinking about a possible topic, Susanna remembered reading in the textbook's introduction that Dickinson "did not write for publication and was easily discouraged from it." Only eight of her nearly 1,800 poems appeared in print during her lifetime. This point had also been made (changing eight to six) in *The Oxford Companion to American Literature*, a standard background resource which Susanna had consulted.

In lectures, her instructor had painted a fascinating picture of this remarkable woman, and Susanna had no trouble finding an account of Dickinson's life in the biographical dictionary *Notable American Women*. Once Susanna felt she knew a fair amount about her subject, she reviewed her notes and discovered that one idea for a topic persisted in her thoughts about the poet and her work: *her failure to publish her poetry.* Susanna naturally wondered why such a great poet had published so few of her works. Consulting her instructor, she learned that the question had not been decisively resolved, so Susanna confidently chose as her topic, *Emily Dickinson's reluctance to publish her poems.*

Our third student, Anita Barrone, became interested in the subject of increasing human life expectancy after reading an article in a 1983 issue of *U.S. News and World Report,* which she picked up in her dentist's waiting room. The article consisted of an interview with Roy Walford, a scientist dedicated to slowing down the aging process. The reporter's questions focused on the chances for extending healthy human life beyond the limits nature seems to have imposed on us, and Walford's responses were decidedly optimistic. The interview was so brief that Walford could mention but a few of the life extension theories now being investigated. But Anita's curiosity was aroused. Her instructor encouraged her to look into the subject as a possible research project, and she was on her way.

Because most of the work in this field had been performed so recently, Anita's background reading in a handbook of biological science gave her little more than an overview of the biology of aging. But after looking up "Walford" in the card catalog and reading the introduction to his book, *Maximum Lifespans,* she felt certain her topic was an excellent one: *extending human life: a dream or a real possibility?*

Forming a Hypothesis

We have been discussing the choice of a topic as though you had to make this decision before moving on to the next step: forming a hypothesis. In practice, however, you should begin to form a hypothesis while you are choosing your topic. This is only natural when you consider that the topic involves unanswered questions, and the hypothesis predicts possible answers.

The key to successful research lies in forming a reasonable hypothesis as early as possible, for you cannot rely entirely on the topic to guide you through this complex process. The problem is that the topic by itself offers very little help when you are trying to decide whether a potential source is useful or not. Although your research may uncover a great deal of information that touches on your topic in some way or other, unless you have a clear idea of where you are going, all these ideas and facts will seem only loosely related to each other. Any notes you take would look like a "grocery list." If you tried to write a paper based on such materials, the result would be lacking in focus and direction. Your readers would become confused and feel no sense of having learned something valuable. Such a paper would do little more than show you had spent a lot of time in the library.

To avoid getting lost, look ahead to the writing stage, when you will need a thesis, just as you do for most other kinds of writing. It would be nice to know the thesis from the beginning so that you could limit your reading in each source to just those passages that relate directly to it. Of course, this is not possible, but you can give some direction to your investigation by thinking about your topic in terms of a possible thesis, or hypothesis.

There are two good reasons for starting out with a hypothesis, even if it may prove to be somewhat inaccurate. First, a hypothesis points you in the right direction by indicating the specific questions you need answers for. As you look for information that either agrees or disagrees with your hypothesis, you move closer to the "truth"—and that will be your thesis.

Second, the hypothesis can test the thoroughness of your research. If your conclusions are to be considered valid, you must consult a variety of sources, representing different viewpoints. You should not try to defend your hypothesis by using only those sources that support it. Your mission is to present readers with the full picture so they will have enough information to evaluate your conclusions.

Let's look at an example. If you are investigating the theory that intelligence (IQ) is inherited, you cannot restrict your search to the work of Arthur Jensen, E. O. Wilson, and other advocates of this theory. You need to find additional experts, such as Steven Rose and Stephen Jay Gould, who are less than enthusiastic, if not downright opposed to this theory. Of course, your thesis might eventually state either that Jensen and his supporters seem to be right, or that Rose and other critics have proved them wrong, or even that the issue has not yet been satisfactorily resolved. But the paper would have to show that you weighed all sides of the question before reaching your conclusion. For some topics, you will find that expert opinion is divided into several camps, in which case, you must fairly represent them all in your paper.

In short, you have a limited amount of time to spend finding sources and then reading and taking notes. A carefully limited topic will ensure that you will be working with a manageable number of sources; but you will need a hypothesis to help you decide what ideas and facts in each source will be most useful in your effort to cover the topic thoroughly, intelligently, and efficiently.

FORMING A HYPOTHESIS BY BRAINSTORMING

Here are two examples of writers moving from subject to topic and then to a hypothesis by combining brainstorming with background reading. In the first example, the student who had brainstormed about dinosaurs was able, after a little background reading, to reject several potential topics. (She discarded *the basis of our knowledge* and *what dinosaurs really were* because she was not very interested in either one, and the extinction problem seemed likely to lead to some exciting ideas, some of which had been mentioned in her background reading.)

After this student had settled on *causes for their extinction* as her topic, another brainstorming session helped her form a hypothesis. Here are her notes.

> Did the evolution of smaller, smarter animals somehow lead to the extinction of the slow-witted dinosaurs? Were these new creatures mammals? Or did major climatic changes bring about the extinction by eliminating the tropical swamplands in which the dinosaurs thrived? How fast might such changes take place? Could a meteor striking the Earth cause such a change? Or did deadly radiation from an exploding nearby star do them in? In that case, wouldn't some have survived? Or did dinosaurs become so large they could not find enough food in their environment?

All these ideas made sense—her background reference materials did not take a stand on the question, and she had not yet read her sources closely enough to be able to judge the relative merits of the theories. She decided, therefore, to go with the newest idea—"radiation from an exploded star caused the Great Extinction." This became her hypothesis. (Her thesis, however, took another turn. After reading all her sources, she believed equal support had to be given to the theory that a meteor hit the Earth 65 million years ago, drastically cooling the atmosphere and killing off the dinosaurs. Thus, she left resolution of the puzzle up to future research paper writers who would probably have more evidence to go on.)

After some background reading, another student narrowed the subject *alcoholism* to the topic: *treatment of alcohol addiction*. A bit of brainstorming at that point produced the following notes:

> How well do support therapies, such as Alcoholics Anonymous, work in their efforts to cure alcoholism? Does the addict have to be religiously inclined for such therapies to work? How successful are aversion therapies that use chemicals to make liquor repellent? Doesn't the effect wear off? How effective are cognitive therapies that try to get alcoholics to stop drinking by showing them films of their own drunken behavior? Is psychotherapy able to cure alcoholism by helping the patients understand the unconscious reasons for their drinking? How would knowing why you drink help you stop?

Again, we find someone faced with several possible answers to his research question. However, this student could see no grounds for choosing any one of them while still in the preliminary research stage. Also, he had personal reasons for doubting whether any method offered a sure cure. So, he took a neutral position that expressed his intuition: "Of the four most common alcoholism therapies, none seems to have convinced its critics that it offers a strong likelihood of success."

The student did not feel committed to this pessimistic view; he hoped that his sources would show him good reason to believe that one of the approaches was definitely on the right track. Considerable research into this problem, however, did not fulfill this hope. His thesis read: "The success of a particular alcoholism therapy depends almost entirely upon the personality of the individual addict."

THE THREE STUDENTS FORM THEIR HYPOTHESES

What about the writers of our sample research papers? George was able to form a hypothesis at the same time he was choosing his topic. He had always regarded Jefferson Davis as something of a hero, but the articles in the encyclopedia were rather negative regarding Davis's achievements as president of the CSA, so George assumed that the majority of Civil War historians would hold this view. This conclusion led him to adopt the hypothesis, "Jefferson Davis's weaknesses as a leader contributed significantly to the defeat of the South." He hoped to find new evidence had been uncovered that could change this view of a man he admired, but he was ready to accept history's traditional verdict. The hypothesis was a good one in that it neatly focused George's research efforts on just those sources and the passages within them that supported or disputed the idea that Davis had acted (or failed to act) in ways that injured the South in the war against the North.

Susanna thought she had a good topic, *Emily Dickinson's reluctance to publish*, but her background reading offered only a vague suggestion that the poet's not publishing her poems grew out of her eccentric character. If that was the only answer to the question, then Susanna's topic was too weak to pursue. So, she brainstormed a bit to see whether she had good reason to continue. Finding a hypothesis would indicate that the topic was worth the effort. Here are a few notes from her brainstorming.

Why didn't she publish most of her poems? Why would any poet do that? Did she think they weren't good enough? Didn't she know how great her poems were? Or did she write them for her own pleasure only? Was she too shy to let other people see her thoughts? Who did she let read them? her family, her friends, or other writers? What did these readers say? Did she ever *try* to have the poems published? Why did she write poetry anyway? What did writing mean to her? What might publication have done for her, or her poems? How did the poems get published eventually?

These notes did not immediately yield a hypothesis, but as Susanna looked them over, she sensed that the answer might be found in Dickinson's idealistic attitude toward the art of poetry and toward herself as an artist. Upon reviewing her lecture notes, Susanna recalled the instructor's saying that these themes run through many of the poems. Susanna then reread some of the poems in the textbook and read some others in a collection of Dickinson's poems she had borrowed from the library. These lines caught her eye: "The Soul selects her own Society—/Then—shuts the Door—. . . ." Remembering her background reading notes, which said the poet was extremely shy, Susanna decided upon the hypothesis: "Emily Dickinson chose not to publish her poems because she was a shy, reclusive person, not interested in public praise." This hypothesis seemed good because it would force Susanna to focus her reading of sources on those comments and facts which shed light on the poet's character and her motivation regarding the poems and their publication.

As for Anita, having been influenced by the optimism expressed in a magazine interview with a leading gerontologist, Roy Walford, she quickly formed this hypothesis: "Science will soon make it possible for us to live for 100 years or more." Anita fully expected to find a wealth of articles, and perhaps even a book or two, that would support her rosy hypothesis. A trip to the reference room added to her knowledge of the aging process but gave little indication of the exciting work presently under way in this field. So, leaving her hypothesis intact, Anita compiled a solid working bibliography and started skimming the potential sources. She had not gone very far into this step before she began to suspect that Walford had been too enthusiastic about the prospects for lengthening the human life span. To be sure, a variety of approaches to the problem were being pursued with interesting results, but none seemed to have the answer firmly in hand. Furthermore, a number of informed observers said it was not presently within the power of science to extend life expectancy by more than several years.

As Anita prepared for a close reading of those sources that survived skimming, she became noticeably more cautious. Her revised hypothesis read: "The varied experiments performed in the last decade have yielded such promising results that a number of scientists believe people may soon be living considerably longer and healthier lives."

As you have seen, none of these students' hypotheses proved to be entirely accurate. In each case, the student's research into specific sources disclosed additional information and persuasive reasons for coming to a somewhat different conclusion (thesis). Nevertheless, their hypotheses served them well as guides through the difficult steps of finding sources and extracting useful information from them.

Some General Reference Sources

Here are some reference books which you will find in many college libraries and which you can use for background reading in your subject.

GENERAL ENCYCLOPEDIAS

Collier's Encyclopedia. 24 vols. with annual supplements. New York: Macmillan Educational Corp., 1981.
Encyclopedia Americana. 30 vols. with annual supplements. New York: Encyclopedia Americana, 1978. Emphasizes subjects related to the United States.
McGraw-Hill Encyclopedia of Science and Technology. 4th ed. New York: McGraw-Hill, 1977.
New Columbia Encyclopedia, The. 4th ed. New York: Columbia University Press, 1975.
New Encyclopaedia Britannica, The. 15th ed. 32 vols. with annual supplements. Chicago: Encyclopaedia Britannica, 1985. Editions prior to the current edition emphasized subjects related to Great Britain and Europe.
Van Nostrand's Scientific Encyclopedia. Ed. Douglas M. Considine. Princeton: Van Nostrand Reinhold, 1976.

ART AND ARCHITECTURE

De La Croix, Horst, and Richard G. Tansey. *Art Through the Ages*. 2 vols. 7th ed. New York: Harcourt Brace Jovanovich, 1980.
Encyclopedia of American Art. Chanticleer Press. New York: Dutton, 1981.
Encyclopedia of World Art. 15 vols. New York. McGraw-Hill, 1959–1968.
McGraw-Hill Dictionary of Art. Ed. Bernard S. Myers and Shirley D. Myers. 5 vols. New York: McGraw-Hill, 1969.

ASTRONOMY

Cambridge Encyclopedia of Astronomy. The Institute of Astronomy, University of Cambridge. New York: Crown, 1977.
Encyclopedia of Astronomy. Ed. Gilbert E. Satterthwaite. New York: St. Martin's, 1971.

BIOGRAPHY

Chambers's Biographical Dictionary. Ed. J. O. Thorne. Rev. ed. T. C. Collocott. 2 vols. New York: Two Continents, 1974.
Current Biography. New York: H. W. Wilson, 1940–present. Published monthly with annual and ten-year cumulations into volumes.
Dictionary of American Biography. 10 vols. New York: Scribner, 1980.

Dictionary of Canadian Biography. Toronto: University of Toronto Press, 1966. (Supplemented.)

Dictionary of National Biography. Ed. Leslie Stephen and Sidney Lee. 22 vols., 1882–1953; rpt. New York: Oxford University Press, 1981. Including supplements through 1970. Ed. George Smith. Detailed biographies of deceased Britons.

Index to Women of the World from Ancient to Modern Times: Biographies and Portraits. Ed. Norma O. Ireland. Westwood, MA: Faxon, 1970.

Notable American Women 1607–1950: A Biographical Dictionary. Ed. Edward T. James and Janet W. James. 3 vols. Cambridge, MA: Belknap Press, Harvard University Press, 1971.

Webster's Biographical Dictionary. Rev. ed. Springfield, MA: Merriam, 1976.

Who's Who. London: A. & C. Black; New York: St. Martin's, 1849–present (annual). Mainly British.

Who's Who Among Black Americans. 2nd ed. Northbrook, IL: Who's Who Among Black Americans, Inc., 1978.

Who's Who in America. Chicago: Marquis-Who's Who, 1899–present (biennial).

Who's Who in the World. 5th ed. Chicago: Marquis-Who's Who, 1980.

Who's Who of American Women. Chicago. Marquis-Who's Who, 1958–present.

BIOLOGICAL SCIENCES

Encyclopedia of Biological Sciences. Ed. Peter Gray. 2nd ed. New York: Van Nostrand Reinhold, 1970.

McGraw-Hill Dictionary of the Life Sciences. Ed. D. N. Lapedes. New York: McGraw-Hill, 1976.

BUSINESS

Dictionary of Business and Economics. Ed. Christine and Dean S. Ammer. New York: Free Press, 1977.

VNR Dictionary of Business and Finance. New York: Van Nostrand Reinhold, 1980.

CHEMISTRY

Lange's Handbook of Chemistry. Ed. John A. Dean. 12th ed. New York: McGraw-Hill, 1979.

COMPUTER SCIENCES

Belzer, Jack. *Encyclopedia of Computer Science and Technology.* 14 vols. New York: Dekker, 1980.

Spencer, Donald. *Computer Dictionary for Everyone.* New York: Scribner, 1981.

DANCE

Concise Oxford Dictionary of Ballet. Ed. Hurst Koegler. New York: Oxford University Press, 1977.
Encyclopedia of Dance and Ballet. Ed. Mary Clarke and David Vaughn. New York: Putnam, 1977.

DRAMA

Matlaw, Myron. *Modern World Drama: An Encyclopedia.* New York: Dutton, 1972.
McGraw-Hill Encyclopedia of World Drama. 4 vols. New York: McGraw-Hill, 1972.
The Oxford Companion to the Theater. Ed. Phyllis Hartnoll. 3rd ed. New York: Oxford University Press, 1967.

ECONOMICS

Dictionary of Economics and Business. Ed. Erwin E. Nemmers. 4th enl. ed. Totowa, NJ: Littlefield, 1978.
Greenwald, Douglas, and Associates. *McGraw-Hill Dictionary of Modern Economics: A Handbook of Terms and Organizations.* 2nd ed. New York: McGraw-Hill, 1973.

EDUCATION

Dictionary of Education. Ed. Carter Victor Good. 3rd ed. New York: McGraw-Hill, 1973.
Encyclopedia of Education. Ed. Lee C. Deighton, et al. 10 vols. New York: Macmillan, 1971.
Page, G. Terry, and J. B. Thomas. *International Dictionary of Education.* Cambridge, MA: MIT Press, 1980.

ENGINEERING

Jones, Franklin D., and Paul B. Schubert. *Engineering Encyclopedia.* 3rd ed. New York: Industrial Press, 1963.
Perry, Robert H. *Engineering Manual: A Practical Reference of Design.* 3rd ed. New York: McGraw-Hill, 1976.
Schenck, Hilbert. *Introduction to the Engineering Research Project.* New York: McGraw-Hill, 1969.

ENVIRONMENTAL SCIENCE

Encyclopedia of Ecology. Ed. Bernhard Grzimek. New York: Van Nostrand Reinhold, 1976.
Encyclopedia of Environmental Science. Ed. Daniel N. Lapedes. New York: McGraw-Hill, 1974.

FILM

Bawden, Liz Anne. *The Oxford Companion to Film*. New York: Oxford University Press, 1977.

New York Times Film Reviews, The. New York: The *New York Times* and Arno Press, 1977. (Supplemented.)

GEOGRAPHY

Brewer, J. Gordon. *The Literature of Geography: A Guide to its Organization and Use*. Hamden, CT: Shoe String, 1978.

Monkhouse, F. J. *A Dictionary of the Natural Environment*. Ed. John Small. Rev. ed. New York: Halsted, 1977.

HEALTH

Foundations of Physical Education. 8th ed. St. Louis: Mosby, 1981.

Menke, Frank G. *Encyclopedia of Sports*. 6th ed. New York: Barnes and Noble, 1978.

Tver, David F., and Percy Russell. *Nutrition and Health Encyclopedia, The*. New York: Van Nostrand Reinhold, 1981.

HISTORY

An Encyclopedia of World History: Ancient, Medieval, and Modern Chronologically Arranged. Comp. and ed. William Leonard Langer. 5th ed. Boston: Houghton Mifflin, 1972.

Cambridge Ancient History. Ed. J. B. Bury, et al. 2nd ed. 12 vols. New York: Macmillan, 1923–1939. (Third edition in progress.)

Cambridge Medieval History. Ed. H. M. Gwathin, et al. 8 vols. New York: Macmillan, 1911–1936. (Second edition in progress.)

Martin, Michael, and Leonard Gelber. *Dictionary of American History*. Rev. ed. Totowa, NJ: Littlefield, 1978.

New Cambridge Modern History. Ed. G. R. Potter. 14 vols. New York: Cambridge University Press, 1970.

See also Political Science.

LANGUAGE (ENGLISH) AND LINGUISTICS

Hayes, Curtis W., Jacob Ornstein, and William W. Gage. *The ABC's of Languages and Linguistics*. Rev. ed. Silver Spring, MD: Institute of Modern Languages, 1977.

Pyles, Thomas. *The Origins and Development of the English Language*. 2nd ed. New York: Harcourt Brace Jovanovich, 1971.

LITERATURE

Cassell's Encyclopedia of World Literature. Ed. J. Buchanan-Brown. Rev. ed. New York: Morrow, 1973.

Columbia Dictionary of Modern European Literature. Ed. Jean-Albert Bede and William Edgerton. 2nd ed. New York: Columbia University Press, 1980.

Crowell's Handbook of Classical Literature. Ed. Lillian Feder. New York: Thomas Y. Crowell, 1964.

Hart, James David. *The Oxford Companion to American Literature.* 4th ed. New York: Oxford University Press, 1965.

Oxford Companion to Canadian History and Literature, The. New York: Oxford University Press, 1967. (Supplemented, 1973.)

Oxford Companion to English Literature, The. Ed. Paul Harvey. Rev. ed. Dorothy Eagle. New York: Oxford University Press, 1967.

Oxford History of English Literature, The. 12 vols. New York: Oxford University Press, 1947–1978. Other volumes in preparation.

Penguin Companion to World Literature, The. 4 vols. New York: McGraw-Hill, 1971. Includes European, American, Oriental, and African literature.

Rush, Theresa G., et al. *Black American Writers, Past and Present: A Biographical and Bibliographical Dictionary.* Metuchen, NJ: Scarecrow, 1975.

The Literary History of the United States. Ed. Robert E. Spiller, et al. 4th ed. 3 vols. New York: Macmillan, 1974.

Whitlow, Roger. *Black American Literature: A Critical History.* Totowa, NJ: Little-field, 1974.

MATHEMATICS

VNR Concise Encyclopedia of Mathematics. Ed. W. Gellert, et al. Florence, KY: Reinhold, 1977.

MEDIA

Educational Media Year Book 1980. 6th ed. Ed. James W. Brown and Shirley N. Brown. New York: 1980. Annual review of developments in educational media.

Rivers, William L., et al. *The Mass Media and Modern Society.* 2nd ed. New York: Holt, Rinehart and Winston, 1971.

MUSIC

New Grove Dictionary of Music and Musicians. 20 vols. Ed. Stanley Sadie. Washington, D.C.: Grove's Dictionaries of Music, 1980.

The Oxford Companion to Music. Ed. Percy A. Scholes. 10th ed. Rev. ed. John Owen Ward. New York: Oxford University Press, 1970.

Westrup, J. A., and F. L. Harrison. *New College Encyclopedia of Music.* Rev. ed. Conrad Wilson. New York: Norton, 1976.

PHILOSOPHY

Angeles, Peter A., *Dictionary of Philosophy*. New York: Harper & Row, 1981.
Copleston, Frederick. *A History of Philosophy*. 9 vols. New York: Paulist Press, 1976.
Encyclopedia of Philosophy. Ed. Paul Edwards. 4 vols. New York: Macmillan, 1973.
Reese, William. (see "Religion")
Russell, Bertrand. *History of Western Philosophy*. New York: Simon and Schuster, 1945.

PHYSICS

Encyclopedia of Physics. Ed. Robert M. Besancon. 2nd ed. New York: Van Nostrand Reinhold, 1974.
Encyclopedia of Physics. Ed. E. Fluegge. 54 vols. New York: Springer-Verlag. 1956–present.

POLITICAL SCIENCE

Plano, Jack C., and Milton Greenberg. *American Political Dictionary*. 5th ed. New York: Holt, Rinehart and Winston, 1979.
Worldmark Encyclopedia of the Nations. 5th ed. 5 vols. New York: Worldmark Press and Harper & Row, 1976.
Yearbook of World Affairs. Published under auspices of London Institute of World Affairs. Boulder, CO: Praeger/Westview, 1947–present. (annual)

PSYCHOLOGY

Beigel, Hugo G. *Dictionary of Psychology and Related Fields*. New York: Ungar, 1974.
Encyclopedia of Psychology. Ed. H. J. Eysenck. 2nd ed. 3 vols. New York: Continuum, 1979.
Encyclopedia of Social Work. Ed. John Turner. New York: National Association of Social Workers, 1977.
The Encyclopedia of Human Behavior: Psychology, Psychiatry, and Mental Health. Ed. Robert M. Goldenson. 2 vols. New York: Doubleday, 1974.

RELIGION

Adams, Charles J. *A Reader's Guide to Religions*. 2nd ed. Riverside, NJ: Free Press, 1977.
Concise Encyclopedia of Living Faiths. Ed. Robert C. Zaehner. New York: Hawthorn, 1959.
Encyclopedia of Religion and Ethics. Ed. James Hastings. 12 vols. New York: Scribner, 1961.
Reese, William. *Dictionary of Philosophy and Religion, Eastern and Western*. Atlanta: Humanics, 1981.

SOCIAL SCIENCES

Dictionary of Sociology and Related Sciences. Ed. Henry Pratt Fairchild. Totowa, NJ: Littlefield, 1977.
International Encyclopedia of the Social Sciences. Ed. David L. Sills. 8 vols. New York: Free Press, 1977.
Reader's Guide to the Social Sciences. Ed. Bert F. Hoselitz. Rev. ed. New York: Free Press, 1972.

SOCIOLOGY

Bart, Pauline B., and Linda Frankel. *Student Sociologist's Handbook.* 3rd ed. Glenview, IL: Scott, Foresman, 1981.
Encyclopedia of Sociology. Ed. Gayle Johnson. Guilford, CT: Dushkin Press, 1974.

WOMEN'S STUDIES

Baker, M. A., et al. *Women Today: A Multidisciplinary Approach to Women's Studies.* Monterey, CA: Brooks/Cole, 1979.
Index to Women of the World from Ancient to Modern Times: Biographies and Portraits (*see* Biography).
Lerner, Gerda. *Black Women in White America.* New York: Pantheon, 1972.
Notable American Women 1607–1950: A Biographical Dictionary. (See "Biography")
Oakes, Elizabeth H., and Kathleen E. Sheldon. *Guide to Social Science Resources in Women's Studies.* Santa Barbara, CA: ABC-Clio, 1978.
Who's Who of American Women. Chicago: A. N. Marquis, 1958–present.

Review Questions

1. Explain the difference between a subject and a topic, as the terms are used in this book.

   • What is your primary concern when choosing a subject?
   • What must be your first concern when looking for a topic?

2. Which of the following items seem likely to work out well as topics for research papers? Explain why you reject each item that seems to have poor potential. (Some are too broad for a paper seven-to-ten pages long; others would lead no further than an encyclopedia for a full investigation; yet others are too deeply involved with personal values or deal with areas in which there is no hard knowledge.)

   • working women in America today
   • the way FM radio signals are sent and received

- the CIA's role in Nicaragua
- the invention of gunpowder
- the cause of measles
- the cause of cancer
- the British colonization of Africa in the nineteenth century
- programs for prevention of child abuse
- the *real* author of Shakespeare's plays
- the cause of teenage alcoholism
- the generation gap
- the role of computers in business today
- automation in heavy industry
- the effectiveness of capital punishment in reducing the crime rate
- the arms race as a threat to peace
- the effect of illegal immigration on the economy of the Southwest
- the effect of high salaries on the quality of baseball being played today
- the ability of some people to see the future in their dreams

3. What is the value of brainstorming? At what point(s) in the research process is this activity likely to help you?
4. What is the purpose of background reading? If you know your topic from the start, should you skip this step?
5. Why is it a good idea to look for a controversy of some sort when trying to come up with a topic?
6. Why do you need to form a hypothesis if you have an excellent topic? How does a hypothesis help at various stages of research?

Exercises

1. Read this article on Emma Goldman, which comes from *Notable American Women*, an excellent background resource for topics in women's studies. Take notes, much like those that accompany the Jefferson Davis article on pages 12–19, identifying several potential topics suitable for a seven-to-ten-page research paper. For each topic, think of a reasonable hypothesis.

    GOLDMAN, Emma (June 27, 1869–May 14, 1940), anarchist rebel, lecturer, and publicist, agitator for free speech and popularizer of the arts, feminist and pioneer advocate of birth control, was born in Kovno, Russia (Kaunas in modern Lithuania). Born to ride whirlwinds, as someone once said, she appropriately came from the Baltic, a region notorious for its political and social tensions, and from a ghetto Jewish family in which all these tensions were intensified. She was the first child of the marriage of Abraham and Taube (Bienowitch) Goldman. Taube Goldman, who had two girls from a previous marriage, responded coldly to her new husband and looked upon her infant daughter as an additional burden. Abraham Goldman, a lower-middle-class shopkeeper, was embittered by his wife's attitude, by an initial business failure, and then by the birth of a daughter instead of a son. Even after he subsequently had two sons, he could not forgive his daughter her sex. His choleric disapproval and her mother's unsympathetic brusqueness clouded Emma's earliest experiences in Kovno and later in the small village of Popelan, where her father kept the inn and managed the government stagecoach.

After her family, dogged by failure, moved to Königsberg, Prussia, Emma Goldman attended *Realschule* for a few years. Her teachers successfully instilled in her a distaste for their own cruel pedantry. Only a teacher of German took an interest in her, helped develop her taste for literature and music, and guided her preparations for the Gymnasium examinations. Her justifiable pride in passing these was cut short by the refusal of her religious instructor to give her the requisite certificate of good character. In St. Petersburg, where the Goldmans moved in 1881, her formal schooling lasted only six months more. But even her work in a cousin's glove factory did not keep her from meeting nihilist and populist university students and reading widely in the new radical literature which had the capital in a ferment. The free-spirited Vera Pavlovna, heroine of Nicolai Chernyshevsky's *What Is to Be Done?* (1863), became the model for her own life.

In 1885, gladly escaping her father's demands that she submit to an arranged marriage, she emigrated to America with her half sister Helena Zodokoff. She settled in Rochester, N.Y., with another half sister and found work in a "model" clothing factory at $2.50 a week. She soon became a critic of the capitalism which prompted German Jews, like her employer, to welcome their Eastern brethren to Rochester only to exploit them in their factories and shops. In early 1887 she was married to Jacob Kersner (also Kershner), a fellow factory worker and naturalized citizen, and was shocked to discover that he was impotent. Each passing month made more obvious the hopelessness of their relationship, which, after a divorce and a reconciliation, ended finally in a permanent divorce.

In later years she always said that her life really began in August 1889 when she moved to New York City, met Johann Most, editor of the inflammatory paper *Freiheit*, and

Alexander Berkman, a young émigré Russian revolutionist, and joined them in the anarchist movement. Her experiences had indeed prepared her for this moment: the harsh parental authority of her home; the rich ethical demands of the prophetic strain in Judaism; brutal Russian anti-Semitism and her vantage point on the margins of two cultures; her contacts with radical literature and students in St. Petersburg; the gap between the ideality and the reality in America; the judicial murders in 1887 of the so-called Haymarket rioters in Chicago; her own native intelligence, which led her to seek intellectual solutions to her problems—all readied her for her role as one of America's outstanding rebels. The anarchism of Peter Kropotkin, the brilliant Russian scientist and social philosopher, had an appeal which she could hardly resist, for it promised to replace authoritarian social hierarchies, the coercive political state, and supernaturalistic religion by a society of equals, a polity of small organic organizations in free cooperation with each other, and a warm humanism rooted in a concern for decency and justice in this world. Never a seminal social or political thinker, she made only one serious attempt to contribute to anarchist theory: at the Amsterdam Anarchist Congress of 1907 she presented a paper wherein she maintained that true anarchism meant both Kropotkin's emphasis on the community and Henrik Ibsen's emphasis on the strong, independent individual.

Her most serious mistake was an early acceptance of the tactic of individual acts of violence. During the Homestead conflict of 1892 she helped Berkman prepare to kill Henry Clay Frick and regretted that a lack of funds prevented her from being at her comrade's side when the attempt was made. Though Frick survived, Berkman disappeared for fourteen years behind the heavy gates of Pennsylvania's Western Penitentiary. In 1893 Emma herself began a one-year term on Blackwell's Island in New York, convicted of advising a Union Square audience of unemployed men that "it was their sacred right" to take bread if they were starving and their demands for food were not answered. Her prison work as a practical nurse led her to study midwifery and nursing at the Allgemeines Krankenhaus in Vienna in 1895–96. Meanwhile her ideas on individual violence were gradually changing as she came to reject the fallacy that great ends justify any means. By 1901, when President McKinley was shot by Leon Czolgosz, a demented young man possessed by the delusion that he was an anarchist with this particular personal mission, she could sympathize with both the pathetic assassin and the stricken president. Notwithstanding the most energetic efforts of the authorities, no evidence was ever unearthed to establish her complicity. Aside from a few chance remarks on another occasion, Czolgosz had heard her talk only once, and then she had vigorously maintained that anarchism and violence had no necessary connection.

In the opening decades of the new century, Emma Goldman involved herself in a wide range of activities. Perhaps the most accomplished, magnetic woman speaker in American history, she crisscrossed the country lecturing on anarchism, the new drama, the revolt of women. Subject to stubborn and sometimes brutal police and vigilante attempts to censor her remarks or to silence her completely, she joyfully waged countless fights for free speech. As the editor, along with Berkman, of the radical monthly *Mother Earth* (1906–17) and the publisher of numerous pamphlets, her own book *Anarchism and Other Essays* (1911), and Berkman's important *Prison Memoirs of an Anarchist* (1912), she aroused the concern of radicals and liberals over threats to freedom of expression and such cause célèbres as the Tom Mooney case. Roger Baldwin, whose professional interest in civil liberties dated from the influence of her lectures, hardly overstated the case when he said: "For the cause of free speech in the United States Emma Goldman fought battles unmatched by the labors of any organization."

As an integral part of her libertarian message she discussed the works of Ibsen, Shaw, Strindberg, and other playwrights. Her lectures, begun as early as 1897, were published in 1914 under the title *The Social Significance of the Modern Drama*. Though she was not primarily responsible for making Shaw known in the United States, as Rebecca West has suggested, nor a "distinguished critic of the drama," as the *New York Times* once observed, she was a great popularizer of new literary currents.

Her concept of the New Woman owed something to Ibsen's influence, as seen in her attacks on the "conventional lie" of marriage and her advocacy of "free love." By the latter she did not mean a promiscuous "wild love," as some of her critics seemed to think, but the uncoerced mutual regard and affection of two mature persons for one another. She agreed with such feminists as Charlotte Perkins Gilman in rejecting for women the role of a mere "sex commodity," but criticized their "narrow, Puritanical vision" which sought to banish "man, as a disturber and doubtful character, out of their emotional life." The suffrage demand she dismissed as a mere fetish. For over two decades a public advocate of voluntary motherhood and family limitation, in 1915 she was moved by Margaret Sanger's arrest to lecture on preventive methods; one such lecture the following year brought her fifteen days in jail. Her efforts influenced Mrs. Sanger and prepared the way for a systematic birth control campaign. With some reason, then, the *Nation* insisted in 1922 that the name of Emma Goldman should be on any list of "the twelve greatest living women."

Government officials had long had a quite different view. In 1908 they deprived her of her citizenship by denaturalizing the missing Jacob Kersner. It was decided not to make her a party to the court proceedings against Kersner, for that, as Secretary of Commerce and Labor Oscar S. Straus confidentially wrote the Attorney General, "would too obviously indicate that the ultimate design . . . is not to vindicate the naturalization law, but to reach an individual . . ." (Feb. 11, 1909, National Archives). In June 1917 she and Berkman were arrested for their leadership of the opposition to conscription and sentenced to two years in prison. After her release from Jefferson City Penitentiary in September 1919, immigration officials, with the energetic aid of J. Edgar Hoover, took advantage of wartime legislation to order her deported to Russia. Three days before Christmas 1919 Emma Goldman and Alexander Berkman, along with 247 other victims of the postwar Red Scare, sailed back past the Statue of Liberty aboard the transport *Buford*.

Two years later she expatriated herself from Russia. An early supporter of the Bolsheviki, she had soon discovered their suppression of all political dissent. From Sweden and later Germany she lashed out at the emergent totalitarianism in newspaper articles and in her book *My Disillusionment in Russia* (1923). The egregious myopia of the liberals and radicals who cried out against the suppression of civil rights in the West and remained silent about much worse in Russia was the target of her sharpest attacks. In 1925 she married James Colton, a Welsh collier, to obtain British citizenship. Fearful of economic dependence, she sought to establish herself through her lectures and royalties from her autobiography, *Living My Life* (1931). When she was not touring England or Canada, she lived in Saint-Tropez, France, where friends had helped her buy a small cottage. In 1934 she was granted a ninety-day stay in the United States, but her visit made her return to exile more a torment than ever. In 1936 Berkman, seriously ill and despondent over his forced inactivity, committed suicide. Emma Goldman was saved from utter despair over his death by an urgent request from Barcelona that she come help combat Franco and help advance the social revolution. Apart from three visits to Catalonia during the Spanish Civil War, she stayed in London to enlist understanding and support for her Latin comrades. In 1939 she went to Canada to raise some money for the lost cause. As she had wished, she went out fighting: in February 1940 she suffered a stroke, and three months later she died in Toronto. Since she was now merely a dead "undesirable alien," United States officials allowed her body to be returned for burial in Chicago's Waldheim Cemetery, near the graves of the Haymarket martyrs.

When "Red Emma" was in her twenties, reporter Nellie Bly (Elizabeth Cochrane Seaman) was surprised to discover that she was attractive, "with a saucy turned-up nose and very expressive blue-gray eyes . . . [brown hair] falling loosely over her forehead, full lips, strong white teeth, a mild, pleasant voice, with a fetching accent." Four decades later the English novelist Ethel Mannin saw her as "a short thickset scowling elderly woman with grey hair and thick glasses." Throughout her life, Emma Goldman had an extraordinary capacity for close, lasting friendships, though she could be imperious and, on occasion, insensitive to the feelings of others. Offering an invaluable counterstatement to the pragmatic faith of progressives and socialists in the omnicompetent state, she fought for the spiritual freedom of the individual at a time when the organizational walls were closing in. When she died, radicals had almost unanimously rejected her message, but hers was, in the words of the novelist Evelyn Scott, "the future they will, paradoxically, hark back to in time."

[The principal holdings of Emma Goldman's papers are in the Labadie Collection, Univ. of Mich. Library; the N.Y. Public Library; and the Internat. Institute for Social Hist., Amsterdam. There is important material also in the files of the Dept. of Justice, Dept. of State, and Post Office Dept. in the Nat. Archives, Washington. For a fuller description and bibliography, including a list of her own writings, see Richard Drinnon, *Rebel in Paradise: A Biog. of Emma Goldman* (1961). See also Frank Harris, *Contemporary Portraits, Fourth Series* (1923); Eunice M. Schuster, *Native Am. Anarchism* (1932); Margaret Goldsmith, *Seven Women against the World* (1935); Ethel Mannin, *Women and the Revolution* (1939) and *Red Rose: A Novel Based on the Life of Emma Goldman* (n.d.); Van Wyck Brooks, *The Confident Years* (1952).]

2. Using the list of subject areas below, choose one subject area, and then do sufficient background reading to find two or three potential topics for a seven-to-ten-page research paper.

- Asian or Italian or Irish immigration to the United States
- the banking industry and the Great Depression
- endangered species
- European colonization of Africa (or Asia)
- environmental controls on large industries
- safety and the automobile industry
- group therapy for emotional problems
- the US judicial system's problems
- the welfare system
- causes of urban decay
- religious cults of the 60s and 70s
- organized crime in America
- genetic experimentation

- government's role in medical care
- pre-Columbian American peoples
- Ethel and Julius Rosenberg, spies executed in the 50s
- Theodore Roosevelt, conservationist, imperialist
- Marcus Garvey, Black nationalist of the 20s
- Martin Luther King, Jr.
- Malcolm X, militant Black leader of the 60s
- Huey Long, powerful populist senator of the 30s
- James Hoffa, union leader accused of being involved with organized crime
- Theodor Herzl, Zionist of early twentieth century
- Mother Jones, union organizer of early twentieth century
- Susan B. Anthony, women's rights activist of early twentieth century
- Elizabeth I, queen of England in a crucial era
- Catherine the Great, empress of Russia
- Eleanor Roosevelt, humanitarian
- V. I. Lenin, leader of Russian Revolution of 1917
- Mao tse-Tung, leader of Chinese Revolution of 1949
- Mohandas Gandhi, leader of Indian independence movement
- Winston Churchill, leader of England during World War II
- Japanese businessmen: their customs, their ethics, their relations with labor and government
- South Africa's system of racial segregation, apartheid
- Brazil, growing pains of a Third World nation of enormous potential
- OPEC, the troubles that come with instant wealth
- Harry Truman, controversial President in critical post-war period, 1945–52
- Pope John XXIII and the New Catholicism

3. Start your own research paper now, following these steps:

   1. Choose a subject—one of the above or any other that meets the requirements of this course (also see the list in Review Question 2;

2. go to three or more background sources and find two to five potentially workable topics (record the titles of the sources, and take some notes as you read through them);

3. select the topic that seems most interesting and/or most workable.

3
Using the Library

After you have chosen a research topic and formed a hypothesis, you are ready to take the next step: finishing your list of sources dealing with your topic. You began your list by noting possible items you found listed in bibliographies of general reference works you read when choosing your topic. To add to the list, you must search for sources on a wider scale, and this means becoming familiar with the resources and services of your library. Find out what materials your library has on hand. Investigate whether you can use the services of your library to locate sources in other libraries.

Working with Librarians

One of the most valuable sources of information in a library is the reference librarian. It is a good idea to introduce yourself early to the reference librarian and to describe your project briefly. Librarians are professionals. They are trained not only to manage libraries but also to keep abreast of existing sources. Their job is to help people with research projects on any subject. This expert can tell you about any special resources your library offers and can often help you to solve problems quickly that might take hours to solve on your own. The research librarian might even have helped someone else working on a topic related to yours and could give you tips and suggestions leading you to valuable sources you might otherwise miss.

Nevertheless, you must remember that although most librarians are quite willing to assist you with your research, they are not obliged to do your research paper for you. Do not go to the librarian and announce, "I have a paper to do for my American history course, but I don't know what to write about. Can you help me to get some books?" The librarian has not attended your classes or read your textbooks and cannot invent a topic for you. If you are at a loss for a topic, see your instructor, not your librarian.

Kinds of Sources

In your research you will be working mainly with books and periodicals. (A periodical is a publication that appears regularly under the same title: *Washington Post, Newsweek, Science News, Publications of the Modern Language Association [PMLA]*, and so on.) Books are cataloged and shelved in one way, periodicals in another, and most of this chapter describes how to find sources of each kind.

Although many students think of library research as being limited only to books, periodical articles offer several important advantages. Periodicals can be more current. A book takes many months or even years to write, and months more to be published, so that it may be at least partly out of date by the time it first appears, and still more so by the time you read it. Articles can be published much more quickly, so in some fields where information and interpretations change rapidly, such as science and technology, articles have replaced books as the primary way professionals exchange information and ideas. Even in fields such as history and literature you need to check the periodical indexes to make sure your research is up to date. And subjects in current affairs, such as *government energy policy* and the *Equal Rights Amendment*, will have to be heavily researched in such periodicals as newspapers, news magazines, and journals of political commentary.

Another frequent advantage of periodical articles is their depth. They usually focus on a specific topic in a narrower but more detailed way than a book. For example, a book about the world's food supply might include a chapter on innovative proposals for increasing agricultural production, and only a paragraph or two might be about "farming" the ocean floor. But in your library you can probably read several recent articles on ocean farming which cover the topic in much greater detail and depth. Furthermore, since a periodical article usually focuses on a specific topic, its title can often tell you exactly what that topic is, and you save time in your search for relevant sources. If you were planning a paper on ocean farming, titles like these would immediately catch your eye:

"A Proposal for Implementing Ocean Farming Off the Southeastern Coast of the United States"

"Ocean Farming: The Crop Will Not Cover the Cost"

In addition to books and periodicals, your library probably has materials available on microfilm—film on which books, periodicals, indexes, and other sources are reproduced in miniature. To read microfilm, you use a special machine that expands the tiny print and projects it onto a screen for easy viewing. In some libraries an aide is in charge of setting up the microfilm reader. In other libraries you can load the reader yourself, following instructions posted nearby. Using such readers is simple, and you should get the hang of how to operate one after a couple of attempts.

Your library may also contain unpublished sources such as manuscripts, letters, and business and personal diaries that can prove valuable in certain kinds of research projects.

In addition, most libraries carry non-print sources such as sound recordings and pictorial material. The reference librarian knows what special sources the library holds and whether or not these sources will help you in your research.

Library Systems—Traditional and Computerized

In all fields where the storage and retrieval of information play important roles, computers are becoming increasingly valuable tools. So it is with libraries. Take time to find out just what computer-assisted services your library offers to make your search for sources easier and more efficient.

Because technological change occurs at different rates across the country, libraries in the 1980s are in different stages of computerization. Your school library may be one of those in the process of transferring traditional systems to computerized ones, leaving you to discover—in cooperation with your instructors and librarians—how computers can help your research. We expect that most large libraries will eventually carry out their main information storage and search procedures electronically. More likely, however, your school library maintains much of its traditional system while adding computerized systems for special purposes.

We write on the assumption that, for the most part, the basic concepts and tools of the traditional system—card catalogs and periodical indexes, for example—will form the essentials of computerized systems, and that a working knowledge of these tools prepares you to use present and future computer systems.

The Library Card Catalog

You are probably already familiar with the card catalog. This catalog is an alphabetical index, usually made up of three- by five-inch file cards, but sometimes published in book form, that contains information about all the books in the library. Actually the card catalog has more cards than the library has books because at least two cards, and often more, are filed, each with a different way of presenting information about a book:

1. an *author* card
2. a *title* card
3. one or more *subject* cards (optional)
4. *cross-reference* cards (optional)

In some libraries the author and title cards are in one set of cabinet drawers and the subject cards in another. In other libraries all the cards are interfiled.

All books are listed under more than one heading. For example, in one library, you will find cards for Bruce Catton's *Grant Takes Command* under these headings:

1. (author) CATTON, Bruce
2. (title) *Grant Takes Command*
3. (subject) Grant, Ulysses S. (1822–85)
4. (subject) Civil War—Military Leaders

FINDING A CARD

When you are compiling a list of sources, which card should you consult first? You will often begin looking for subject cards whose subjects are related to your topic. For example, if you are looking for sources about the Civil War, you might first look under "Civil War." There you will probably find only a cross-reference card telling you to look under "U.S.—HISTORY—CIVIL WAR." Looking under the letter U in the subject cards, you will find a number of cards like the one in Figure 3–1.

Subject heading is typed at the top of the card.

> E
> 468   U.S.--HISTORY--CIVIL WAR
> R27   Randall, James Garfield, 1881-1953.
>   The divided Union ₍by₎ J. G. Randall ₍and₎ David Donald
>   Boston, Little, Brown ₍1961₎
>
>   xvi, 572 p. illus., ports, maps. 24 cm
>   Based on "the late J. G. Randall's The Civil War and Reconstruction."
>   Bibliography: p. ₍533₎-548.
>
>
>   1. U.S.–Hist.–Civil War.   I. Randall, James Garfield, 1881-1953.
>   The Civil War and Reconstruction.   II. Donald, David Herbert, 1920–
>   III. Title.
>
>   E468.R27   973.7   61-9295

Figure 3–1. A subject card

If your topic is more specific, such as Jefferson Davis, you would probably do better to look for a subject card on Davis himself: "Davis, Jefferson, 1808–89."

To locate an author card, look in the author catalog under the first letter of the author's last name; then, if necessary, use his or her other names. The author card for *The Divided Union* is shown in Figure 3–2.

Except for the heading, the author card is identical to the subject card. It is filed under the heading, the author's name.

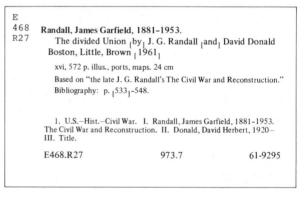

> E
> 468   Randall, James Garfield, 1881-1953.
> R27   The divided Union ₍by₎ J. G. Randall ₍and₎ David Donald
>   Boston, Little, Brown ₍1961₎
>   xvi, 572 p. illus., ports, maps. 24 cm
>   Based on "the late J. G. Randall's The Civil War and Reconstruction."
>   Bibliography: p. ₍533₎-548.
>
>
>   1. U.S.–Hist.–Civil War.   I. Randall, James Garfield, 1881-1953.
>   The Civil War and Reconstruction.   II. Donald, David Herbert, 1920–
>   III. Title.
>
>   E468.R27   973.7   61-9295

Figure 3–2. An author card

The author card looks virtually the same as the subject card, except that it lacks the subject heading typed across the top. It is filed under *Randall*.

To locate a title card, look for the first word in the title of the book, omitting the words *A*, *An*, or *The*.

The title card looks the same as the author card except that the title is typed across the top. It is filed under *Divided Union*—not under *The*. See Figure 3–3.

The title card is
identical to subject and
author cards except for
the title typed at its top.

```
E        The divided Union.
468      Randall, James Garfield, 1881-1953.
R27          The divided Union ₁by₁ J. G. Randall ₍and₎ David Donald
         Boston, Little, Brown ₍1961₎

             xvi, 572 p. illus., ports, maps. 24 cm
             Based on "the late J. G. Randall's The Civil War and Reconstruction."
             Bibliography: p. ₍533₎-548.


             1. U.S.–Hist.–Civil War.   I. Randall, James Garfield, 1881-1853.
             The Civil War and Reconstruction.  II. Donald, David Herbert, 1920–
             III. Title.

             E468.R27                   973.7                   61-9295
```

Figure 3–3. A title card

Here are two alphabetical rules that might save you some time.

1. Abbreviations are alphabetized as if they were spelled out. For example, *St.* is filed under *Saint*.

2. *Mc*, as in *McAllister*, is alphabetized as if it were spelled *Mac*.

The card catalog most likely also includes cross-reference cards that list subject headings under which you can find related materials. Look for a cross-reference or "see also" card, such as that in Figure 3–4, at the end of a set of subject cards.

If you were interested
only in the Civil War,
you would not consult
"Reconstruction
period" or
"PRESIDENTS."

```
         GRANT, Ulysses S.    (1822-85)

             see also

         U.S.--HISTORY--CIVIL WAR
            Military leaders
            Reconstruction period
         U.S.--PRESIDENTS
```

Figure 3–4. A cross-reference or "see also" card

A cross-reference card can lead you to sources that you might otherwise miss. For example, let's say you are planning a paper on the topic *Grant's new style of warfare*. A book titled *Lincoln Finds a General* could be quite useful, for the book deals with Lincoln's search for a commander who would wage the war in a particular way—and of course Grant was his choice. This book, however, might well be found in the subject cards only under "CIVIL WAR—Military Leaders" and not under "GRANT." Consult the cross-reference cards; you can discover valuable sources.

UNDERSTANDING A CATALOG CARD

The organization of information on a catalog card is standardized, so if you understand the format and the significance of the various pieces of information, the card can help you. On the following author card, ten key pieces of information are identified. See Figure 3–5.

Three items—call number, author's name, and book title—are essential to your search for sources. The remaining seven items may also be useful to you when you evaluate sources for possible use in your research paper.

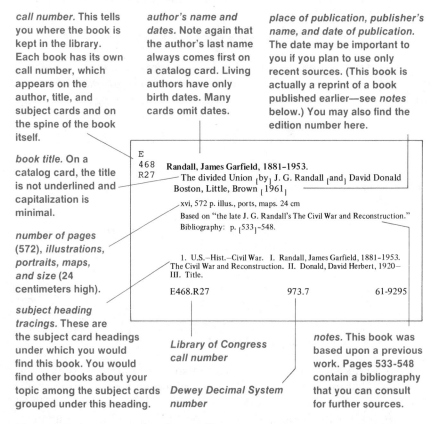

call number. This tells you where the book is kept in the library. Each book has its own call number, which appears on the author, title, and subject cards and on the spine of the book itself.

book title. On a catalog card, the title is not underlined and capitalization is minimal.

number of pages (572), *illustrations, portraits, maps, and size* (24 centimeters high).

subject heading tracings. These are the subject card headings under which you would find this book. You would find other books about your topic among the subject cards grouped under this heading.

author's name and dates. Note again that the author's last name always comes first on a catalog card. Living authors have only birth dates. Many cards omit dates.

place of publication, publisher's name, and date of publication. The date may be important to you if you plan to use only recent sources. (This book is actually a reprint of a book published earlier—see *notes* below.) You may also find the edition number here.

```
E
468    Randall, James Garfield, 1881–1953.
R27       The divided Union ₍by₎ J. G. Randall ₍and₎ David Donald
          Boston, Little, Brown ₍1961₎
          xvi, 572 p. illus., ports, maps. 24 cm
          Based on "the late J. G. Randall's The Civil War and Reconstruction."
          Bibliography: p. ₍533₎–548.

          1. U.S.–Hist.–Civil War.  I. Randall, James Garfield, 1881–1953.
          The Civil War and Reconstruction. II. Donald, David Herbert, 1920–
          III. Title.

          E468.R27                         973.7              61-9295
```

Library of Congress call number

Dewey Decimal System number

notes. This book was based upon a previous work. Pages 533-548 contain a bibliography that you can consult for further sources.

Figure 3–5. An annotated author card

COMPUTERIZED CATALOGS

A knowledge of the traditional card catalog system should make it easy for you to use catalogs that are arranged and maintained by computers. If your library owns a Computer Output Microfilm Catalog (COMCAT), then printed catalog cards may no longer be used in your library. Instead, card catalog information has been put on microfilm and you will have to use a microfilm reader to search for sources. The COMCAT readers may be in a special room, or they may be placed in strategic spots throughout the library. Instructions about how to use the microfilm catalog will be posted on or near each reader.

For the most part, the information you see on a microfilm catalog reader will be similar to that found on a traditional file card in a card catalog. If you bring *Writing Research Papers* with you when you use the microfilm catalog the first time, you should be able to identify the various pieces of information that the microfilm reader projects about a source. The placement of information may differ a bit from the traditional format of a card catalog file card, but you should have no trouble in spotting the call number and the other information you need to find the source you want.

However, not all libraries that have COMCAT have transferred their complete catalog to microfilm. Thus, you may find yourself using both COMCAT and the traditional card catalog in the course of your research. Your librarian will be able to tell you which will be most helpful to you, given your particular topic. And even if your library has gone completely to COMCAT, there may be a gap of several months before new library acquisitions are listed in the microfilm system. If you do not locate the information about a recent source, check with the librarian. The information you need may be filed in a special place, awaiting the update period to be incorporated into the microfilm catalog.

Some libraries have replaced the traditional card catalog with on-line computer catalogs. *On-line* means that a computer directly taps information in one or more data bases. A data base is a collection of printed materials, such as periodical indexes, scientific abstracts, and government reports that have been fed into the memory bank of a central computer. This means that all that printed material can be recalled electronically by a person using a computer in a library that has a ''hookup'' or is ''on-line'' with the central computer.

When you use a computer terminal instead of alphabetized file cards, you type in requests on the keyboard, asking the computer about one or more sources at a time, depending upon how the system is programmed. The computer's response appears on the screen. If your library does not have the material you want, the computer lets you know. If your library does have it, the on-screen information will be similar to what you would find in card catalogs. But the computer searches through data far more quickly than you can when you flip through a card catalog.

A library's on-line system may be connected to data bases that provide information about the holdings in other libraries, especially the libraries of colleges and universities that form a state system. This hookup can tell a researcher if another school's library has a source unavailable in his school library. In more extensive on-line systems, a library's computer system may subscribe to data bases covering the holdings in libraries in many parts of the country.

On-line systems connected to outside data bases allow for computer searches. A computer search—typed pages containing the information you would see on the screen—provides a researcher with a printout of possible sources, including the names and locations of the libraries where each of the items is available. Such searches are usually ordered by professionals or graduate students undertaking a research project that might require looking at hundreds of sources and would result in an article for a scholarly or technical journal or in a book or a dissertation. A computer search must be carried out by a computer expert, and a researcher generally pays a hefty fee for the expert's time and for the time the computer takes to perform the search.

Sources available in the college or in nearby libraries, as well as sources available in various institutions in the community, should provide the undergraduate researcher with ample materials to carry out a successful research project.

Locating Books

Once you have decided which books you should read, locating those books within the library is relatively easy.

STACKS

Some libraries allow you to enter the *stacks*—the shelves where the books are kept; others do not. In order to get books in libraries where stacks are closed to you, you must fill out a *call slip* and give it to a library employee, who will find the book and give it to you. On the call slip, you supply basic information which you copy from the catalog card for the book.

CALL NUMBERS

In the stacks books are shelved according to the call numbers you found given with each book's name. Call numbers are of two major classification systems: the *Library of Congress* or the *Dewey Decimal*.

The Library of Congress system uses a combination of letters and numbers to arrange books by subject area and within the subject area. The Dewey Decimal system uses numbers to designate major subject areas, and then a combination of letters and numbers to designate subdivisions under the major classifications. You do not have to memorize the codes for the system your library uses, and you need no specialized knowledge to use it yourself. However, if you have access to the stacks, familiarizing yourself with the call numbers for your particular field will enable you not only to locate the books you have found listed in the card catalog, but also to browse in appropriate sections for other books that may prove valuable. As always, your librarian is the professional to turn to if you have any problems understanding the organization and location of materials in the library.

BOOKS ON RESERVE

Most college libraries have a *reserve reading room* or a *reserve shelf*. In this area you find books that instructors have asked a librarian to pull out of the stacks and set aside for particular classes. However, the books remain available for anyone to use, with certain restrictions. A book placed on reserve must be checked out only for use in the library, or, at best, can be taken out overnight.

When a book is put on reserve, a librarian usually notes that on the catalog cards that list the book. Should you discover that a book you need for your research has been put on reserve, plan to read it and take notes on it in the library. Try to use reserve books as early in the term as possible, for you can be sure that other students will soon be competing with you to consult the same books.

Periodical Indexes

Titles of specific articles published in periodicals are not listed in the library's card catalog but in guides known as *periodical indexes*. Recent articles are cataloged at intervals throughout the year in paperbound supplements to the past year's index. At the end of the year complete annual indexes appear as one or two hardbound volumes. These volumes, as well as the periodical supplements, are usually kept available on shelves or tables in the reference room of the library and must be used there.

In a periodical index you will find subject entries and, sometimes, author entries, condensed into abbreviations to save space. The indexes are not standardized. Different indexes use different formats and abbreviations and include somewhat different amounts and kinds of information. At the beginning of each volume each abbreviation is explained; you should consult these explanations before using the index. In this chapter you will have a chance to examine typical entries.

Once you have found an index entry for an article that promises to be a good source for your paper, you need to find out whether your library has a copy of the periodical in which that article appeared. In some libraries, periodicals the library subscribes to are listed, alphabetically by title, in the card catalog or in a separate periodicals card catalog. In others, you might consult pamphlets, loose pages at the main desk, or computer printouts. Whatever system your library uses, find out from the librarian how it operates.

The library's periodical list normally tells you how long the library has been accumulating issues of each magazine, so you will need to see if the dates you want are covered. The list also gives the location in the library of each periodical and will usually indicate if some or all issues are available only on microfilm.

Types of Periodicals

Periodicals fall into two broad categories—popular and professional—according to their intended audiences. Within each category you may have to use several indexes, most of which you will find in the reference room of your library.

Some of the most frequently used indexes to periodicals are the following:

popular periodicals (magazines and newspapers)	*Readers' Guide to Periodical Literature* *New York Times Index* *Book Review Digest*
professional periodicals (often called journals)	*Humanities Index* *Social Sciences Index*

In addition, many indexes have been published for periodicals in specific fields, such as art, medicine, and psychology. (A list for your convenience is provided at the end of this chapter.)

Indexes to Popular Periodicals

THE *READERS' GUIDE TO PERIODICAL LITERATURE*

The *Readers' Guide to Periodical Literature*, or *Readers' Guide*, is an index to articles on a wide variety of subjects published in periodicals aimed at a cross section of American readers. Some periodicals, such as *Newsweek, Reader's Digest,* and *National Geographic,* appeal to general interests; others, such as *Aviation Week, Business Week,* and *Art in America,* appeal to special interests. Here is a sampling of the 175 magazines indexed by *Readers' Guide* and the subjects they cover:

The American City—architecture, city planning, urban problems

Atlantic Monthly—current affairs, short fiction

Consumer Reports—evaluations of the performances of commercial products for the general consumer

Cosmopolitan—features, fashions, primarily for career women

Ebony—features, fashions, of particular interest to black readers

Foreign Affairs—political topics, aimed at readers up on current events

House and Garden—architecture, interior decoration, landscaping

National Review—political issues, aimed at politically conservative audience

New Republic—political issues, aimed at politically liberal or moderate audience

Psychology Today—reports on recent research in all branches of psychology, designed for the general reader

Scientific American—reports of recent scientific research, aimed at scientifically informed readers

Sports Illustrated—sports and excellent photographs for the general public

Time—news items from the current week for the general public

United Nations Monthly Chronicle—issues pertaining to the work of the United Nations

Vital Speeches of the Day—transcripts for those who want to know *exactly* what was said

The *Readers' Guide* has been published, since 1900, as a series, each volume covering one or more years (the *Guide* year currently runs from March through February). (If you need material from the nineteenth century, go to *Poole's Index to Periodical Literature*, which covers 1802 to 1906.) Consult the *Readers' Guide* for social science subjects—modern history, economics, political science, and sociology. It is especially valuable for topics that concern public reaction to an event at the time it was happening, such as Franklin Roosevelt's attempt to alter the composition of the Supreme Court, and for the latest articles on current events not yet included in books, such as changing attitudes toward old age in the United States from 1970 to the present.

For scientific topics the *Readers' Guide* offers relatively few useful sources. Scientific subjects were not even included in this index until 1953. Because magazines for the general public must avoid highly technical discussions, their science writers may oversimplify and occasionally distort some of the ideas they present. (Remember Anita's experience with the longevity article.) If you begin your investigation of a scientific topic with a popular magazine, be sure to turn to books and scholarly journals that deal with the same topic in more depth and detail.

The *Readers' Guide* lists both authors and subjects alphabetically. Regardless of whether you are looking for a subject or an author, use this index as you would a dictionary.

For example, if you were looking for articles published in the last ten years on a particular subject—say, the siege of Vicksburg—you would look at several volumes of the *Guide,* checking listings under "Civil War." In the 1977–1978 *Guide,* you would find the cross-reference shown in Figure 3–6.

CIVIL service pensions
Burden of generosity. L. Aspin; discussion.
Harpers 254:4 + F '77
Rising cost of public pensions—can taxpayers
afford them? il U.S. News 82:84-6 Ja 24 '77
Washington memo; key Republicans urge merger
with Civil Service Retirement Fund to save
social security. R. D. Westgate, Ret Liv 17:
60-2 N '77
See also
Municipal employees—Pensions

Finance
See Pensions—Finance
CIVIL war
See also
Lebanon—Civil War, 1975-
Spain—History—Civil War, 1936-1939
CIVIL War (United States) See United States—
History—Civil War, 1861-1865
CIVILIZATION
Terror of the wilderness; spread of Western
civilization; excerpt from The cost of living.
F. Turner. il Am Heritage 28:58-65 F '77
Toward a day of reckoning: the poor vs. the
rich worlds. H. Brown. Current 191:23-9 Mr '77
Tutankhamun and Star trek; address, July 29,
1977. C. L. Babcock. Vital Speeches 43:744-7
O 1 '77
Visions of futures past; Lindisfarne Association.
S. Helgesen. il Harpers 254:80-6 Mr '77
See also
Acculturation
Animals and civilization
History
Popular culture
Renaissance
Social change
Social sciences
Technology and civilization
also subhead Civilization under names of
countries, e.g. France—Civilization

The *Guide* directs you to another heading to find articles on the Civil War. The *Guide* uses the same subject headings as the library card catalog.

Figure 3–6. From the *Readers' Guide*

Following the cross-reference directions of the *Guide,* you would turn to the "United States—History" heading, find "Civil War, 1861–1865—Campaigns and battles" subheading, and copy the information you need (Figure 3-7).

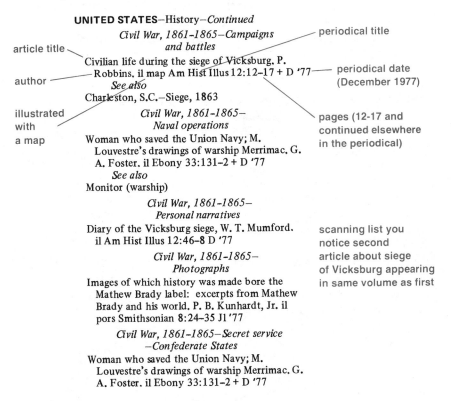

UNITED STATES–History–*Continued*

article title — *Civil War, 1861–1865–Campaigns and battles* — periodical title

Civilian life during the siege of Vicksburg. P.
author — Robbins. il map Am Hist Illus 12:12–17 + D '77 — periodical date
See also — (December 1977)
Charleston, S.C.–Siege, 1863

illustrated with a map — *Civil War, 1861–1865–Naval operations* — pages (12-17 and continued elsewhere in the periodical)
Woman who saved the Union Navy; M.
Louvestre's drawings of warship Merrimac. G.
A. Foster. il Ebony 33:131–2 + D '77
See also
Monitor (warship)

Civil War, 1861–1865–Personal narratives
Diary of the Vicksburg siege, W. T. Mumford.
il Am Hist Illus 12:46–8 D '77 — scanning list you notice second article about siege of Vicksburg appearing in same volume as first

Civil War, 1861–1865–Photographs
Images of which history was made bore the
Mathew Brady label: excerpts from Mathew
Brady and his world. P. B. Kunhardt, Jr. il
pors Smithsonian 8:24–35 Jl '77

*Civil War, 1861–1865–Secret service
–Confederate States*
Woman who saved the Union Navy; M.
Louvestre's drawings of warship Merrimac. G.
A. Foster. il Ebony 33:131–2 + D '77

Figure 3–7. From the *Readers' Guide*

To find an author's work in the *Readers' Guide,* look alphabetically for the author's last name. Under the author's name you will find all articles by the author arranged alphabetically according to title, disregarding *A, An,* and *The.* (The word *about* above an author's name indicates that the author is the subject of an article written by someone else.)

THE *MAGAZINE INDEX*

This index covers articles from more than 400 magazines. It is available in some libraries as part of the computer system and in other libraries as a microform system. The microform system consists of a console with a large viewing screen and an operating knob. You need only turn the knob to move the microform swiftly in search of subjects or authors, both indexed alphabetically. The *Magazine Index* is most useful for locating articles that have appeared in magazines during the past five or six years. However, because the index provides information from so many magazines, it includes publications that your instructor may think inappropriate for serious research. Check with your instructor or your librarian if you have any doubts about the research value of a magazine with which you are unfamiliar. In addition, your library will almost certainly subscribe to only a relatively small percentage of the 400 magazines.

THE *NEW YORK TIMES INDEX*

The *New York Times* is generally agreed by professionals in all fields to be the most important newspaper in the United States. You can find listed, in annual volumes of the *New York Times Index*, all major news accounts and feature articles that have appeared in the *Times* since 1913, arranged alphabetically according to subject. To locate articles on a specific topic or event, select the volumes that cover the relevant time period and then look alphabetically in the volumes for the subject. To check the *Index* for very recent events, use the supplements published every two weeks. At the year's end, these supplements are republished as the new annual volume of the *Index*.

Newspaper articles are particularly useful for topics that require you to know precisely what facts and impressions were reported at the time an event occurred or to sample public opinion over a particular period of time. Here are some examples of such topics:

attitudes toward Prohibition at the time the Eighteenth Amendment was being ratified (1917–19)

reactions throughout the South to the Supreme Court decision of 1954 outlawing segregation in public schools

the extent to which the American public was misinformed about the testing of atomic bombs in Nevada after World War II

While researching public opinion preceding an event, such as an election or the ratification of a constitutional amendment, be sure to check the *Index* volume that covers not only the calendar year of the event but also the previous year, especially if the event took place early in its year. Similarly, when investigating the reactions to an event, check the *Index* volume for the year of the event and the following year.

Even if your library does not subscribe to the *Times* on microfilm, consult the *New York Times Index* for the year the event occurred; then you can find the exact days on which important events were reported. Use those dates to locate information in newspapers that your library does have, since most newspapers usually publish important stories at the same time. Every daily issue of the *New York Times*, beginning with the very first in 1851, has been reproduced in microfilm, and many libraries have a complete set. Find the date, section, and page number of a particular news item in the *Index*, then request a filmstrip of the *Times* for that date, and run it through a microfilm viewer.

The *New York Times Index* offers another convenient feature: its brief summaries of many articles may help you decide whether to spend time searching for and reading a particular story.

Figure 3-8 shows a sample from the *New York Times Index*. The entry, "DAVIS, Jefferson," in the annual bound volume of the *New York Times Index* for 1977 indicates that two articles about Jefferson Davis appeared in the newspaper in 1977. Notice that the birth date given for Davis here

an article dealing with restoration of Davis's citizenship appeared in section IV, page 9, column 4 of the April 24 issue of the *Times*; "(S)" indicates article was short; medium-length articles are identified "(M)," long articles by "(L)"

an article about the FBI's recovery of objects that once belonged to Davis appeared in May ("My"), on the fifteenth ("15"), on page 51 ("51"), in the third column (":3"); "(S)" indicates article was short

DAVIS, I G. **See also** Gambling–NJ, Mr 3, My 5, Je 3
DAVIS, Issa, **See also** Fires–NYC, Jl 16
DAVIS, J B, **See also** Culture–US, N 3
DAVIS, James (Suspect), **See also** Murders–NYC, Aguilles, Christian (Ptl), Mr 21
DAVIS, Jefferson (1809–89)
   Sen Judiciary Com approves bill restoring Jefferson Davis's citizenship (S), Ap 24, IV, 9:4; FBI recovers Jefferson Davis's pipe and case, which was stolen from display at Casement Museum, Ft Monroe, Va, 6 days ago and found in Augusta, Ga, in hands of private individual; no arrests reptd (S), My 15,51:3
DAVIS, John H. **See also** Straus, Roger W Jr, N 27
DAVIS, John M (Judge). **See also** King, M L, Jl 16
DAVIS, John W 3d (Judge). **See also** Wallace, George Corley (Gov). S 24, Wallace, George Corley (Mrs). N. J. Wallace, George Corley (Gov). D 6
DAVIS, Joseph (Prisoner). **See also** Capital Punishment, S 8 Murders–California, N 19 Murders–NYS, Woods, Harold (Ptl), S 8, N 16 D 10.20
DAVIS, Karen (Dr). **See also** Brookings Institution, Ap 3. Med–US, Ja 6, N 8, Med–US–Health Insurance, Ja 2
DAVIS, Leon. **See also** Housing–NYC–Cooperatives, F 28
DAVIS, Lewis Carlton. **See also** Ballet Theater Foundation, Je 13
DAVIS, Lynn. **See also** US–Defense Dept. Ja 22
DAVIS, Margy-Ruth, **See also** USSR–Pol. Ap 20
DAVIS, Mark. **See also** Murders–NYC, Robinson, Steven, Jl 13
DAVIS, Martha. **See also** Drug addiction–NYC–Therapy, O 24,25
DAVIS, Martin S. **See also** Athena Communications Corp. Jl 25, Gulf & Western Industries Inc. Jl 26
DAVIS, Martin S. **See also** Baseball–AL, Oakland Athletics, D 15,16.24,29,31
DAVIS, Mendel J (Repr). **See also** Louisiana–Elections, O 5
DAVIS, Michael (Ford Motor Co). **See also** Transit Systems–US, Ag 28
DAVIS, Michael (Shipping Exec). **See also** Antiques, O 20

Figure 3–8. From the *New York Times Index*

(1809) differs from that correctly given (1808) on page 12 in the encyclopedia article, probably the result of a printing error. If this sort of information is important to your research, be sure to go to a third source.

The *New York Times Index* is most useful for social science subjects,
such as modern history, economics, and political science. The *Times* also
reports extensively on literature and the arts.

THE *NEWSPAPER INDEX*

A valuable addition to periodical guides is the *Newspaper Index*, which
began publication in 1972. This index provides information on articles
that have appeared in four of the nation's largest newspapers: the *Chicago Tribune*, the *Los Angeles Times*, the *New Orleans Times-Picayune*, and
the *Washington Post*. As you might gather from the titles of the newspapers included, this index can be especially useful for looking up regional
news and opinion, as well as national and international news.

THE *BOOK REVIEW DIGEST*

The *Book Review Digest* publishes excerpts from book reviews that appeared within a year after a book was first published. The *Book Review Digest* does not cite every published review, but only a sample of critical responses, both favorable and unfavorable.

Each annual volume of this digest (beginning in 1905) indexes reviews
of several thousand books, according to both title and author. To use the
Book Review Digest, you need to know the year in which a book was first
published. Then you should look up the title or the author in the volumes both for that year and for the next year because some books are not
reviewed during the calendar year in which they are published: a book
published in November 1966, for example, might not have been reviewed until January 1967.

The *Book Review Digest* presents the initial critical reactions to a book,
helpful especially if you wish to compare immediate responses with later
judgments made by critics and scholars after the work has had a chance
to influence other writers or after public tastes have changed. Examples
of research assignments requiring you to use the *Digest* would be "Initial
Critical Reactions to Ernest Hemingway's *The Sun Also Rises*," and
"Changing Critical Evaluations of Willa Cather's *My Antonia*."

The *Book Review Digest*'s value is not limited to literary topics. For example, you might want to know how reviewers reacted to a book that
presented a new view of a well-known person or event or that unveiled a
new social or scientific theory, such as evolution, relativity, or psychoanalysis.

Finally, check a book you want to use as a source in the *Book Review Digest*; you can find out very easily whether the reviewers thought that book informative and reliable.

Indexes to Scholarly and Professional Journals

THE *HUMANITIES INDEX* AND THE *SOCIAL SCIENCES INDEX*

These two indexes may well provide an undergraduate with all the sources needed for research papers in the social sciences or the humanities. These indexes are more specialized than those discussed so far, for each indexes not general magazines but scholarly journals in a variety of fields.

Since 1974 the *Humanities Index* and *Social Sciences Index* have appeared as separate volumes. From 1965 to 1974 the two indexes were combined in the *Social Sciences and Humanities Index*, and from 1920 to 1965 its title was the *International Index to Periodicals*. From 1907 through 1919 the single index was titled *Readers' Guide Supplement and International Index*.

Together, the *Humanities Index* and the *Social Sciences Index* cover articles published in more than 500 scholarly and professional journals. (Many of these journals, however, are not available in small libraries.) The *Humanities Index* lists articles according to subject in the following academic disciplines:

archaeology
classical studies
area studies
folklore
history (not included until 1974)
language and literature

literary and political criticism
performing arts
philosophy
religion
theology

The *Social Sciences Index* lists articles according to subject in the following academic disciplines:

anthropology
area studies
economics
environmental science
education
law and criminology

medical science
political sciences
psychology (not included between
    1945 and 1974)
public administration
sociology

SPECIALIZED INDEXES

The *Humanities Index* and the *Social Sciences Index*, though highly valuable resources, cover only a small fraction of all the scholarly and professional journals published in the humanities and the social sciences. Because the number of specialized scholarly articles published each year is enormous, each field has its own annual index to specialized periodicals. Even so, areas such as English literature cannot be contained within a single annual index, so there are still more specialized indexes.

All of the indexes to scholarly and professional journals will lead you to very difficult materials. Most authors of scholarly articles are writing for fellow experts and therefore assume that their readers have a strong background in the field; many articles focus on very narrow topics and employ a highly specialized terminology. You may find much scholarly writing hard to understand, but you should become acquainted with such materials and perhaps work through an article with your instructor so you can incorporate some specialized scholarly sources into your research paper if such sources strengthen your thesis. Later in college, especially in your major field, the information in scholarly journals will become increasingly accessible and valuable to you.

At the end of this chapter is a selective list of indexes to scholarly and professional journals in many major fields. If you need to find additional sources, consult the *Bibliographic Index: A Cumulative Bibliography of Bibliographies*. This work briefly describes all the periodical indexes you will probably ever need.

Locating Periodicals

Most libraries have a periodical room where you can find the current issue of each magazine and newspaper to which the library subscribes. Most of your research, however, will involve back (previous) issues, and these may be kept elsewhere.

Libraries usually have back issues of periodical magazines and journals gathered by year—or, if the periodical is published very often or is bulky, into shorter periods—and permanently rebound in hard covers. These bound volumes are then shelved chronologically, either in the periodical room or in the stacks. Back issues that are not in the periodical room may be in the library offices awaiting rebinding or actually at the bindery; ask a librarian for any issues you cannot find.

Back issues of daily and weekly newspapers are kept unbound for one or more years. Then, in many libraries, they are thrown away. However, the Sunday magazine and book review sections may be kept much longer and may be bound for permanent storage. A librarian at your library can tell you what its policy is.

Additional Resources

Although you can produce a fine research paper based entirely on books and periodicals found through the card catalog and the major periodical indexes, there are other resources both in the library and outside it where you may find still more information and ideas.

IN THE LIBRARY

Specialized Collections. Some libraries maintain separate special collections of materials such as books, periodicals, personal letters, and manuscripts. A special collection sometimes relates to special areas of interest: a particular author's works, the history of a particular place, or a fairly narrow field (cave exploration, Broadway musicals, or aviation engineering). Other special collections are kept separate from the main collection because their holdings are fragile, rare, or otherwise unusual. The catalog for each special collection is usually separate and kept in a special section of the library.

Microforms. To save space, save wear and tear on delicate holdings, and increase usefulness, many source materials have been preserved on microforms, mainly microfilm or microfiche. The most common resources on microforms are periodicals; others include old and rare books and even facsimiles of manuscripts. Some sources, such as graduate dissertations, may be published only on microforms.

Vertical File Index. Some printed sources may not be classified either as books or as periodicals, and so will not appear in either the card catalog or the periodical indexes. Such materials include pamphlets, brochures, and clippings from hard-to-get periodicals on specialized topics. You can find these resources by using the Vertical File Index. A librarian can explain how to use this index.

Audiovisual Materials. Many libraries now contain media sections which house films, videotapes, pictures, slides, and sound recordings. If your topic concerns the performing or visual arts, architecture, or the social or natural sciences, you will often find materials useful to your research in the audiovisual collection. In addition to materials on the arts, you can find valuable documentaries, especially in those fields having to do with human and animal behavior and society.

Interlibrary Loan. If you discover a source which you believe to be crucial to your research, and your library does not have a copy of it, you may be able to borrow the source through an interlibrary loan arranged by a librarian. (**Warning:** It normally takes several weeks for the source to arrive at your library, and it may take longer. Allow sufficient time for the loan to be arranged.)

OUTSIDE THE LIBRARY

Other Libraries. Large colleges and universities may have separate, specialized libraries attached to particular graduate schools or departments, such as law, medicine, engineering, music, and art. Off campus, museums and professional societies devoted to such fields often operate their own small but excellent libraries. You may have to apply formally to use such facilities; often simply verifying your school affiliation will be enough. The public library in your city may also be a useful resource. Some, like the New York Public Library, are among the greatest research facilities in the world, but even the most modest public library may have the particular periodical or book you need.

Special Printed Materials. Private businesses, nonprofit organizations, special interest groups, and various levels of government publish reports and pamphlets in great numbers. Usually these materials can be obtained free of charge by writing to the organizations. In most cases there will be no catalog to which you can refer, so you may be able only to describe what you are looking for and hope the answer meets your needs. The United States Government Printing Office (GPO) *Monthly Catalog* lists all publications by the federal government that are available to the public, their prices, and the addresses from which they may be ordered. Your library should have a copy, and you can ask your librarian where it is kept. Be warned, however, that delivery is not overnight: one GPO distribution center in Pueblo, Colorado, alone handles some 80,000 requests every week, and you may wait a month or more for materials ordered.

Television and Radio Programs. The Public Broadcasting System (PBS) regularly presents documentaries about the performing and graphic arts and also the natural and social sciences. These programs are often repeated several times, so you may be able to watch broadcasts originally shown before you started your research project. If your topic has to do with a current issue, be alert for interviews and documentaries scheduled on any station. Transcripts of regularly scheduled news interviews are often available from the stations or networks that produce or broadcast them. Because transcripts usually require four to six weeks' delivery time, you will in most cases have to make your own transcription. If possible, record the program and later transcribe those portions of it you want to use word by word, rather than trying to take notes during the program.

Interviews. You may want to set up an interview with a person whose knowledge and opinions would be useful to your research project. Perhaps a faculty member is an authority on your topic, or a local public official administers a program relevant to your research. Depending upon your topic, you may well find that interviews with people who possess special knowledge or who have undergone unusual experiences will yield valuable information.

When you request a personal interview with someone who lives by a busy schedule, prepare the groundwork well. Always write or telephone ahead, informing the authority just why you want the meeting. Specify your field of inquiry as precisely as you can and explain why you think this interview can help you get a better grasp of the topic you are researching. Let the person know that you will limit the interview to a few pertinent questions that will not take up too much valuable time. It is a good idea to review your questions with your instructor. Forming brief questions that will bring out the kind of information you need is a kind of art, and you may need help the first time you plan for an interview. You might even offer to send the questions in advance for consideration before the actual interview. If you would like to bring a tape recorder to the interview, ask whether the potential interviewee minds. If there are objections, don't persist. Diplomatically state that taking notes will serve your recording purposes just as well. And be flexible in arranging the date and time of the interview. If you can arrange a mutually agreeable time, fine. If not, you will have to go out of your way to suit the authority's schedule.

The attitude you assume will be important to the success of your interview. Keep in mind that the authority is a research source, and that your main concern is to find out what the person knows or believes about some aspect of your topic. At the time of an interview you are gathering sources to test the hypothesis you have chosen to guide your research. This means that you have not yet arrived at a particular conclusion regarding your topic. Thus, your job is to listen carefully to the person's responses to your questions and to summarize major points in your notes. If you enter into an interview with a biased point of view, your "source" might catch the tone of your remarks and give you very little—if anything—in the way of useful information or opinion.

Finally, be sure to write a note thanking the person for the interview.

Questionnaires and Surveys. If your topic involves public opinion, particularly the opinions of a particular group such as college students or faculty, the parents of schoolchildren, or senior citizens, you may find that no published poll serves your purposes. Conduct a poll of your own. Whether you conduct your survey in person or by mail through questionnaires, your questions must be carefully stated to make sure that the answers are relevant and meaningful. You should probably ask your instructor to review your list of questions before you begin your poll.

Some General Bibliographies, Periodical Indexes, and Representative Journals

Here are some guides to sources which you will find in many college libraries and which you can use to develop your working bibliography. Also you know to consult the bibliographies that accompany articles in the general reference books you use for background reading.

ART AND ARCHITECTURE

Art Index, The: A Cumulative Author and Subject Index to a Selected List of Fine Art Periodicals. New York: H. W. Wilson, 1933–present. (Quarterly, with biennial cumulations.) In addition to fine arts, index includes architecture, design, and decorating journals.

ASTRONOMY

Sky and Telescope. Cambridge, MA: Sky Publishing, 1941–present. (Monthly.) Publication for non-specialists in astronomy: articles, observations, data, equipment guides, etc.

BIOGRAPHY

Biography Index, The: A Cumulative Index to Biographical Material in Books and Magazines. New York: H. W. Wilson, 1946–present. (Quarterly, with annual and triennial cumulations.)

BIOLOGICAL SCIENCES

Biological Abstracts. Philadelphia: Biosciences Information Service, 1926–present. (Bimonthly.) Abstracts and index of international publications, excludes clinical medicine.
Biological and Agricultural Index, The. New York: H. W. Wilson, 1964–present. (Monthly except August.) Subject index to periodicals about agriculture and biology.

BUSINESS

Business Periodicals Index. New York: H. W. Wilson, 1958–present. (Monthly, except July.)

CHEMISTRY

Chemical Abstracts: Key to the World's Chemical Literature. Washington, DC: American Chemical Society, 1907–present. (Weekly.)

DRAMA

Breed, Paul F., and Florence M. Sniderman. *Dramatic Criticism Index. A Bibliography of Commentaries on Playwrights from Ibsen to the Avant-Garde.* Detroit: Gale, 1972.

Cumulated Dramatic Index, 1909–1949. A Cumulation of the F. W. Faxon Company's Dramatic Index. Ed. Frederick W. Faxon, et al. 2 vols. Boston: G. K. Hall, 1965.

Play Index. 5 vols. New York: H. W. Wilson, 1953–78.

ECONOMICS

American Journal of Economics and Sociology. New York: American Journal of Economics and Sociology, 1941–present. (Quarterly.)

Hughes, Catherine, ed. *Economic Education: A Guide to Information Sources.* Detroit: Gale, 1977.

International Bibliography of Economics. Ed. UNESCO International Committee for Social Science Documentation. Chicago: Aldine, 1952–present. (Annual.)

EDUCATION

Current Index to Journals in Education. New York: Macmillan, 1969–present. (Monthly, with annual and semiannual cumulations.)

Education Index, The. New York: H. W. Wilson, 1929–present. (Monthly, except July and August, with annual cumulations.)

ENGINEERING

Applied Science and Technology Index. New York: H. W. Wilson, 1958–present. (Monthly.)

Engineering Index, The. Ed. American Society of Mechanical Engineers. New York: Engineering Index, 1934–present. (Monthly.)

Malinowsky, Harold R., et al. *Science and Engineering Literature: A Guide to Reference Sources.* 2nd ed. Littleton, CO: Libraries Unlimited, 1976.

ENVIRONMENTAL SCIENCE

Pollution Abstracts. Ed., Oceanic Library and Information Center. Louisville, KY: Data Courier, 1970–present.

ETHNIC STUDIES

Index to Literature on the American Indian. San Francisco: Indian Historian Press, 1970–present. (Annual.)

Index to Periodical Articles by and about Negroes. Ed. Hallie Q. Brown Memorial Library. Boston: G. K. Hall, 1950–present. (Annual.)

Welsch, Ervin K. *The Negro in the United States: A Research Guide.* Bloomington: Indiana University Press, 1965. Discusses books and periodicals.

Woods, Richard D. *Reference Materials on Mexican Americans.* Metuchen, NJ: Scarecrow, 1976.

HEALTH AND PHYSICAL EDUCATION

American Alliance for Health, Physical Education and Recreation. *Abstracts of Research Papers.* Washington, DC: AAHPER, 1971–1975.

HISTORY

America: History and Life. A Guide to Periodical Literature. Santa Barbara, CA: American Bibliographical Center, Clio Press, 1964–present. (Annual.)

American Historical Association. *Guide to Historical Literature.* Ed. George F. Howe et al. New York: Macmillan, 1961.

Guide to the Study of the United States of America, A: Representative Books Reflecting the Development of American Thought. Washington, DC: U. S. Government Printing Office, 1960. Supplements 1956–1965, 1976.

Historical Abstracts: Bibliography of the World's Periodical Literature, 1775–. Santa Barbara, CA: American Bibliographical Center, Clio Press, 1955–present. (Annual.)

International Bibliography of Historical Sciences. New York: International Publications Service, 1930–present. (Annual.)

LANGUAGE AND LITERATURE

Bond, Donald F. *Reference Guide to English Studies.* 2nd ed. Chicago: University of Chicago Press, 1971.

Essay and General Literature Index 1900–1933: An Index to about 40,000 Essays and Articles in 2,144 Volumes of Collections of Essays and Miscellaneous Works. New York: H. W. Wilson, 1934–present. (Biennial supplements.)

Kennedy, Arthur G., and Donald B. Sands. *A Concise Bibliography for Students of English,* 5th ed. Rev. William E. Coburn. Stanford: Stanford University Press, 1972.

Modern Humanities Research Association. *Annual Bibliography of English Language and Literature.* Cambridge: Cambridge University Press, 1921–present.

Modern Language Association of America. *MLA International Bibliography of Books and Articles on the Modern Languages and Literature.* New York: MLA. 1922–1968 as June issue of PMLA. (Formerly *American Bibliography.*) 1969–present.

New Cambridge Bibliography of English Literature, The. 5 vols. New York: Cambridge University Press, 1969–77.

Spiller, Robert E., et al. *The Literary History of the United States.* 4th ed. 2 vols. New York: Macmillan, 1974.

LAW

Index to Legal Periodicals. New York: H. W. Wilson for the American Association of Law Libraries, 1908–present. (Monthly.)

MUSIC

Duckles, Vincent, *Music Reference and Research Materials: An Annotated Bibliography.* 2nd ed. New York: Macmillan, 1974.
Music Index: The Key to Current Music Periodical Literature. Detroit: Information Service, 1949–present. (Monthly, with annual cumulations.)
RILM Abstracts. New York: International Association of Music Libraries. 1967–present. (Quarterly.)

PHILOSOPHY

Philosopher's Index, The: An International Index to Philosophical Periodicals. Bowling Green, OH: Bowling Green University, 1967–present. (Quarterly.)

PHYSICS

Science Abstracts. London: Institution of Electrical Engineers, 1898–present. (Monthly.) Includes abstracts of articles about physics.

POLITICAL SCIENCE

Brock, Clifton. *The Literature of Political Science: A Guide for Students, Librarians, and Teachers.* New York: Bowker, 1969.
Harmon, Robert B. *Political Science: A Bibliographic Guide to the Literature.* Metuchen, NJ: Scarecrow, 1965. Third Supplement, 1974.

PSYCHOLOGY

Harvard List of Books in Psychology, The. 4th ed. Cambridge, MA: Harvard University Press, 1971.
Psychological Abstracts. Lancaster, PA: American Psychological Association, 1927–present. (Monthly.)

RELIGION

American Theological Library Association. *Index to Religious Periodical Literature, 1949/1952–.* Chicago: American Theological Library Association, 1953–present. (Annual.)
Religious and Theological Abstracts. Youngstown, OH: Theological Publishers, 1958–present. (Quarterly.)

SCIENCE AND TECHNOLOGY

Applied Science and Technology Index. New York: H. W. Wilson, 1958–present.
General Science Index. New York: H. W. Wilson, 1978–present.

SOCIOLOGY

Social Sciences Index. New York: H. W. Wilson, 1974–present. (Quarterly.) See p. 57 of this book for a complete description.
Sociological Abstracts. New York: Sociological Abstracts, 1953–present.
White, Carl M., et al. *Sources of Information in the Social Sciences: A Guide to the Literature.* 3rd ed. Chicago: American Library Association, 1973.

WOMEN

Backscheider, Paula R., and Felicity A. Nussbaum. *An Annotated Bibliography of Twentieth Century Critical Studies of Women and Literature, 1660–1800.* New York: Garland, 1977.
Krichman, Albert. *The Women's Rights Movement in the United States, 1848–1970: A Bibliography and Sourcebook.* Metuchen, NJ: Scarecrow, 1972.

Review Questions

1. Suppose you are looking for a particular biography of Queen Elizabeth I of England, *Elizabeth the First* by Paul Johnson. How many entries in the card catalog can you find for this book? How can the card catalog help you locate other books about Queen Elizabeth?

2. How is each of these pieces of information, found on cards in the card catalog, useful to researchers?

author	date of publication
title	number of pages
subject	notation about a
call number	bibliography

3. What kinds of materials are listed in periodical indexes? Why might a researcher need to use several different indexes?

4. For each of the following topics, what additional resources (besides books from the card catalog and periodical articles from indexes) might you look for?

   • the latest government recommendations about energy conservation

- a seventeenth-century book (all known copies are owned by British libraries)
- the inauguration address of President Kennedy
- the jobs located by recent graduates of your school
- the history of the town in which your library is located
- your city's model program for rat control
- the major paintings of a particular artist
- the position on a controversial issue, taken last week by the governor

Exercises

1. Just to feel more at home in your school library, pay a visit there and locate the following:

   - the reference room or reference area
   - the periodical room or area
   - the reserve reading room or reserve desk
   - the card catalog

   If your library provides a diagram or floor plan of its physical layout, obtain a copy and use it to locate these resources. If no diagram is available, draw a rough floor plan of your own, showing the locations of the main sections of the library.

2. Use the card catalog to look up a fairly recent work of fiction by a well-known author, perhaps one you have studied in high school or college. Consult your library's classification guide to find the shelf where the book should be located. Use the *Book Review Digest* to find out if the book was reviewed during the year it was published or the following year. Report your findings.

3. Using microfilms of the *New York Times*, find the most important story reported on the day and year you were born (the ''lead'' story is in the upper right-hand corner of the front page). Then go to the *New York Times Index*, find a listing for this article and the next *Times* article on the same subject. Copy out both listings and convert all abbreviations to the full forms of the words that they represent.

4. Use the *Readers' Guide to Periodical Literature* to locate in your library an article published during the past year about your favorite hobby, pastime, or field of interest. Read it, determine the author's topic

and thesis, and explain briefly why you agree or disagree with this thesis.

5. Choose one of the topics listed on page 37 of this book. Use the subject card catalog to try to find the titles of three books related to the topic. Write out these titles and their call numbers and describe briefly where in the library each is located.

6. Think of a topic in psychology or medical science that interests you. Use the *Social Science Index* to discover how many articles have been written on that topic during the past three years. Record appropriate article and journal titles and any other information provided in the index description. Convert all abbreviations to the full forms of the words that they represent.

4
Searching for Sources

Now that you have a good idea of the research aids available in your library, you can begin the process of searching for sources by developing a *working bibliography*—a list of the books and periodical articles that may become sources of information for your research paper. Once you have collected a substantial list of possible sources, you must locate as many of them as you can and examine each one <u>briefly</u> to see whether it contains information and ideas that will further the investigation of your specific topic. Ultimately, you will use some of the information you find in these sources to support your paper's thesis. Those sources that provide specific ideas and information for the paper will be listed in your *final bibliography*.

Compiling the Working Bibliography

To begin putting together a working bibliography, get a supply of three- by five-inch note cards for *bibliography cards*. Then, whenever you come across the title of a book or article that seems worth checking into, make out a bibliography card for it. Use a separate card for each item and keep the cards in alphabetical order. Cards are handier for this purpose than a simple list because they can more easily be kept in order as you add and drop items from your working bibliography.

THE INFORMATION ON BIBLIOGRAPHY CARDS

For a bibliography card to be useful, it must contain all the information you will need when you prepare the footnotes or endnotes and the bibliography for your paper. In addition, the card should give you whatever information is needed to find the book or article in the library.

BOOKS

To make out a card for a *book*, record the following information (see Figure 4–1):

* name of the author, last name first
* title of the book, underlined
* place of publication
* publisher's name
* date of publication
* library call number (in top right corner)

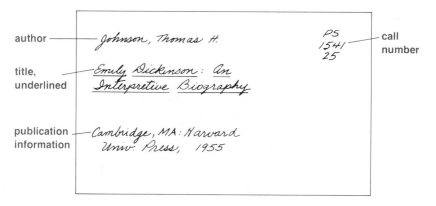

Figure 4–1. Bibliography card for a book

PERIODICALS

For a *periodical article*, follow this guide (see Figure 4–2):

* name of the author
* title of the article (in quotation marks)
* title of the periodical (underlined)
* volume number and date of publication
* numbers of the pages on which the article appears

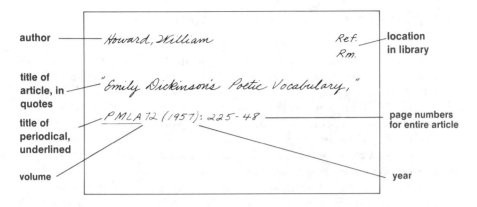

Figure 4–2. Bibliography card for a periodical article

Be sure to place in the upper right corner of every bibliography card the library call number or other "locator" information from the card catalog or catalog-on-line.* Take extra care to copy all bibliographical information accurately onto your cards. Misspellings, incorrect punctuation, careless omissions, and other mistakes in copying can force you to waste time in return trips to the library.

Gathering Sources

You will almost always collect more titles for your working bibliography than will appear in your final list of Works Cited because many potential sources will, upon a close reading, prove to be no help in the investigation of your hypothesis. The problem is that when you are looking through the card catalog or a periodical index, you must try to judge the value of a book or article by its title alone or by the heading under which you found it. Because you do not want to miss a potentially useful source, you must add to your working bibliography every title that sounds even slightly promising. Of course, quite a few of these potential sources will turn out to be worthless for your purposes, so your working bibliography will shrink accordingly. However, while you are dropping disappointing items from your list, you may be adding titles that are mentioned in the useful sources. You should, therefore, expect to be adding and dropping potential sources from your working bibliography throughout your research.

*Throughout our discussion, please keep in mind that we mean to include "catalog-on-line system" anytime we refer to the "card catalog." (More and more colleges are moving into this use of computers to replace the cumbersome card catalog kept in drawers.)

THE THREE STUDENTS GATHER THEIR SOURCES

George Pitman began assembling a working bibliography while taking notes during his background reading. First, he came across several potentially useful titles at the end of the encyclopedia article on "Jefferson Davis." He then went to the card catalog to learn whether those titles were available in his library. Four were, and three of them yielded information that directly supported his eventual thesis. Furthermore, these three books also contained bibliographies which, in turn, led to other useful sources. In this way, George was able to acquire a sizable working bibliography before he began a methodical search through the card catalog and periodical indexes.

Once he had followed up these early leads, George moved on to the card catalog. He looked under subject headings that were obviously related to his topic, such as "Davis, Jefferson, 1808–1889" and "U.S.—History—Civil War 1861–1865." Next, he used several cross-reference cards to find other headings that were not so obvious. (This procedure works slightly differently for catalog-on-line systems. Your instructor or librarian can explain how to go about this work.)

George rejected many items—such as A. H. Abel's *The American Indian as Participant in the Civil War*—without further examination because their titles indicated they were virtually certain to say nothing of value on his topic. However, for the many titles that seemed at all likely to prove useful, he carefully made out bibliography cards. Later, when he examined each of these items closely, he eliminated most of them from his working bibliography because they turned out to be either popular accounts or survey studies, much like textbooks, which repeated the same general information about Davis and his problems as president.

Finally, George searched through several periodical indexes, looking under "Jefferson Davis" and other relevant Civil War headings. Some titles clearly indicated that the material bore little or no relation to his particular topic, so they were left off the working bibliography. Others sounded vaguely useful, but these, too, were rejected when George examined them firsthand, either because they did not relate directly to his topic or because the information they provided had already been recorded in his notes. In fact, George ended up using only one periodical as a source, but that particular article was extremely valuable for its strong evidence of Davis's morality and courage.

Do not be misled by George's citing just one periodical in his paper. His case was fairly unusual. Many papers, especially those dealing with topics in science and the social sciences, list more articles than books as sources. (For example, Anita Barrone's paper on the possibilities of increasing human life span incorporated information from seventeen different periodicals, both popular and specialized.)

The student who researched Emily Dickinson used the same basic strategies for gathering sources but with somewhat different results. Susanna's final bibliography lists several books about Dickinson's life and works, two periodical articles, an essay from a collection of literary criticism, two volumes of the poet's works, and a collection of the poet's letters. Along the way, she found and skimmed numerous other books and articles, but most of these contained analyses of Dickinson's poems, with no useful references to the poet's life.

The search for sources is a journey into the unknown that tests your imagination, perseverance, and ability to plan. Sometimes this search can be frustrating because many clues lead nowhere and seem to waste your time. But do not try to save time by hastily rejecting items whose titles do not indicate a clear and immediate relation to your topic. Ambiguous clues must always be followed up. The possible source that is discarded unseen may be the one that could have helped you the most.

REASSESSING YOUR TOPIC

While searching for sources, you may reach a point where you doubt the topic is workable, either because you are finding far too many potential sources or because you have found too few. If after several hours of intensive searching through various indexes as well as the card catalog, you have discovered only two or three *possible* sources, your topic needs to be broadened. On the other hand, if you quickly find dozens of potential sources, you need to reduce the scope of the topic and/or sharpen the focus of your hypothesis.

We hesitate to talk in terms of specific numbers because the number of sources does not directly indicate how much information you have collected. You might take a couple of pieces of information from just one or two paragraphs in one source, and then take more than a dozen lengthy notes from an entire chapter in another source. The crucial question is whether you have enough sources, for your research cannot be considered complete unless you provide a full range of points of view. For instance, George included those historians who condemned Jefferson Davis, those who praised him, as well as those who took a middle position. And Anita Barrone gave her readers an extensive survey of the current scientific attempts to extend human longevity as well as a fair sampling of those who, for various reasons, question the value of such research.

NARROWING A TOPIC THAT IS TOO BROAD

We saw how one student limited his subject—*Jefferson Davis*—to a reasonable topic—*Davis's performance as president of the Confederacy*—after a conference with his instructor and a background reading session in the library. George's familiarity with his subject made it easy for him to take full advantage of the advice he received. However, another student, who knew relatively little about her subject—*abnormal psychology*—ran into trouble with her topic at a somewhat later step in the research.

Being curious about the many strange paths human behavior often takes, this student decided to concentrate on just one disorder, schizophrenia. It seemed reasonable to plan to discuss its cause and some of the therapies presently practiced in the effort to conquer this puzzling, distressing problem. During her preliminary research, she formed this hypothesis: "Since the exact cause of schizophrenia is not yet known, treatment is often difficult."

Her psychology textbook contained fewer than three pages on the topic, and an encyclopedia covered it in just one column. So the topic did not seem too broad. Only after the student had gotten fairly well into her search for sources did she realize that there were far more books and articles on schizophrenia than she could hope to read. The college library held more than a dozen books and hundreds of articles dealing directly with the causes and treatment of schizophrenia. What she believed to be a topic was actually a subject area, and a broad one at that. What should she do? Go back to the background sources, which had not clearly indicated the trouble she ran into? She checked with her instructor, who recommended that she look through her working bibliography cards to see if the titles might suggest some direction in which she could reasonably move. After all, why waste the time that had gone into the search for those sources?

The student noticed that several of the titles mentioned the *nature of schizophrenia*, others its *causes*, others its *effect on those living with schizophrenics*, and still others its *treatment*. She remembered from her background reading that doctors use several different methods of treatment because of uncertainty regarding the causes of the disorder. Although she was interested in the treatment of schizophrenia, she realized from looking at her working bibliography that this, too, was likely to prove too broad for her paper. So she reviewed her background reading notes and class lecture notes once more and decided to narrow her topic still further, to one kind of treatment. Her new topic became *treatment of schizophrenia in a community setting*. She also needed to form a new hypothesis and decided on "Treating schizophrenia in a community setting is a new idea that works."

In assembling a new working bibliography, the student began with titles from the old one. But something seemed wrong. She could not eliminate very many of the thirty titles in her working bibliography because any book on schizophrenia might refer to the type of treatment she was investigating. Clearly, her hypothesis needed to be revised again, this time to give it sharper focus. Reviewing those background notes that mentioned the new method of treatment, she realized that it was applied only to severe cases. And its proponents did not claim success in all cases, only better results than treatment in institutions. This led her to recast her hypothesis again: "Treating severe schizophrenia in a community setting has in some cases proven more successful than treatment in traditional institutions."

The sharper focus provided by the revised hypothesis saved the student from reading and taking notes on matters that were not directly related to her purposes, such as treatment outside of mental institutions (but not in community settings), the history of treating schizophrenia, or the treatment of mild forms of schizophrenia.

Let's compare the way the two hypotheses are worded. The first contains only two terms, other than "community setting," that give any focus to the topic—*new idea* and *works*. *New idea* refers to a minor point that can be made simply by giving the date of the first use of this method. *Works* gives some focus, but it is rather vague, lacking the sense of scientific validity carried by "has proven more successful." In contrast, the second hypothesis has four key terms—*severe, proven, successful,* and *traditional institutions*—that helped the student to search for sources and read them far more efficiently. The word *severe* warned her to skip over passages about milder forms of the disorder which do not force sufferers to be committed to mental hospitals. *Proven* kept her attention focused on the need to find specific evidence for or against her hypothesis. The term *successful* made her think about finding a valid basis for judging success—a difficult problem in this situation because schizophrenia is rarely, if ever, cured; the sufferer's symptoms only become less distressing. The student had to look closely to find the criteria used by her various sources in order to determine how much improvement could reasonably be considered "success." *Traditional institutions* reminded her that if she wanted to show that this method is successful, she had to compare it with well-established treatments, rather than with other experimental approaches.

REVISING A TOPIC THAT IS TOO NARROW

You may never find yourself in this position, for most newcomers to research tend to come up with topics that are too broad. And, if you remember the warning about topics that can be completely researched by reading just one source—*how bees communicate*, for example—then you are even less likely to err in the direction of "too narrow."

A student who had read an article on "lions" in *Natural History* found himself with no sources beyond that article except for two brief summaries of that article, one in the magazine *Newsweek* and another in the *New York Times*. His topic was *the effect of the severe drought of 1973 on the rearing of lion cubs in the Serengeti Plains of East Africa.* The *Natural History* article provided all the necessary information; *Newsweek* and the *Times* merely reported the story by summarizing the original article, so they could NOT be considered "different" sources, for they did not present any new information or a different point of view.

Stuck, after a long but futile search, the student went back to the step he had previously cut short—background reading. He had done nothing more than read about "lions" in an encyclopedia article on "African wildlife."

As the student read additional background studies, he thought about ways to expand his topic. These ideas passed through his mind: "The lions had trouble due to a drought; are there other more common problems they face as parents? Is there a *mild* drought every year? (The article had dealt with a particularly severe one.) Do they normally have trouble feeding themselves as well as their cubs? Who gets fed first, the parents or the cubs?" His new readings revealed that lions face famine every year in the Serengeti Plains because they do not follow the herds of antelope who migrate each winter to greener pastures.

The student now realized that he should broaden the problem from "the drought of '73" to the "regular shortages of food" due to droughts and the disappearance of the antelopes. He also broadened his focus to include the adult lions as well as the cubs. Thus, he arrived at the topic, *the ways in which lions manage to survive periodic food shortages.* At this point the writer still could not see how to frame a hypothesis, so he deferred that step until he had gathered some sources. He had to hope to find some difference of opinion or at least different sets of data in the sources, or else he would once more be left with a topic that could be handled entirely through one source. After collecting more than a dozen titles of potential sources, he skimmed through them to see what they had to offer. (The next section of this chapter explains how to go about this important step.) Sure enough, other observers of lions clearly had not seen the same thing or had drawn different conclusions about what they saw, especially about the roles played in the hunt by males and females. A quick glance at the sources enabled the student to form a reasonable hypothesis: "In their effort to survive under sometimes difficult circumstances, the female lion plays a more aggressive and critical role than the so-called king of beasts."

Skimming Potential Sources

Once you have compiled what seems to be an adequate working bibliography, you are almost ready to begin reading the sources and taking notes. Before you undertake this challenging work, however, check to see if the sources provide enough ideas and information to allow you to do a thorough job of research. This is best done by skimming each source to gain a rough idea of what it says about your topic. The purpose of skimming is to find out quickly whether a source is useful or not, and if it is, how much relevant information it contains. Skimming not only allows you to avoid a close reading of unhelpful sources, but it also gives you a chance to evaluate your hypothesis. A skimming of his sources told George Pitman that his hypothesis, which placed Jefferson Davis in a poor light, needed to be modified in Davis's favor. He did not make a full U-turn and say Davis had no faults, but he did see that the experts were divided in their judgment of the man.

If skimming leads you to reduce your list of potential sources to fewer than five, go back and look for more sources. If you cannot find any, check with your instructor to see whether you should try to broaden your topic or continue with what you have. Your instructor's advice will depend largely upon how much information the remaining sources offer and how adequately they cover the variety of views that experts have expressed on your topic.

If skimming leaves you with a great many substantial sources, you may want to limit the topic or sharpen the focus of the hypothesis. Of course, several sources may offer much the same information and arrive at the same general judgment; in that case, you need read and take notes on only one of them, thereby reducing the overload of sources. It is not easy, especially when first undertaking research, to judge whether two or more sources duplicate themselves. The main points to keep in mind are that you do not want to miss any valuable information, and you do not want to leave out any of the various viewpoints on your topic.

SKIMMING BOOKS

Skimming a book begins with the table of contents and the index. The table of contents usually presents a broad outline of the book's organization. If the author discusses your particular topic, you may be able to find out from the chapter titles the extent of the discussion and the major points it raises. Briefer discussions within chapters can be found by using the index, which gives page numbers for all references to a topic, however brief they may be.

When you are using an index, take the time to check all the headings that might be relevant to your topic, not just the obvious ones. For example, if your topic were *reading problems of grade-school boys as opposed to those of grade-school girls* (in this age group boys with reading trouble outnumber girls by a ratio of four to one), you would naturally look in a book's index under *reading*, *grade-school*, and *boys*. Some references would probably be listed under *reading*, but the other two terms might not appear in the index. In that case, you could look under synonyms such as *elementary school* and *male*. Do not stop at synonyms, however. Think of different ways to approach the topic which might lead you to other, possibly more fruitful headings, such as *learning disabilities* or *disabilities, learning* and *sex as a factor in learning*.

Finally, if you have reason to believe that a particular book is important to your research, but you have trouble finding what you want, do not give up. Instead, skim through the index, searching for significant headings that may not have occurred to you.

When you locate pages that deal with your topic, skim the first line or two of each paragraph. In this way, you are likely to discover the author's main points, which are often stated in topic sentences. In addition, if the book has chapter summaries, read those that pertain to your topic.

SKIMMING PERIODICAL ARTICLES

Articles rarely come with outlines that might serve as tables of contents, but some of them include abstracts that summarize their theses and major supporting points. If a summary indicates that an article may be worth a close reading, you do not need to skim it. If, on the other hand, the summary does not mention material that is likely to help you, do not discard the source; skim it by reading the first line of every paragraph to pick up the main ideas. You should not abandon the source unless such a skimming uncovers nothing useful. Even then, do not throw away the bibliography card, for if you have to revise your topic, the source might become useful.

TAKING NOTES WHILE SKIMMING

When skimming a potential source, take brief notes that tell you how the source might prove useful, or why it is not useful. Place these notes on the backs of the bibliography cards.

In order to determine how useful a source may be, keep these questions in mind:

* Is this information relevant to my topic?
* How much useful information does it seem to offer?
* Does this source support or contradict my hypothesis?

You do not have to take detailed notes at this time. Simply indicate the possible value of the source.

Keep all the bibliography cards. Do not discard them even if the sources look unpromising. If you are later forced to change your topic slightly, these items may become quite valuable. You will not want to waste time looking up a source you had previously skimmed.

Evaluating Potential Sources

As you skim through potential sources, try to evaluate each one in terms of its possible usefulness to your research. Here are some important points to keep in mind.

Depth of Coverage. Not every book or article that deals with your topic will contribute something meaningful to your investigation. In general, any source that treats the topic in depth will be more valuable than one that covers it superficially. You are looking for sources that give you a clearer, more detailed understanding of some aspect of your topic and thereby provide grounds for accepting, or rejecting, or in some way modifying your hypothesis.

For example, all books on the Civil War mention Jefferson Davis, and many of them sum up his performance as president in a paragraph or two. Such short commentaries are too general to be useful as sources for a paper on *Davis's qualities as a leader.* The conclusions they offer were boiled down from other sources that pursued the topic in greater detail. It is those other, in-depth studies that you want to read. Any writer can state with some justification that "Davis was an ineffective president because he did not always work well with other Southern leaders." Such a sweeping generalization may not necessarily be wrong. In a research paper, however, you are expected to go beyond mere generalization to find specific evidence, in this case, accounts of Davis's troubles with those other leaders. Otherwise, neither you nor your readers will have a sound basis for deciding whether your judgment is well supported.

Variety of Viewpoints. While putting together your working bibliography, remember to include works that express various points of view. A paper that depends mainly on the opinions and interpretations of one writer might well be criticized for being one-sided. For example, look at this list of books for a paper on the topic *Lee and Grant: the old vs. the new style of warfare.*

> **Hypothesis:** "The South's initial military success was due in large part to Robert E. Lee's mastery of the traditional theories of warfare, but the tide of battle turned when Lee was unable to cope with Ulysses S. Grant's new strategy of TOTAL WAR."
>
> **Sources:**   1. *Glory Road,* Bruce Catton
>   2. *Grant Moves South,* Bruce Catton

3. *Grant Takes Command*, Bruce Catton
4. *Mr. Lincoln's Army*, Bruce Catton
5. *The Civil War*, Bruce Catton
6. *Robert E. Lee*, Douglas Freeman
7. *Lincoln Finds a General*, K. P. Williams

This bibliography is so heavily weighted with Catton's works that his views are almost certain to dominate the paper. An experienced researcher would notice this imbalance and take steps to remedy the situation. Maybe some of Catton's books could be dropped if they largely repeated each other in regard to this topic. In any event, other historians' works must be found in order to support or oppose Catton's views.

One further question about "balance" comes to mind when looking over this list of titles. Isn't something wrong when four of the sources deal with Grant while just one focuses on Lee? After all, the topic suggests equal treatment of the two men.

The Problem of Obsolescence. Another important factor to keep in mind when evaluating sources is that some may be out of date. Especially in the natural and social sciences, knowledge is expanding so rapidly that theories, and even facts, are often revised or discarded within a year or two. Even history may be rewritten when new evidence comes to light or when a historian examines an old event from a new angle.

Therefore, if you investigate topics that involve current issues or the developments in a scientific field such as astronomy, you *absolutely must* find the latest possible sources. A book on astronomy, for instance, is partially out of date before it is published. This does not mean that most of what it says is inaccurate, but some of the facts and theories concern phenomena about which new, more powerful telescopes are yielding fresh information daily. Current social problems such as child abuse and issues such as nuclear deterrence also demand that you work with the most recently published sources. Since the information in books can never be totally up to date, you need to rely heavily upon periodical articles when researching these kinds of topics.

PRIMARY VERSUS SECONDARY SOURCES

Another kind of topic may send you back in time for many of your sources. For example, if you picked a topic involving the constitutional amendment that granted women the right to vote, you would probably want to find out what the general public as well as the leading social commentators thought about the issue in the years immediately before its passage in 1920. A recently written historical account of those years would get you started, but you might feel that the account missed something or even slightly distorted the picture of that historic crusade. Fortunately, you could check for yourself by reading some newspaper and periodical articles of that time which have been preserved in libraries, usually on microfilm.

The two sources we just mentioned are referred to as primary and secondary sources. *Primary sources* are those that *secondary sources* write about. The newspapers and magazines published at the time of the event are the sources used by later historians, whose writings then become secondary sources for your research. In literature, the term ''primary'' refers to the literary works themselves, while ''secondary'' refers to biographies and critical studies of the author's work.

If this kind of research sounds interesting, you should be aware that some very good topics focus on the way the literary works of now-famous authors were received when they were first published. For such research, you would use the *Book Review Digest* and a newspaper index. See pages 56–57 in chapter 3.

GUIDELINES FOR WORKING WITH PERIODICALS

In chapter 3, you learned that periodicals fall into two main classes—magazines, which are designed to be read by the general public, and journals, which are written for experts in particular fields. Each class poses distinct problems for research paper writers. The journals, because they are written for experts, are often very difficult to read unless you are familiar with the technical terminology and the special problems the experts are working on. On the other hand, magazines, because they are written for persons having a general educational background, usually avoid specialized terms and do not assume that readers possess an expert knowledge of the subject. The problem with magazines grows out of their effort to make complex ideas understandable. Simplifying sophisticated subjects often leads to some degree of distortion. Also, these magazines tend to leave out what could be important details from your point of view—complex examples, sophisticated theoretical explanations, and descriptions. What is true for this class of periodicals is even more likely to be true for newspapers.

You need to learn how to make the best use of both classes of periodicals if you hope to become a good research paper writer. Here are some guidelines that can help you handle the problems we just described.

If, like Anita Barrone, you were writing a paper for a science course, you would probably have to struggle with several journal articles. In that case, start your search for sources by looking through the *Readers' Guide* and a newspaper index. Magazine and newspaper accounts, which are usually very readable, will give you the general idea behind whatever recent discovery or theory your topic deals with. Then, when you move ahead to reading a journal article, you will be in a stronger position to cope with the technical vocabulary, and you will have become somewhat familiar with the subject.

If, however, your topic focuses on a current social problem, you may not have to resort to an academic journal. Social issues appeal to readers of varied interests, not just to experts in one field. For this reason, you can often find full discussions of an issue in newsstand magazines that are written for an educated but otherwise general audience. For example, the controversy over deployment of the neutron bomb, which destroys people but not buildings, can be understood without expert knowledge of how such a weapon is assembled or how a nuclear reaction takes place. Research into this topic would focus on sources that consider such matters as the bomb's value in the Cold War and the possible outcomes—social, environmental, and political—of its deployment. You don't have to be a nuclear physicist to understand the debate, so you might very well limit your search for periodicals to the *Readers' Guide* and a newspaper index. In any case, it is a good idea to ask your instructor what kinds of sources you will be expected to use, given your particular topic.

REVIEWING YOUR HYPOTHESIS

After skimming and evaluating the sources, review your notes to check the direction your hypothesis is taking. If you see that the sources do not fully support the hypothesis, make whatever modifications are needed to bring it into conformity with the sources. Do not plow straight ahead. Stop and consider what you have just learned through skimming. Revising the hypothesis will bring it into sharper focus and this will make the next step—reading the sources in depth—much easier.

Review Questions

1. What is a working bibliography? How does it differ from the final list of Works Cited?
2. Write out the information for the following sources as you would on a bibliography card:

   • a 1952 book published in New York by Harcourt, Brace, & World called A History of Western Philosophy and written by W. T. Jones.

- an article about the Japanese economy called How Japan Does It, written by Christopher Byron, published in Time magazine on March 30, 1981, and running from page 54 through page 60.
- an article in The Sixteenth Century Journal by N. M. Sutherland called Catherine de Medici: The Legend of the Wicked Italian Queen, running from page 45 through page 56 and published in volume 9 in 1978.

3. Briefly outline the different but related processes of skimming a book and skimming a periodical article.

4. Explain how you can tell whether a potential source is likely to be useful to you. Mention several specific criteria.

5. What signs might warn that a topic is probably too narrow? too broad? What steps can be taken to resolve both problems?

6. After you have found what seems to be an adequate *number* of sources, and you are *looking over the titles*, what should you be looking for if you are concerned that the list might not really be adequate?

Exercises

1. If you are presently working on a research project and have developed a topic and hypothesis, follow the suggestions in this chapter to put together a working bibliography and evaluate the potential sources by skimming them. Turn in your notes (annotated bibliography).

2. In a popular magazine of your choice, read an article about a topic of current interest, such as *new energy sources, genetic engineering, political problems in Central America,* or *space probes of distant planets.* Then, using an appropriate periodical index, find an article on the same topic in a professional journal, and read it. Write a paragraph or two contrasting the approaches used by the authors of the two articles.

3. Choose a nationally controversial topic, such as *the neutron bomb, medicaid payments for abortion, free agency in baseball, nuclear power plants, affirmative action programs,* or any important issue facing your area of the country. Find articles in two different periodicals (newspapers included) that take opposite sides on the issue. Write a summary that points out the major differences in their views and the general tone of each article.

5
Reading the Sources and Taking Notes

Taking good notes is not simply a matter of copying down as much information as you can, as fast as you can. You must be selective. Although you will surely end up with more information in your notes than will ultimately appear in your paper, you don't want to go too far in that direction. Yet you also want to be sure to record everything you will need when it's time to support whatever thesis your investigation leads to. For notes to be effective, then, it is essential to keep your hypothesis firmly in mind at all times.

Practical Aspects of Note-taking

When taking notes, you cannot know just how each piece of information will finally be used in the paper. One thing is certain, however: you will present your information in a different order from that in which you recorded it. Therefore, you will want a flexible method of note-taking that makes it easy to find the best possible arrangement of your information. We can offer two such methods, each having its own advantages.

PREFERRED METHOD

Use four- by six-inch note cards, and record just one idea, or a small group of closely related facts, on each card. Write notes on only one side of each card, leaving the back free for bibliographic information. The main advantage of note cards is that you can spread the cards out on a table and rearrange them until you discover a satisfactory order. Another advantage is that the limited writing space available on a card will encourage you to avoid taking longer notes than you need.

ALTERNATE METHOD

If you still feel more comfortable using a notebook, perhaps because you are worried that a card is too easy to lose, write on just one side of each page and leave a fair amount of space between notes. This will allow you to cut each page into separate notes when you are ready to organize your paper.

Whatever method you use, be a big spender. Do not try to squeeze as many notes as possible into the space available. The satisfaction gained from being thrifty cannot compensate for the frustration of trying to untangle a tightly bunched, loosely connected set of facts and ideas.

ENTERING INFORMATION ON CARDS

We feel it is important to develop a single format for putting information on cards and then to follow it consistently. Later you will want to thumb through the stack of cards looking for a particular piece of information or looking simply to see if there's an appropriate piece of information that fits in with whatever you are doing at the moment. In either case, you want to know at a glance if a card has what you want. Using a set format makes this easy.

1. On the back side of each card, identify the author and title of the source, and be sure to add the numbers of the page or pages from which you are taking the information. We need to stress this seemingly minor point. If you forget to take down this information, you could lose hours retracing your steps.

2. Use only the front side when recording information. Don't be tempted to save a penny by finishing up on the back, for you may miss that piece of information when reviewing your notes.

3. Leave lots of white space to make it easier to review your notes. Main points should easily catch your eye. Minor points should be clearly subordinate to the major ideas they support, so you should use numbers more often than you normally do. Underline *major ideas*. Capitalize KEY WORDS. Use numbers or letters to indicate (1) subordination, (2) sequence. (See Figures 5–1 and 5–2.)

4. Think ahead to the organization of the paper and try to come up with a few likely subtopics. For example, the Jefferson Davis topic

might be broken down into: *military strategy, conflicts with other leaders, poor health, cabinet choices, belief in the Southern cause.* The appropriate subtopic should be written, in pencil perhaps, at the top of each card, using more than one subtopic if a note refers to more than one. Most of the time, you will discover some subtopics while reading the sources. As soon as you see one emerging, start using it. Then, when you take a break from reading, go over the previous cards adding the new subtopic where it fits. Reviewing your earlier notes from time to time can also prove very helpful in keeping the scope of your project clearly in mind.

short bibliographic note

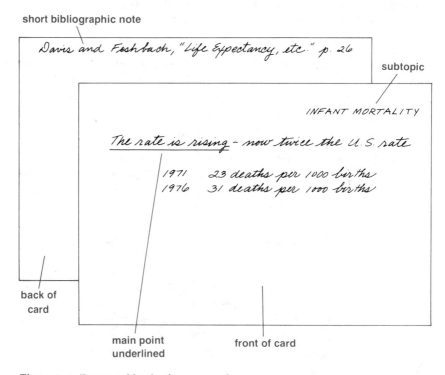

Figure 5–1. Front and back of a note card

The Fine Art of Note-taking

As we have said, effective note-taking consists of more than copying relevant passages out of your sources. In fact, the more direct copying you do, the less useful your notes are likely to be. Here is why.

Note-taking for a research paper has three fundamental objectives:

- to record the general ideas that will form the backbone of your research paper,

- to record specific pieces of information that support the general ideas, and
- to preserve the exact wording of some statements in your sources that you may want to quote directly in the paper.

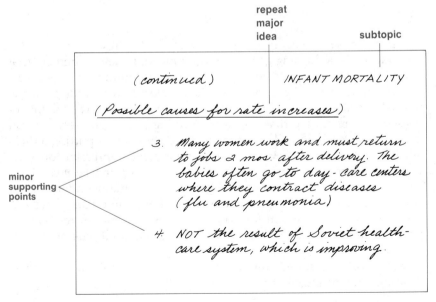

Figure 5–2. A series of notes continued on a second card

Note: Author, title, and page numbers appear on backs of *both* cards in case one becomes mislaid.

Many students waste time copying down long passages, even whole pages, word for word, because they believe, wrongly, that research papers must contain a large number of quotations. This is just not so. In fact, the opposite is true. For most research assignments, you should restrict the use of direct quotation to at most 20 percent of the paper. (This limit does not apply to literature topics for which you must quote from the literary works you are discussing as well as from secondary sources.) For some topics, especially in the natural sciences, excellent papers can be produced without using any direct quotations at all.

One important reason for limiting the amount of direct quotation is that by stating most of the ideas and information in the paper in your own words, you show your readers that you understand what you are talking about. Furthermore, the quotes will come from a wide variety of sources, each written in a distinctive style. Therefore, expressing the ideas in your own style, using consistent vocabulary and sentence patterns, will make it much easier for someone to read the paper. Finally, producing a convincing paper from a collection of quotations is almost impossible. Even though it might seem easier to quote than to paraphrase and summarize, the resulting "paper" would amount to a confusing, loosely related set of statements. Actually, it is easier to express most of the ideas and information in your own words than to try to piece dozens of quotations together into a smoothly flowing, coherent essay.

Paraphrasing

To paraphrase is to express another person's idea in your own words. The value of paraphrasing goes far beyond meeting the requirement that you find your own way of saying what you have found in your sources. For one thing, a good paraphrase usually takes fewer words than the original to convey the essential meaning. Even more important is the increased understanding that comes from trying to paraphrase what you are reading. Psychological experiments have shown that putting a difficult idea into your own words makes a stronger impression on your memory than merely copying the idea word for word. In fact, if you have trouble restating an idea, you probably do not thoroughly understand it. In general, therefore, paraphrase any ideas that go into your notes unless there is a good reason for quoting the exact words in the source. (Several common situations that call for quotation are discussed on pp. 92–94.)

The following examples reveal two benefits to be gained from paraphrasing: brevity and clarity.

original   Will reputable scientists ever accept the claim that extrasensory perception and other paranormal powers really exist? It appears that many of them have.

paraphrase

```
                    Many scientists today believe in the reality of

                    ESP and other paranormal powers.
```

The idea of "reputable" is not needed in your note; you know that you are looking only for real scientists—not those who simply call themselves scientists, as do some who work with ESP.

original

Contrary to popular belief, exercise has never been shown conclusively to prolong life.

paraphrase

```
                    No one has ever proved that exercise lengthens

                    life.
```

poor paraphrase: too close to the original

```
                    Contrary to popular thinking, exercise has never

                    been demonstrated conclusively to lengthen life.
```

There's no need to record "contrary to popular belief" if that is not the point you are interested in. Being careful to exclude unnecessary information from your paraphrase will help you avoid the sort of "partial paraphrase" that can slip into plagiarism, a serious problem discussed at length on pages 109–113.

original

Olfactory receptors for communication between different creatures are crucial for establishment of symbiotic relations.

two reasonable paraphrases

```
                    The sense of smell is essential to cooperation

                    among different animal species.

                    Cooperation between different animal species is

                    made possible by their sense of smell.
```

The original, which comes from a biology journal, shows how difficult such periodicals can be. Obviously, the notetaker had already learned some of the specialized vocabulary of the field or had looked up the meanings of the technical terms. Notice that either paraphrase would be much easier to understand than the original when reviewing notes and organizing information into an essay.

Summarizing

A summary greatly reduces the length of what you have read, which might be anything from a long paragraph to an entire magazine article.

Writing effective summaries requires good judgment, for you must decide what can be left out of your notes without losing or distorting the basic idea.

If you are working on a single paragraph, you may find that it contains a clearly stated topic sentence aptly supported by several details. In that case, you can simply paraphrase the main idea and then decide whether you need to note briefly any of the details, either for use in your paper or to reinforce your understanding of the main idea. In the following example, the main idea is stated in the first sentence, as is the case in much professional writing.

original

Zoologists define *species* as a category of animals whose members are capable of mating and producing offspring which are also able to reproduce. Thus, dogs constitute a species because even males and females of the most dissimilar breeds can produce mongrels that can, in turn, reproduce. However, the mating of a horse and a donkey, though the two are more similar in appearance than, let us say, a poodle and a boxer, yields a mule, which is always sterile. Thus, they are placed in separate species. A lion and a tiger, though of different species, can produce a "liger" or a "tiglon," which in very rare cases may be fertile. This exception betrays a slight weakness in our definition of the term *species*.

summary
note card

Whether or not you should include details in your note depends on your hypothesis. If your use for this source goes no further than the definition of *species*, you probably do not need the parenthetical examples. If you intend to develop the concept of *species* in your paper, you may need them. The example of the "liger" and the "tiglon" would be needed only if you planned to discuss the fact that a scientific term can be less precise than most of us believe.

Often your summary of a paragraph will consist of a general idea that you have derived from several details in the paragraph which directly relate to your hypothesis. Assume when reading the next example that you are gathering information related to the hypothesis, "Most scientists now believe that life probably exists on planets circling other stars in the universe."

original
The sun is accompanied on its journey through space by a retinue of nine planets, thirty-two natural satellites revolving around the planets, hundreds of comets and thousands of asteroids. Do other stars have similar arrays of companions? At present there is no direct way of telling, because if such a collection of bodies were associated with a nearby star, the most powerful telescopes on the earth could not detect them. The feeble light reflected from the companions would be lost in the brilliant glare of the central star.

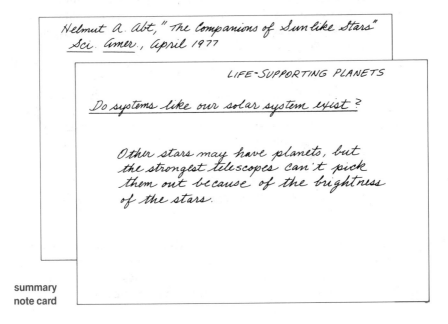

Helmut A. Abt, "The Companions of Sun like Stars"
Sci. Amer., April 1977

LIFE-SUPPORTING PLANETS

Do systems like our solar system exist?

Other stars may have planets, but the strongest telescopes can't pick them out because of the brightness of the stars.

summary note card

The background information at the beginning of the original paragraph has been left out of the summary because you do not need it to understand the main idea—that even if other stars have planets on which life might exist, these planets cannot be seen by our telescopes. This example illustrates another way to keep your notes brief. If some of the background information had been new to you, you might have been tempted to add it to your notes, just because it was unfamiliar. Doing so would not have helped you when you came to write your paper. Use your hypothesis to guide you in deciding whether such information is truly relevant to your purposes.

Quoting

Once you accept the principle that you should paraphrase or summarize most of the ideas that go into your notes, you will be better able to judge when quotation can be both appropriate and effective. There are four common reasons for quoting from your sources—*conciseness, accuracy, memorable language,* and *authority.*

Sometimes your best efforts at paraphrasing will produce a version that is either longer and clumsier than the original or else somewhat inaccurate. In either case, you should quote all or part of the original statement. On other occasions, a source may express an idea so brilliantly that you want to preserve its beauty and power. Finally, you may want to support an idea or one of your conclusions by quoting a key statement or two from an established authority on the subject. None of these reasons for quoting is, however, an excuse for avoiding the effort necessary to create a successful paraphrase. You must learn to recognize those special times when these reasons are likely to be valid.

Examples of four situations in which direct quotation is desirable are presented below, along with some further advice on when to quote rather than paraphrase or summarize. The examples consist of note cards and of excerpts from research papers that show how the quotations were eventually put to use.

Conciseness: *You find that you cannot paraphrase an idea without using many more words than the source.*

A common instance of this occurs when you decide to introduce a specialized term into your paper. You think it should be defined, but your attempts to paraphrase a definition are long and awkward. In that case, you should quote at least part of the definition from the source.

excerpt from paper   Noam Chomsky can be considered a reductionist--
someone who believes that ''all complex phenomena
are ultimately explained and understood by

analyzing them into increasingly simpler and
supposedly more elementary components'' (Pronko
497).

Works Cited entry

Pronko, N. H. <u>Panorama of Psychology.</u> Belmont, CA:
Wadsworth, 1969.

(The note refers to the source of the definition, a textbook that the student used solely for the definition and not for any information related to Professor Chomsky. That textbook, however, must be included in the list of Works Cited for the research paper, and the student therefore made out a bibliography card for the source as well as a note card for the quotation.)

Accuracy: *You find that you cannot effectively paraphrase an idea without distorting the author's meaning.*

If, for example, a writer said that "virtually all women have experienced fantasies in which they were born as men," any paraphrase is likely to be more or less inaccurate.

questionable
paraphrases

Most women wish they were men.

The majority of women have dreamed that they were
men.

Almost every woman has a dream or daydream in
which she had been born a male.

The first paraphrase grossly distorts the meaning; the second comes closer, but is not entirely accurate; the third is accurate but longer than the original. In such cases, you would do much better to quote the source and let your readers draw their own conclusions. Then, they can compare their interpretations with those you put forth in your paper.

Memorable language: *You believe that the words or ideas expressed by your source are so vivid or powerful that the meaning cannot be captured in a paraphrase.*

Restrain yourself in this matter; beware of quoting someone merely because you feel you cannot say it so well. An example of brilliant language that cries out for quotation comes from a speech by Winston

Churchill, in which he refers to the behavior of Russia as "a riddle wrapped in a mystery inside an enigma."

In the same vein, you should quote famous remarks whether or not the word choice is brilliant or difficult to paraphrase. President Harry Truman once advised timid politicians, "If you can't stand the heat, get out of the kitchen."

Finally, you may come across a remark which is so startling that your readers deserve to see the original. The outstanding biologist J. H. S. Haldane described Albert Einstein as "the greatest Jew since Jesus." Such a striking comment would surely lose a great deal if paraphrased.

Authority: *You want to support a conclusion you have reached in your research by quoting the words of an expert on the subject.*

The authors of many of your sources are probably experts on their subjects, at least in the sense that their ideas have been thought authoritative enough to be published. Still, you need to be a little selective in this regard. Choose those writers whose credentials are known. A reporter for *Newsweek* or the *Washington Post* is an expert only on journalism, though he or she may be very well-informed on the topic you are dealing with. A person referred to in your other sources (or in a biographical sketch accompanying her article in *Scientific American*) as "a leading gerontologist" can be treated as an expert in the study of aging. In general, however, even experts should be quoted only when their words are more concise, accurate, or memorable than any paraphrase or summary you can make.

At any rate, remember that you cannot rely entirely upon expert opinion, whether quoted or paraphrased. You must also work to support your conclusions with hard facts and clear reasoning.

QUOTING OUT OF CONTEXT

Since you are always quoting just a small part of any source, you must take great care to see that everything *which you did not quote* agrees with the idea which you did quote. This principle applies to paraphrasing as well, of course. The next example shows how someone could read a passage hastily and then produce a serious misrepresentation of its author's meaning.

student's source   It is currently very fashionable among popular social critics to blame television for the recent widespread increase in juvenile crime statistics. The argument usually pursues this line of reasoning: Many parents today neglect their children by allowing them complete freedom in watching TV. The shows these children choose to watch often present violence in an attractive form, and some have even gone so far as to depict clever ways of committing crimes. Many of these children later re-enact the violent acts they have witnessed on TV in order to recapture the thrills.

    I contend, however, that this widely accepted explanation of a serious social problem is too simplistic. . . .

Anyone who read that passage and then produced the following quotation would be grossly distorting the author's meaning.

quotation out of context

Sociologist Jane Doe joins those persons who denounce violence on TV as the primary cause of the sharp increase in the number of crimes committed by young people: ''Many . . . children later re-enact the violent acts they have witnessed on TV in order to recapture the thrills'' (41).

Apparently, the student missed the signal that tells the reader that the writer disagrees with the points listed. (''It is currently very fashionable among popular social critics . . .'' carries a mocking tone.) Then, the student completely ignored the clearcut assertion that opens the next paragraph: ''I contend, however, that this . . . is too simplistic.''

BLENDING QUOTATION WITH PARAPHRASE

The most effective way to avoid quoting too many words is to combine quotation with paraphrase. A good guideline says to quote only that part of a passage that relates directly to your hypothesis. Below, you can read the context surrounding Churchill's famous remark about Russia, and you will see the advantage of quoting just the most pertinent part of a source. Churchill was attempting to alleviate Britain's fears that Russia might not enter the war against Nazi Germany. Part of that speech is presented here, along with a note card showing how quotation can be blended with paraphrase or summary. (The student's hypothesis was, ''Before and during World War II, Churchill demonstrated a clear understanding of other nations and the ways their leaders thought.'')

original speech by Churchill

I cannot forecast to you the action of Russia. It is a riddle wrapped in a mystery inside an enigma; but perhaps there is a key. That key is Russian national interest. It

cannot be in accordance with the interest or safety of
Russia that Germany should plant itself upon the shores
of the Black Sea, or that it should overrun the Balkan
states and subjugate the Slavonic peoples of Southeastern Europe. That would be contrary to the historic life interests of Russia.

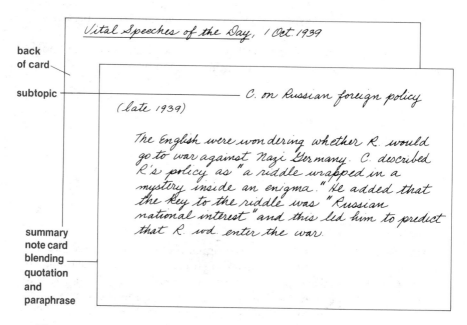

back of card *Vital Speeches of the Day, 1 Oct. 1939*

subtopic C. on Russian foreign policy

(late 1939)

The English were wondering whether R. would
go to war against Nazi Germany. C. described
R's policy as "a riddle wrapped in a
mystery inside an enigma." He added that
the key to the riddle was "Russian
national interest" and this led him to predict
that R. wd. enter the war.

summary note card blending quotation and paraphrase

The note supplies a connection between Churchill's words and the
student's hypothesis—that when others were confused (in this case,
about Russia), Churchill's intuition or plain old political savvy led him to
the truth. The note shows this point better than a lengthy quotation from
the speech.

ENTERING QUOTATIONS ONTO NOTE CARDS

When writing a note, you must be extremely precise in placing the
quotation marks and absolutely accurate in recording the author's
words. This need for super accuracy when quoting can be better understood if we examine some problems that can occur when reviewing notes
in preparation for writing the paper.

Problem 1
Since quotation marks are small, they can be
overlooked when you are transferring information
from your notes to your paper. To avoid missing a
quotation mark or two, use very heavy strokes or

even the marks « and » (guillemets). This will insure against your confusing quotations with paraphrases.

Problem 2   If a note summarizing several pages of a source
includes a quotation, you must record the page
number where the quotation appeared, as well as
the page numbers of the full passage being summarized. Be sure to record the page number of
each direct quotation.

back
of card

page numbers
of section being
summarized

Herman Arthur, "To Err Is Huperson; to Forgive, Divine," Amer. Educator, Winter 1980, pp. 30-32.

SEXISM

Correcting sexism in language

summary with
direct quotation
clearly marked

In getting rid of sexism, teachers must avoid awkward and ugly constructions such as he/she. « Like badly tattered fig leaves, they call attention to what they are trying to conceal. » (30).

page number
of quotation

Three suggestions (1) Do away with most feminine suffixes, such as -ess and -ette; (2) Provide substitutes for man and woman suffixes, ex: mail deliverer instead of mailman; (3) Avoid he/she and him/her constructions by using it when sex is not specified.

summary
card with
quotation

Problem 3   Sometimes, you will want to leave some words
out of the middle of a quotation because they are
not relevant to your purpose. A reader is entitled to
know about such an omission, so you must use an
ellipsis, which consists of three dots in place of the
omitted words. The example shows a quotation
that was shortened by ellipsis. (The passage also
demonstrates a smooth blend of quotation and
paraphrase.)

student's source   Literature is slow to register its own historical moment. Only in the past few years has a literature an-

nouncing the end of the 1960s emerged. It isn't generally a literature *about* that decade; apart from the novels of Marge Piercy and a few scenes in Mary Gordon's *The Company of Women*, there isn't much description of the tableaux that represent the sixties: rock concerts, riots, campus demonstrations. Purposeful collective acts have

omitted words

given way to private anomie. The predominant mood in the novels and stories of Jayne Anne Phillips, Richard Ford, Mary Robison, Ann Beattie, and Raymond Carver—to mention five younger writers who have begun to command an audience—is indifference, depression, even criminality. Such is fiction's bleak requiem for that turbulent era.

excerpt from student's paper

The critic James Atlas believes that "a literature announcing the end of the 1960s" has only come into being as we move into the 1980s, and it does not present those public events that marked "that turbulent era," such as student demonstrations against the war, riots in the inner cities, and rock concerts. "Purposeful collective acts have given way to private anomie.

ellipsis

The predominant mood . . . is indifference, depression, even criminality" (96).

Works Cited entry

Atlas, James. "Less to Less." Atlantic Monthly June 1981: 96-98.

The two partial quotations give readers the maximum chance to understand Atlas's points. The only word Atlas used to describe the 1960s was "turbulent." With so little else to go on, the student decided not to risk distorting the meaning by looking for a synonym for that word. The other partial quotation describes a theme of recent literature, represented metaphorically—we doubt these novelists actually said, "the 60s are over!" The "end of the 60s" refers to the end of a way of thinking about life and its problems. Conciseness and accuracy were the motives for quoting Atlas's major point.

Notice that you must leave spaces around the dots of an ellipsis. Also, occasionally, the ellipsis will fall at the end of your own sentence. When that happens, you must add a fourth dot, which is really the period that ends *your* sentence.

Problem 4

One last problem occurs when you want to quote a remark that was quoted by your source. The possible danger here is that when you review your notes you might become confused. You must clearly indicate whether the quotation marks enclosed your source's words or those of the person your source was quoting. Devise a format that leaves no doubt in your mind when you review the notes. We believe the easiest solution is to add a parenthetical note on your card if there is any chance of mistake.

student's source

    Of all the Concord circle, Emerson was perhaps the most widely read in science. He was familiar with Sir Charles Lyell's work in geology and was well aware that Christian chronology had become a mere ''kitchen clock'' compared with the vast time depths the earth sciences were beginning to reveal. ''What terrible questions we are learning to ask,'' brooded the man sometimes accused of walking with his head in the clouds. He saw us as already divesting ourselves of the theism of our fathers.

back of card

Loren Eiseley, "Man Against the Universe." The Star Thrower (New York: Harcourt Brace Jovanovich, 1978) p. 212

RWE / Science / Faith

Religion vs. Science

Emerson knew a good deal about current scientific advances, e.g. Sir Charles Lyell's geological theories. E. believed that ≪ Christian chronology had become a mere "kitchen clock" compared with the vast time depths the earth sciences were beginning to reveal. "What terrible questions we are learning to ask," ≫ said E., who realized Americans were moving away from the ≪ theism of our fathers. ≫

(NOTE: ≪ ≫ mark Eiseley's words)

these words help make it clear, but the note at bottom leaves no chance for error

summary card with quotations

An Extended Example of Effective Note-taking

To illustrate the process of note-taking, an article that served as a source for a paper on ESP follows. Accompanying the article is a full set of note cards derived from it. First, notice how the student's hypothesis limits the amount of information that has to be recorded. Also note the student's reasoning for deciding what to quote, paraphrase, or summarize.

Student's hypothesis: "Modern scientific techniques are being used to investigate ESP, and the results have convinced some leading scientists that parapsychology is a valid field of study."

Note: As mentioned in chapter 2, ESP is one of those subjects, like UFOs and the "Bermuda Triangle," which must be handled with great caution. Far too much of the writing in these areas consists of personal, *unverified* accounts. These cannot be taken as *proof* of any kind, and are *evidence* only of what some people are claiming, for a variety of reasons. This student stuck to verifiable materials, the work of professional scientists, trying to discover validity in some areas of ESP.

Arguing the Existence of ESP

By MALCOLM W. BROWNE

Browne's thesis takes the form of a question and its answer. The research that went into this article may have grown out of that question.

This is a restatement of the thesis, so no note is needed.

WILL reputable scientists ever accept the claim that extrasensory perception and other "paranormal powers" really exist?

It appears that many of them already have.

Not only do some of the world's most honored scientists believe in parapsychology, but a newly published survey suggests that a majority of American scientists accept at least the possibility that extrasensory perception really exists.

This states the controversy; no note needed.

A rash of new parapsychology experiments drawing ideas from the physics of atomic particles has rekindled an old controversy over whether parapsychology is a legitimate science or merely a pseudoscience created by charlatans to snare the naïve.

Results Are Reported

We are coming closer to specific details, but we can wait until the writer goes into them more precisely.

Some experimenters claim that the natural process of radioactive decay can be influenced by mental concentration, and that results of their latest work demonstrate the contention. Other experiments purport to show that mind power alone can change the temperature of supersensitive thermometers and the separation between objects. Some respected scientists have turned to meditation as a means of seeking truth.

No note should be recorded. This information is interesting, but it is not directly related to the student's hypothesis.

Various laboratories have sought to either confirm or debunk the legitimacy of parapsychology since the controversial 1930s experiments by Dr. Joseph Banks Rhine of Duke University. Dr. Rhine had his subjects try to use supposed paranormal powers to "see" the designs on special cards concealed from them.

His results proved, he contended, that extrasensory perception permits subjects to pick the right cards significantly more often than chance alone would allow.

Conclusions Challenged

Other scientists challenged this conclusion, noting that Dr. Rhine and other parapsychologists routinely reject data from subjects who are not performing well. If all the data from extrasensory perception tests were preserved and reckoned into the statistics, critics say, the statistics would show a result no better than pure chance.

The parapsychologists have argued that paranormal abilities cannot be turned on or off like laboratory apparatus, and that it is fair to discard results from subjects who are not "on."

No note is needed. The sentence merely restates the article's thesis.

The dispute over this key question has never been resolved, and belief in parapsychology, like religion, remains a matter of faith. Despite that, belief by scientists in psychic phenomena seems to be far more widespread than many had suspected.

note card 1

poll of scientists re ESP

poll   conducted by Dr. Mahlon Wagner, psychologist
State Univ. of N.Y., Oswego

published in Zetetic Scholar, journal that
often attacks claims of ESP.

Wagner: 《 "I used to be a total skeptic...
but I've become a little more accepting
because there are good, honest scholars
in the field." 》
                    ⌐ (of parapsychology)
          (continued)

note card 2

poll of scientists   re ESP

poll sent to 2,100 professors across country
          1,188 answered

of the 《 natural scientists 》 who answered —

9% 《 accepted extrasensory perception as
        an "established fact" 》
45% 《 described ESP as a "likely
        possibility." 》

note card 3

Scientists researching in parapsych.

1. Dr. Robert G. Jahn, dean of engineering
and applied science at Princeton
— can mental powers change a thermometer
reading or the distance between objects?

2. Dr. Peter F. Phillips, physicist, Washington
Univ. (St. Louis)
received grant of $500,000 for 《 psychic
research 》 from McDonnell Douglas
Corp. foundation.

See note cards 1 and 2.

This journal seems objective; that is the kind of evidence you are looking for.

The hypothesis points directly to such scientists and their views.

See note card 3.

Hypothesis focuses on modern scientific techniques, so this is valuable.

No note is needed. The information is interesting but not relevant to the student's hypothesis.

See note card 4.

Once more we learn what tough-minded scientists are thinking.

Dr. Mahlon Wagner, a psychologist at the Oswego campus of the State University of New York, recently published in the journal Zetetic Scholar the results of a poll he conducted. The journal, whose name is derived from the Greek word for skeptic, publishes scholarly papers, most of which attack claims of paranormal phenomena.

Dr. Wagner sent questionnaires to 2,100 professors at colleges and universities throughout the country, and received 1,188 responses. Of the natural scientists who responded, he said, 9 percent said they accepted extrasensory perception as an "established fact," and 45 percent described ESP as "a likely possibility."

How does Dr. Wagner himself feel about his results?

"I used to be a total skeptic," he said, speaking of parapsychology, "but I've become a little more accepting because there are good, honest scholars in the field."

Research in parapsychology has been spurred by a number of recent financial grants.

Backed by private donors, Dr. Robert G. Jahn, dean of engineering and applied science at Princeton University, has undertaken a psychic research program based on some experiments that suggested mind power might change a thermometer reading or the distance between two objects.

Another physicist, Dr. Peter F. Phillips of Washington University in St. Louis, was awarded a $500,000 grant several months ago for psychic research. The grant, one of the largest ever made for psychic research, was from a foundation established by the McDonnell Douglas Corporation.

There have been hints that American intelligence organizations have experimented with ESP, and Soviet security officials interrogated and expelled an American news correspondent for allegedly receiving a secret research report on parapsychology.

At the annual meeting of the prestigious American Physical Society last year, a special session on parapsychology was held for the first time, and al-

note card 4

recognition of parasych. by
scientific world

American Physical Society

1979 annual meeting held special session
on parapsychology, though most
attending were skeptical.

Dr. Helmut Schmidt described his
experiments with ESP.

see Schmidt cards

---

note card 5

Radioactive decay experiments
SCHMIDT

S. built machine in which radioactivity
randomly turns on lights, one at a
time. Lights are arranged in a circle.

《 Subjects are asked to try to influence
the direction in which the lights
come on. 》
Results —
《 Significant correlation between subjects'
mental efforts and the observed
results. 》

---

note card 6

Radioactive decay experiments
SCHMIDT

Variation on experiment

Machine lit lights _before_ the people were
asked to use their ES power, but people
weren't told about it.

Results —
Same as on first test. Schmidt says this
seems to show that ES power can work
《 " backward in time, and that is an outrageous
idea from a conventional standpoint." 》 May be
due to some 《 quantum effects 》 scientists don't
understand.

See note card 5.

More modern techniques.

See note card 6.

More modern techniques.

See note card 7.

Though this tough-minded scientist runs counter to hypothesis, you need his views to balance your research.

though most of those attending were deeply skeptical, some 500 scientists listened attentively to such parapsychologists as Helmut Schmidt of the Mind Science Foundation of San Antonio, Tex., an institution maintained by grants from William Thomas Slick Jr., a Texas oil magnate.

Dr. Schmidt, a physicist by training, uses devices called random-number generators in his experiments. These machines are actuated by the random quantum-mechanical process of radioactive decay, producing a continuous series of numbers.

Describing his experiments in an interview, Dr. Schmidt said one of his machines has a ring of lights arranged like a clock dial, and the radioactive process randomly illuminates one of these lights at a time. Subjects are asked to try to influence the direction in which the lights come on. The results, he asserted, demonstrated a significant correlation between his subjects' mental efforts and the observed results.

In another type of experiment, Dr. Schmidt said he gave subjects the same instructions, but unknown to them, the machine had already produced its random series of numbers the previous day. Electronic recordings had been made of the numbers and stored in a safe without being examined. Copies made from them were then played for the subjects, who believed they were watching the machine in action rather than a mere recording.

Again, Dr. Schmidt said, there was correlation between their mental efforts and the results, even though the results had been obtained beforehand. "The implication seems to be that the effect can work backward in time," he said, "and that is an outrageous idea from a conventional standpoint. But it may be that some quantum effects not yet understood could account for just such an outcome."

The chairman of the parapsychology session, Paul Horowitz of Cambridge, Mass., a physicist, asserted that Dr. Schmidt was "probably wrong." "But it's important that the investigation of

radioactive decay experiments
SCHMIDT

Criticism of Schmidt's conclusions

Paul Horowitz, physicist, Chairman of the
Amer. Physical Soc. parapsych. session –

Schmidt « probably wrong » but
H. believes that scientists should continue to investigate parapsych.

Scientists attack ESP

John A. Wheeler, physicist working on black hole theory

parapsych is a «"pretentious pseudoscience"»
when its experiments are examined by
rigorous scientific methods. They «prove
nothing.»

Wheeler wd. like Parapsych. Assn. to lose status
as Amer. Assn. for the Advancement of
Science affiliate.

Scientists attack ESP

John G. Taylor, mathematician at King's Coll.,
London, once believed but now does not.
1975 book, Superminds, supported parapsych.

T. had been convinced that Uri Geller,
Israeli psychic, could bend spoons and
move objects solely by mental power.

After Geller's tricks were exposed, Dr. Taylor
wrote two papers recanting his earlier
position.

See note card 8.

This enemy of the believers causes you to realize that only "some" leading scientists believe there is something to be said for ESP.

See note card 9.

This case is especially relevant and interesting because he became a believer, then went back to his original skepticism.

See note cards 10 and 11.

Here are bona fide believers among the leading scientists.

parapsychology be kept within the structure of science where it can be examined critically," he said.

Some scientists are outraged by such thinking.

Among them is John A. Wheeler, an American physicist specializing in the theory of gravitational collapse and "black holes."

Contending that parapsychology is a "pretentious pseudoscience," he has sought for the past year to have the Parapsychological Association based in Alexandria, Va., deprived of its status as an affiliate of the American Association for the Advancement of Science.

Dr. Wheeler and other scientific critics of parapsychology maintain that when results from psychic experiments are scrutinized according to accepted scientific and statistical tests they turn out to prove nothing.

Despite such objections, scientists are as often duped by charlatans and hoaxsters as are nonscientists, skeptics assert.

A case in point, they say, is that of John G. Taylor, a distinguished mathematician at King's College, London, who wrote a popular book in 1975 called "Superminds." The book, which was essentially a testimonial for parapsychology, recounted how Dr. Taylor had become convinced by the demonstrations of a self-styled psychic from Israel named Uri Geller. Mr. Geller claimed to be able to bend spoons, transport objects through the air and perform many other tricks by mental power alone.

Later, when Mr. Geller's feats were revealed as mere tricks of stagecraft, Dr. Taylor published two papers in the scientific journal Nature, recanting his earlier endorsement.

But many similar cases over the years have failed to shake the convictions of a number of distinguished scientists, including two giants of physics, Sir William Crookes and Wolfgang Pauli.

Dr. Brian Josephson, a 40-year-old British scientist who was awarded the Nobel physics prize in 1973, has increasingly turned toward parapsychology during the past 10 years in his research at Cavendish Laboratory, Cambridge Uni-

note
card 10

Scientists support ESP

Sir William Crookes
Wolfgang Pauli

《 giants of physics 》

Still believe in spite of numerous
exposures of psychics like Uri
Geller.

note
card 11

Scientists support ESP
JOSEPHSON
Brian Josephson — Nobel prize in physics, 1973
Cambridge Univ.

《 has increasingly turned toward parapsych.
during the past 10 years in his research. 》

is 《 "99% convinced" 》 that 《 "remote
viewing" 》 and 《 metal bending 》 are real.

note
card 12

Scientists support ESP
JOSEPHSON
《 "to some extent . . . parapsych. lies within
the bounds of physical law." 》
《 "but physical law itself may have to be redefined . . . It may be that some effects in
parapsych. are ordered - state effects
of a kind not yet encompassed by
physical theory." 》

In this sense, the study of parapsych. is
similar to the study of intelligence
and consciousness.

versity, England. (The latter institution awarded its first doctorate in parapsychology last year.)

In a telephone interview, Dr. Josephson said he was "99 percent convinced" of the reality of the paranormal effects, notably "remote viewing" and mental metal bending.

No note is needed since scientists are expected to think rigorously.

Dr. Josephson's mastery of quantum mechanics and other hard physical principles led him to discovery of the Josephson effect, by which electrical conductivity in an ultra-cold environment can be switched on or off with a magnetic field. Super computers of the coming decade are expected to be based on it. Is the rigorous technique of thought that discovered the Josephson effect compatible with parapsychology?

See note card 12.

Here you get a carefully measured acceptance of the belief without acceptance of many ESPers' specific claims.

"You ask whether parapsychology lies within the bounds of physical law," Dr. Josephson said. "My feeling is that to some extent it does, but physical law itself may have to be redefined in terms of some new principles. It may be that some effects in parapsychology are ordered-state effects of a kind not yet encompassed by physical theory.

"My interest is not only in parapsychology but in the nature of intelligence and consciousness. These are also ordered processes which are not yet understood," he said. "It may be that an understanding of intelligence and consciousness lies outside the paradigm of physics. It may be that more can be learned about the nature of reality through meditative processes."

But he did not expect the results of such work to be universally persuasive.

"It is clear," he said, "that you can never satisfy a skeptic except by enrolling him directly in an experiment, and you can't do that with every skeptic."

The Problem of Plagiarism

The subject of plagiarism can be very perplexing because students often have trouble seeing it from the instructors' point of view. Many tend to feel that teachers exaggerate the seriousness of the offense, and some teachers think students treat the problem lightly because avoiding plagiarism sometimes takes too much effort. But the fact of the matter is that teachers do consider plagiarism a serious offense, and therefore, students need to beware of getting into trouble through carelessness.

The problem reduces to one of trust and personal integrity. Teachers want to believe that you will give proper credit where it is due, and they want to give you credit for your own judgments concerning the significance of the evidence you gathered. Readers assume that all ideas and judgments which are not accompanied by a note are yours. Only when a teacher has good reason to doubt that an idea is yours will he or she raise the question of plagiarism. As a matter of personal integrity, you must acknowledge any idea that comes from a source as well as the wording that was used to express that idea.

By "acknowledging sources" we mean that when you use an idea, for instance a critical judgment, that appeared in one of your sources, you must give that writer credit with a note telling readers who proposed the idea and just where you found it. Even if you arrived at the same judgment on your own, you need to acknowledge that the writer also came up with the idea.

It is possible to plagiarize by accident. In using an idea from a source, you might carelessly fail to insert a sourcenote, and so it would appear that you were trying to claim that idea was your own or that you had discovered the information through your own efforts. Such an oversight is easy to discover. Simply reread your paper, with your note cards at hand, and check each significant concept or fact against your notes to see whether you have given proper credit. Add any source citations you omitted. (Note: Chapter 8 provides specific guidelines for determining what kinds of information require notes.)

The problem of plagiarizing another author's language may not be so easy to deal with. Many of your notes will consist of paraphrases and summaries; therefore, you might accidentally treat one of your direct quotations as though it, too, had been written in your own words. If in taking notes you followed our suggestion and marked off the quotations with large quotation marks, or « and », then you can easily check your paper against your notes to be sure all quotations are identified as such. If the markings on your note cards are not clear, however, you must go back to the actual sources to determine which words in your notes are quotations and which are your own.

The problem of plagiarizing language, however, usually goes beyond copying full sentences or even paragraphs from a source without using quotation marks and notes. Some students find themselves suspected of plagiarism because the wording of their paraphrases is so close to that of the original passages that they are practically quoting. Only a few words are changed, and the sentence patterns are virtually identical to those in the sources. Here is an example.

This passage comes from a description of George Washington's plan for saving his forces from the British army, which had trapped him into defending a fortress on the shore of Long Island. The only means of escape required moving the men in small boats (Source was Flexner, James T. *The Young Hamilton*. Boston: Little, Brown, 1978.)

original passage   The other necessity, and this seemed the impossible one, was for Washington to find some way to get his army away without tremendous loss. The problem was that, when part of the force was on water, the rest, unable adequately to defend the fortifications, would become easy prey for the enemy. Unless he could somehow slip secretly away, Washington would have to sacrifice half his army.

a case of laziness or deliberate plagiarism?   The other need, which seemed to be impossible, was for Washington to discover some means of getting the army away without enormous losses. His problem was that, when some of the soldiers were on the water, the others would be unable to defend their land position adequately and could be easily defeated by the British. Unless Washington could manage to slip away in secret, he would lose half his forces (Flexner 110).

Perhaps the only crime here is laziness, but the fact remains that this student relied very heavily upon the original sentence structure and only "translated" the passage by finding synonyms for a few words. The flow of thought is a direct echo of the original. Although the note tells the reader where the information came from, there is no indication that the wording is not entirely the student's own work.

Perhaps this plagiarism was unintentional. The student may have thought that since the two versions are not *exactly* the same, no plagiarism occurred. But his version sounds too much like the original. In order to repair the damage, he would have to rewrite the entire paragraph, changing the sentence structure and finding different word choices. (Remember that a paraphrase restates the author's idea in your own words.)

acceptable paraphrase   Washington's brilliance as a field commander is shown by his plan for the army to escape by water

before the British knew what was happening.
Obviously, the soldiers could not simply board
boats and sail away, because, if the British
attacked in the middle of the operation, most of
the troops would be in no position to defend
themselves (Flexner 110).

This paraphrase is distinctly different from the source, as it should be. Of course, a note is still essential—to credit the author as the source of the information. (Remember that ideas, opinions, judgments, all must be acknowledged, even after you express them in your own words.)

It is not always easy to know how different from the original your paraphrase must be if you are to avoid plagiarism. A possible rule would be to enclose any words found in a source within quotation marks, but this could lead to absurdities in many common situations. For instance, how would you paraphrase the following sentence without using the italicized words?

original

The typical *Inuit igloo* offers superior insulation against *temperatures* that fall as low as − *50° F.*

There are no synonyms for most proper nouns, such as *Inuit,* just as there are no synonyms for most numbers (exceptions: *dozen* for *12; score* for *20; decade* for *ten years*). As for *igloo,* the substitution of *ice house* or *house made from blocks of hard-packed snow* would be either inaccurate or very clumsy, and *temperature* can only be replaced by a slightly different idea, such as *coldness* or *freezing weather.* If you put quotation marks around these words in your paraphrase, the result would look rather silly:

absurd use of
quotation marks

A well-made ''Inuit igloo'' can protect its
occupants even when ''temperatures'' outside reach
''-50° F. ''

Obviously, any rule must be flexible enough to prevent this ugliness. In general, then, you can safely repeat specific numbers (− *50° F., 21 percent, 5,280 feet, seven million people, $524.52*), special terms for which there are no simple synonyms (*igloo, gross national product, income tax, influenza, touchdown, amphetamine*), and even very simple words that would require bizarre substitutions (*horse, ocean, atmosphere, lung, father, high school, temperature*).

Remember, however, that sometimes even a single word taken from a source requires quotation marks if it is especially colorful or represents the writer's judgment. The following summary of an article quoted just two isolated words, "ridiculous" and "absurd."

student summary of article

In 1912, H. H. Goddard, director of research at Vineland Institute for Feeble-minded Girls and Boys in New Jersey, was commissioned by the U.S. Public Health Service to survey mental deficiency among immigrant populations at Ellis Island. According to paleontologist Stephen Jay Gould, Goddard's study employed "ridiculous" criteria which led to "absurd" conclusions regarding the native intelligence of Jews and other unpopular European minorities. Goddard's work played a significant role in the passage of the Restriction Act of 1924, which, according to Allan Chase, author of The Legacy of Malthus, barred millions of Jews from entering the United States and thereby escaping the Nazi holocaust (Gould 14-15).

Works Cited shows

Gould, Stephen Jay. "Science and Jewish Immigration." Natural History Dec. 1980: 14-19.

As you can see, the problem of plagiarism concerns not only individual words, but also the flow of thought and the presentation of ideas, all of which combine to give a piece of writing its style and originality. The research paper measures, among other things, your ability to express ideas effectively. Although this challenge can be frustrating at times, you are expected to maintain a personal integrity that will prevent your surrendering to the temptation to borrow even "just a little bit here and there" from your sources.

Review Questions

1. How does a hypothesis help you to read sources and take good notes?

2. What kind of information *must* be recorded on every note card to avoid problems at later stages in the process? Where should this information be entered on a card?

3. Why do successful note-takers keep each note as brief as possible?

4. What is the difference between a summary and a paraphrase? How are they similar?

5. What are the advantages of paraphrasing and summarizing rather than copying passages from sources?

6. When paraphrasing, do you have to change every word that appeared in the original? Explain your answer.

7. For what reasons might you quote rather than paraphrase a statement found in a source?

8. Why might plagiarism become a problem even for very honest writers of research papers?

Exercises

1. Take a full set of notes on the following excerpt from a lecture.* Be sure to follow the direction indicated by the hypothesis when deciding what information belongs in your notes. Remember not to put too much information on individual cards. If you quote something, mark it clearly, and, in parentheses, give a reason for quoting—accuracy, memorable words, conciseness, authority.

Topic: *the causes of violence in America today*

Hypothesis: "Although some observers blame violence on TV and the economy, the cause may lie in our past, going back to the lawless West and to Prohibition."

It is commonly assumed that violence is part of our frontier heritage. But the historical record shows that frontier violence was very different from violence today. Robbery and burglary, two of our most common crimes, were of no great significance in the frontier towns of the Old West, and rape was seemingly nonexistent.

Bodie, one of the principal towns on the trans-Sierra frontier, illustrates the point. Nestled high in the mountains of eastern California, Bodie, which boomed in the late 1870s and early 1880s, ranked among the most notorious frontier towns of the Old West. It was, as one prospector put it, the last of the old-time mining camps.

*Roger D. McGrath, "The Myth of Frontier Violence," *Harper's*, February 1985, 26–28, an excerpt from a lecture given November 1984 at California State University, Long Beach.

Like the trans-Sierra frontier in general, Bodie was indisputably violent and lawless, yet most people were not affected. Fistfights and gunfights among willing combatants—gamblers, miners, and the like—were regular events, and stagecoach holdups were not unusual. But the old, the young, the weak, and the female—so often the victims of crime today—were generally not harmed.

Robbery was more often aimed at stagecoaches than at individuals. Highwaymen usually took only the express box and left the passengers alone. There were eleven stagecoach robberies in Bodie between 1878 and 1882, and in only two instances were passengers robbed. (In one instance, the highwaymen later apologized for their conduct.)

There were only ten robberies and three attempted robberies of individuals in Bodie during its boom years, and in nearly every case the circumstances were the same: the victim had spent the evening in a gambling den, saloon, or brothel; he had revealed that he had on his person a significant sum of money; and he was staggering home drunk when the attack occurred.

Bodie's total of twenty-one robberies—eleven of stages and ten of individuals—over a five-year period converts to a rate of eighty-four robberies per 100,000 inhabitants per year. On this scale—the same scale used by the FBI to index crime—New York City's robbery rate in 1980 was 1,140, Miami's was 995, and Los Angeles's was 628. The rate for the United States as a whole was 243. Thus Bodie's robbery rate was significantly below the national average in 1980.

Perhaps the greatest deterrent to crime in Bodie was the fact that so many people were armed. Armed guards prevented bank robberies and holdups of stagecoaches carrying shipments of bullion, and armed homeowners and merchants discouraged burglary. Between 1878 and 1882, there were only thirty-two burglaries—seventeen of homes and fifteen of businesses—in Bodie. At least a half-dozen burglaries were thwarted by the presence of armed citizens. The newspapers regularly advocated shooting burglars on sight, and several burglars were, in fact, shot at.

Using the FBI scale, Bodie's burglary rate for those five years was 128. Miami's rate in 1980 was 3,282, New York City's was 2,661, and Los Angeles's was 2,602. The rate of the United States as a whole was 1,668, thirteen times that of Bodie.

Bodie's law enforcement institutions were certainly not responsible for these low rates. Rarely were robbers or burglars arrested, and even less often were they convicted. Moreover, many law enforcement officers operated on both sides of the law.

It was the armed citizens themselves who were the most potent—though not the only—deterrent to larcenous crime. Another was the threat of vigilantism. Highwaymen, for example, understood that while they could take the express box from a stagecoach without arousing the citizens, they risked inciting the entire populace to action if they robbed the passengers.

There is considerable evidence that women in Bodie were rarely the victims of crime. Between 1878 and 1882 only one woman, a prostitute, was robbed, and there were no reported cases of rape. (There is no evidence that rapes occurred but were not reported.)

Finally, juvenile crime, which accounts for a significant portion of the violent crime in the United States today, was limited in Bodie to pranks and malicious mischief.

If robbery, burglary, crimes against women, and juvenile crime were relatively rare on the trans-Sierra frontier, homicide was not: thirty-one Bodieites were shot, stabbed, or beaten to death during the boom years, for a homicide rate of 116. No U.S. city today comes close to this rate. In 1980, Miami led the nation with a homicide rate of 32.7; Las Vegas was a distant second at 23.4. A half-dozen cities had rates of zero. The rate for the United States as a whole in that year was a mere 10.2.

Several factors contributed to Bodie's

high homicide rate. A majority of the town's residents were young, adventurous, single males who adhered to a code of conduct that frequently required them to fight even if, or perhaps especially if, it could mean death. Courage was admired above all else. Alcohol also played a major role in fostering the settlement of disputes by violence.

If the men's code of conduct and their consumption of alcohol made fighting inevitable, their sidearms often made it fatal. While the carrying of guns probably reduced the incidence of robbery and burglary, it undoubtedly increased the number of homicides.

For the most part, the citizens of Bodie were not troubled by the great number of killings; nor were they troubled that only one man was ever convicted of murder. They accepted the killings and the lack of convictions because most of those killed had been willing combatants.

Thus the violence and lawlessness of the trans-Sierra frontier bear little relation to the violence and lawlessness that pervade American society today. If Bodie is at all representative of frontier towns, there is little justification for blaming contemporary American violence on our frontier heritage.

2. Take a full set of notes on this magazine article.* Be sure to follow the direction indicated by the hypothesis when deciding what information belongs in your notes. Remember not to crowd information on your cards. If you quote something, mark it clearly, and, in parentheses, give your reason for quoting—accuracy, memorable words, conciseness, authority. Also, make up bibliography cards for any potential sources you discover in this article.

Topic: *preservation of world's forests*

Hypothesis: ''The continued loss of the world's forests will have disastrous effects on both nature and civilization.''

The End of Eden

Man is fast destroying the rain forests.

Most Americans think of the environment—if they think of it at all—as whatever affects their own backyard. Oil spills, toxic-waste dumps, the Disneying of the national parks: all draw impassioned debate and criticism. In a broader context, however, such ''parochial'' concerns amount to not seeing the forest for the trees. The worst ecological disaster now

*Annalyn Swan, *Newsweek*, February 18, 1985.

facing mankind, as four timely new books attest, is the relentless eradication of the world's rain forests—those magnificent green expanses that are, as conservationist Norman Myers writes in *The Primary Source (399 pages. Norton. $17.95)*, "the finest celebration of nature ever known on the planet."

Until recently, no one really thought much about saving rain forests. Millions upon millions of acres of them girdled the equator, many unseen by human eye. In the last two decades, however, that seemingly infinite resource has dwindled at a terrifying speed. Every minute of every day, writes journalist Catherine Caufield in *In the Rainforest (304 pages. Knopf. $16.95)*, an exhaustively researched report from the front line, almost 30 acres vanish forever. Each year an area the size of England, Scotland and Wales is razed. By the turn of the century, if this rate of destruction continues, most major rain forests (they exist primarily in Central and South America, the Congo basin and such eastern islands as Sumatra, Borneo and Papua New Guinea) may well be reduced to degraded patches. The war is on, waged by loggers eager for valuable timber, poor farmers hungry for land to call their own, Latin American ranchers who, often for the prestige of being a weekend *caballero*, clear vast tracts to run cattle.

It is hard for most people to envision what is being lost; few Americans will ever see a rain forest. Hence the value of books like Adrian Forsyth and Ken Miyata's *Tropical Nature (248 pages. Scribners. $16.95)*, which seeks "to provoke curiosity" about the forests—not just provide facts about them—and succeeds splendidly. Written by two biologists—one of whom, Miyata, was tragically killed on a fishing expedition before its publication—"Tropical Nature" evokes the magic and wonder of a world completely contained within itself.

On first seeing a rain forest, write the authors, the overwhelming impression is of green stillness and luxuriant life. Far above the ground is the forest canopy, through which little sunlight penetrates to the forest floor. Everywhere one looks are huge lianas or vines snaking toward the light. Tree trunks drip masses of epiphytes—ferns, mosses, orchids. There are thousands upon thousands of plant, animal and insect species, almost half the planet's species in only 2 percent of its area. Nothing is as it seems: in the high-stakes game of survival, many plants and insects have assumed the appearance or coloration of similar species that are inedible or even deadly. Some really *are* deadly, including the sinister pit vipers that use infrared sensors, located between their eyes, to track their victims through the darkness. At night, contrary to the Tarzan myth of a jungle echoing with screams and roars, the forest interior takes on a slightly foreboding stillness.

Drought: It's difficult to believe that such richness cannot be converted into prime farmland. The fact is, however, that most rain-forest soil is among the world's oldest and poorest. What's more, the forest acts like a giant sponge. If it is cut down, the result is not only flooding in the rainy season but drought in the dry; studies have shown that the forests retain and recycle as much moisture into the air as comes from the clouds. Destroy a rain forest and you wind up, at best, with a few years of crops gleaned from the temporary nutrients that come from burning trees. Then the soil is exhausted. And, since each species is interdependent with so many others in the great chain of being, the forest cannot easily regenerate itself. Where once there was exuberant life there is barren wasteland.

And still the misguided schemes to make the rain forest "productive" continue. In the forthcoming *Dreams of Amazonia (192 pages. Viking. $17.95)*, Roger Stone, a former Time-Life bureau chief in Brazil and now vice president of the World Wildlife Fund, chronicles one mistaken effort after another to turn Amazonia into El Dorado. The most famous venture of the 1970s was American billionaire Daniel K. Ludwig's ill-fated Jari, for which enormous paper mills were floated up the Amazon. Few people now remember Henry Ford's equally ambitious Fordlândia, which preceded Jari by four decades. This was a huge rubber plantation that limped along for years until Ford finally sold the land back to the Brazilian government in 1945. The most recent schemes, to resettle small farmers and clear vast tracts for cattle, have foundered on the poverty of the soil. Now the Brazilian government has launched a vast mining project, Grande Carajas, that dwarfs all of its predecessors. It will cover a sixth of Amazonia—the biggest rain-forest area left in the world—with huge mines and dams. The first, Tucuruí Dam, which is already under construction, will alone flood 800 square miles of virgin forest. It is far too big an area to clear; the trees will simply be left to rot. As for the Indians who have settled there, they'll be uprooted yet again and forced ever nearer to extinction.

Species: What's distressing about such destruction is not simply the loss of the world's most beautiful forests; it is the possibly disastrous side effects. At worst, the carbon released from the burning and decaying forest could have a "greenhouse effect" on the earth, melting part of the polar ice caps and causing floods worldwide. The world's gene pool will dwindle as species become extinct; wild plants are regularly interbred with domestic crops to strengthen them against blight and pests. Most tragic of all, perhaps, is the annihilation of species as yet undiscovered, which might well have proven invaluable to mankind. Of the plants known to have anticancerous properties, for example, more than 70 percent are rain-forest species. "Few environmental disorders cause irreversible damage to our biosphere," writes Myers in "The Primary Source." "But the extinction of species is a different ballgame. When a species is gone, it is gone forever."

Is there any way to save the forests, or at least significant chunks of them? Of the four books, "The Primary Source" is the most optimistic. Its proposals range from tree plantations planted with fast-growing species to limiting timber cutting to selected secondary, or previously logged, forest to a U.S. boycott of Central American beef. In the end, it is just as unlikely that Americans will deprive themselves of the cheap beef used by convenience-food giants as that rain-forest countries will welcome foreign intervention. In many countries, the destruction of the forest is a direct result of national poverty. In others, it is a matter of machismo or pride—"our moon shot," as one Brazilian proudly proclaimed to Stone. What chance does the forest stand against that? As an official of Eletronorte, the builders of the Tucuruí Dam, told Caufield, "Any dam is economic, most of all if you consider that the land is free. The only price is the environmental one." That price, sadly, will be paid by us all.

6

Preparing to Write the Paper

You are now ready to enter the writing phase of the assignment, having completed virtually all the research and having read the sources. Of course, you may have to go back and reexamine one or more sources if you suspect you missed some useful information. Or, after you have begun to write the paper, you may hear of another possible source and want to check it out. Research is seldom a straightforward procedure. Retracing your steps is frequently necessary.

The writing of the paper is complicated by the large amount of information which must be organized into a logical sequence. In order to cope with this complexity, you must review all your findings to obtain a clear overview of what your research has uncovered.

Organizing Your Note Cards

An easy way to get such an overview is to lay all your note cards out on a table, arranging them into groups according to subtopics. Now you can see the advantage to having each note on its own card, for you can shift a note from one group to another as you try to find the best way to organize the information. By looking over the notes in this manner, you can begin to see possibilities for arranging the information into a coherent essay.

No one can tell how many subtopics you will end up with, but you can usually expect to find between ten and twenty groups of cards on the table. In order to come up with a rough outline of the paper, you should consolidate some of the small groups into fairly large ones representing major divisions of the essay.

For his paper on Jefferson Davis, George took the cards he had assigned to relatively small subtopics and joined them to form one major subdivision of his rough outline.

small groups: *vision of South's greatness; previous administrative experience; service as U.S. senator; achievements as army officer; views on individual liberty; convictions about states' rights.*

major division: *Davis's strong points.*

This was not the last rearrangement, however. Later, when George constructed a detailed outline for his paper, he broke this major division down into three headings:

Davis's vision of South's greatness;

Davis's personal and political convictions;

Davis's military and political experience.

Another objective of this overviewing process is to determine whether your research is complete. If you feel you do not have enough evidence from which to draw a valid conclusion, you need to do more research—either find more sources or go back and get more information from sources you have already examined. A student writing on *dinosaur extinction* saw she had just one very brief note on a theory that is not widely held. Her research would not have been considered complete without a reasonably thorough account of that theory, which would give readers a fair chance to judge its validity. So back she went to the library.

Determining Your Thesis

Occasionally, your original hypothesis will clearly not fit the results of your research, and you will have to revise it several times during the research process. But once you finish your reading of the sources and feel confident the research is complete, your hypothesis must be evaluated to determine just how closely it fits all the information you have discovered. Out of this evaluation of the hypothesis comes your thesis.

One method for performing this analysis is to sketch out your findings on a sheet of paper so you can easily weigh the evidence and arrive at a valid conclusion. Whenever you are dealing with different sides of an issue or different approaches to a problem, some of the information can be arranged in columns, as in a business ledger. George used this method to check his hypothesis against the various opinions he had collected in his reading.

Hypothesis: "Davis's weaknesses as a leader contributed significantly to the defeat of the Confederacy."

From this sketch, you will see that the case against Davis is not nearly so one-sided as George's background reading had led him to believe.

Positive	Negative
Strode—unselfish, principled, didn't compromise on civil liberties the way Lincoln did	some minor flaws in personality
Pollard—"distinguished personal devotion"	squandered South's resources, administration was "imbecile and barren," great vanity
Nevins—vision of South's greatness, dignity and integrity, experience in government	obsession with details, involvement with military, worked poorly with other leaders
Randall/Donald—military and administrative accomplishments	vs. weaknesses in those areas

Catton—tragic view, based on the North's overwhelming strengths and the South's internal problems

Barney—Davis no better, no worse than Lincoln as a war leader

Patrick—We tend to make scapegoats of leaders of losing causes, even when the chances for victory were slight.

Rabun—didn't concede to special interests (good and bad); an opponent (Stephens) made problems much worse

Writing the Introduction

After you have arrived at your thesis and arranged your note cards into a rough, preliminary outline for the paper, your next step is to write the introduction. The introductory paragraph* not only states your thesis,

---

*For long essays, such as the sample paper on extending the human life span, two paragraphs may be needed.

but it also indicates the major subdivisions of the paper and the general nature of your sources. By putting together your major subtopics in what amounts to a preview of the whole paper, you gain a sense of control over the writing. This feeling of control will help you to see the significance of each detail as you try to find a place for it in the overall essay.

Before writing the introduction, jot down the major points you expect it to include. For the paper on Davis, these main points were:

Topic: *Jefferson Davis's leadership of the Confederacy*

Major Subtopics: comparison to Lincoln; problems with other leaders; overwork and poor health; personal strengths; South's hopeless situation

Sources: biographies and historical studies, from just after the war to now; emphasis on recent works

From these items, George prepared a rough draft of his introductory paragraph:

topic	For a long time, historians have blamed Davis for the South's loss of the Civil War. But a modern
subtopic	writer compared Davis to Lincoln and showed that Lincoln also made serious mistakes and had as many faults. Of course, the North won, so Lincoln
thesis (brief)	became a hero and Davis a scapegoat. Some writers today see Davis as a very able leader faced with an impossible task. Sure, Davis had his faults.
subtopic	Having been a successful army officer, he often tried to run the fighting of the war, angering the
subtopic	generals and causing confusion. He also fought bitterly with several political opponents, creating needless tension and confusing issues.
subtopic	As for administration itself, he spent too much time on details, and his weak health suffered.
sources	Older writers on Davis and the war felt these character faults contributed a great deal to the
thesis	loss of the war. Some recent writers, however, having more evidence to work with plus a fresh approach, have found Davis a first-rate leader in spite of his personality problems.

This paragraph needs polishing, but it fulfills the basic aims of an introductory paragraph—it gives readers a clear idea of what the writer is trying to do and how he means to do it. The final version, which follows, was not produced until the rest of the paper had been written. Note in particular the structural changes. The thesis is stated just once, at the end of the paragraph where it carries the most weight. The addition of a quotation from one of the sources provides a nice touch. Finally, several of the subtopics are presented in more general terms so that readers will not be distracted by the details.

For many years after Robert E. Lee surrendered at Appomattox, historians tended to lay much of the blame for the South's crushing defeat upon the president of the Confederacy, Jefferson Davis. However, one writer, in comparing Davis to Lincoln, claims that Davis's reputation would have been quite different if he had been on the winning side. When a leader fails to achieve victory, even if his cause was doomed from the start, his ''errors and defects and limitations of character . . . stand out as do a few spots of ink on a white sheet of paper.''[1] This does not mean that Davis had no faults. Almost all historians agree that

main subtopics the man suffered from character flaws. He spent far too much time on administrative details; he often interfered in purely military matters; and he allowed himself to be drawn into bitter controversies with other political leaders. The question all Civil War analysts must answer is this: To what extent did Davis's failings contribute to the defeat of the Confederacy? A survey of modern studies of Davis and the Civil War reveals a softening in the historical judgment

nature of sources of Davis as a leader. Most historians today conclude that Jefferson Davis, despite his personal shortcomings, was probably the most capable president the South could have chosen.

thesis statement Indeed, given the enormous problems the

```
Confederacy faced, Davis was a definite asset in
the struggle to secede from the Union.
```

Constructing the Outline

Once you have drafted your introductory paragraph, your next concern is the structure of the paper. An outline is essential if you expect to control all the information that lies spread out on the table before you. Outlining can be done in several stages, culminating in a detailed plan for the paper, in which each note card has been assigned its appropriate place. (Examples of such an outline are included with the sample research papers in chapter 9.)

Your first outline for a paper can be very simple—just take your major subtopics and figure out a reasonable order in which to present them. The original plan for the Jefferson Davis paper looked like this:

Introductory paragraph
1. Davis's strengths—why he was chosen
2. Davis's weaknesses—why he has been criticized
3. The traditional view of Davis—emphasis on faults
4. The latest assessment of his leadership—the best man available
5. Comparison with Lincoln
   Conclusion

A rough outline such as this gives you a chance to think about the shape of the paper without being confused by all the details you have collected in your research. Next, you should mark down those sources that go with each proposed section, in order to see how well you are utilizing your major sources. In this example, the third item seems likely to repeat the second one to a large extent, so revision is required. The revised brief outline, on which the complete final outline was based, follows:

1. Davis's weaknesses—the traditional view (Pollard)
2. Davis's strengths—why he was chosen (Strode)
3. Two moderate views (Nevins; Randall and Donald)
4. Defense of Davis based on the South's problems (Catton)
5. Davis's weaknesses compared with Lincoln's (Barney; Rabun)
   Conclusion

The next stage, constructing a detailed outline, depends on a careful evaluation of your materials. First, arrange the piles of note cards in the same order as the subtopics in your brief outline. Then, read through your notes again, to be sure they are both relevant and usable. You may want to eliminate a note that no longer seems relevant, to reassign a minor subtopic to a different major subtopic, or perhaps even to return to the library and look for information on an important subtopic about which you have not uncovered enough information.

Now you are ready to put your full set of cards in the precise order you expect to follow when writing the paper. Start by arranging the minor subtopics within the major subtopic to which you have assigned them. Then, arrange all the note cards within each minor subtopic in a logical sequence. By arranging your entire collection of notes in this way, you will have laid out on the table an organizational pattern for your paper. This is, in effect, a physical outline, and from it you can prepare the detailed written outline that will guide your writing of the first draft.

THE MATTER OF BALANCE

As you put your groups of note cards into sequence, look for possible imbalance. No subtopic should outweigh or overshadow other equally important subtopics. For example, suppose you were writing about Martin Luther King, Jr. and had arrived at the thesis, "Martin Luther King's success resulted from three major factors—his courage, his intelligence, and his charisma." Your outline, which determines the shape of the paper, would be strongly unbalanced if you devoted one section to "courage," one to "intelligence," and then six sections to "charisma." If your general impression from reading the sources was that all three factors contributed equally to King's success, then you would need to return to your sources or find new sources, looking for more information about the two briefly covered factors. If, however, you now realize that most of the sources had indeed emphasized charisma, you must revise your thesis. It might well read, "Martin Luther King's success depended on three factors—courage, intelligence, and charisma—of which charisma was by far the most important." Whatever direction you take, be sure to correct an unbalanced outline before you start to write. You will find it much harder to make such a change later.

THE TRADITIONAL OUTLINE FORMAT

In constructing an outline, use whatever format you feel comfortable with, unless your instructor specifies a particular one. One of the most common formats combines letters and numbers to designate the various levels of classification. Even if you are already familiar with this format, take time now to be sure you understand the subtle distinctions between those levels.

This list indicates the relative difference between levels:

Roman numerals (I, II) represent major subtopics, each covering a large section of the paper.

Capital letters (A, B) represent minor subtopics, each occupying at least one, sometimes several paragraphs.

Arabic numerals (1, 2) represent major details that support a minor subtopic.

Small letters (a, b) represent minor details that support a major detail.

The longer the paper you are writing, the broader the area covered by the highest category (Roman numerals) and the greater the chance that you might need a fifth set of symbols to represent the smallest details in the paper (small Roman numerals—i, ii, iii).

Notice the use of these levels of classification in the following segment of the outline for the Davis paper. (This kind of outline is sometimes called a "phrase" outline because each entry in it is a phrase rather than a sentence.) You may find it helpful to indicate the source in parentheses next to material drawn from it.

	Introductory paragraph, including the thesis statement
major subtopic	I. Extreme views of Davis's leadership
minor subtopic	A. Negative (Pollard)
major detail	1. Responsibility for loss of the war
minor details	a. Squandering of South's resources
	b. An "imbecile and barren" administration
	c. Personal vanity
major detail	2. Pollard's bias
minor details	a. Personal dislike of Davis
	b. Need for a scapegoat (Patrick)
minor subtopic	B. Positive (Strode)
major detail	1. Davis's strengths
minor details	a. Unselfishness and integrity

b. Minor nature of his flaws

c. Refusal to play politics at
   expense of civil liberties

major detail   2. Superiority to Lincoln in regard to
                                      civil liberties

minor details   a. Implied comparison
                                      b. Direct comparison (Dodd)

major detail   3. Nobility of Davis in a doomed cause

There are, however, two sensible rules for constructing outlines.

Rule 1: *Never break down a category into just one subdivision. To do so is il-
logical.*

wrong: only one detail   I. Difficulties faced by Diego Rivera in early
supports subtopic A.   years

                                 A. Childhood problems
                                    1. Grave illness from typhus and scarlet
                                       fever
                                 B. Adolescent problems

At some point, childhood problems must have seemed an important
subtopic, but in this outline it looks trivial. Perhaps information about
another childhood problem has been assigned to a different subtopic
and could be moved into this one. Or perhaps another trip to the library
would produce information about a second childhood problem accidentally omitted during note-taking. The outline might then look like this:

correct   I. Difficulties faced by Diego Rivera in early
                                 years

                                 A. Childhood problems
                                    1. Grave illness from typhus and scarlet
                                       fever
                                    2. Dangers arising from father's radical
                                       politics
                                 B. Adolescent problems

On the other hand, if Rivera's only significant childhood problem had been illness, the outline might be revised to look like this:

correct

    I. Difficulties faced by Diego Rivera in early
       years
       A. Childhood illnesses
       B. Adolescent problems

(It is not necessary to add arabic numerals under *A* for the specific illnesses, unless your note cards treat them extensively and you mean to discuss them in detail.)

Rule 2: *Use the same grammatical form for words at the same level of classification. By doing so, you produce parallel structure, that is, a pleasing and easy-to-understand ordering of ideas.*

wrong; the subdivisions are not grammatically parallel

    A. Symptoms of senility
       1. Forgetting recent events
       2. Mistakes in simple arithmetic
       3. Occasional hallucinating
       4. Inappropriate responses in social
          situations

correct; each subdivision is a gerund phrase

    A. Symptoms of senility
       1. Forgetting recent events
       2. Making mistakes in simple arithmetic
       3. Hallucinating occasionally
       4. Responding inappropriately in social
          situations

SENTENCE OUTLINES

Some instructors may require you to submit a *sentence outline*, in which you must express each category as a complete sentence. A sentence outline usually takes more time to write than a phrase outline, but it offers you an important advantage. The sentences that make up the outline can often be used almost word for word when you start to write your full paper. Whatever outline form you use, be consistent. Do not mix phrases into a sentence outline or sentences into a phrase outline.

Here is a sample section from a sentence outline:

complete sentences
appear at each level of
entry

A. Diego Rivera suffered from a number of
    childhood problems.
    1. Rivera contracted typhus at nine and
       nearly died from scarlet fever at eleven.
    2. Rivera faced dangers resulting from his
       father's radical politics.

UNCONVENTIONAL OUTLINES

The major reason for constructing an outline is to organize your thoughts and notes into a logical pattern before you write your research paper. The conventional outline formats you have studied thus far have been used for many years by many writers to organize their thoughts before undertaking an extensive piece of writing. However, some writers prefer to devise their own approaches to outlining which both satisfy their personal sense of organization and work well as guides to the creation of logical essays.

The following outline—developed by Anita Barrone for her research paper "Increasing Maximum Life Expectancy: Myth or Reality?"—is an example of an unconventional outline approach. As you look it over, you may want to refer to the finished paper in chapter 9 now and again to see how Anita used her personal format to guide her writing of the paper.

Increasing Maximum Life Expectancy: Myth or Reality?

1. Introduction
    Make point that human beings have always dreamed of extending
    their life spans
    --Ponce de Leon example
    Today, we look to science, not magic
    Thesis: Gerontologists carrying out experiments that may or may
            not help to extend life span. Many are optimistic about
            being on right track.
2. Tell what gerontologists mean by "increasing life expectancy"
    --not just more people living longer
    --quote Rosenfeld on life span of Ancient Greeks--some Greeks
      lived ripe old ages, same as today

--Use Alexander Leaf article to refute belief that people in certain areas of world have longer life spans

3. Explain "Hayflick limit"--quote Hayflick on "maximum proliferative capacity . . . rarely, if ever, reached by cells in vivo." (Explain difference between in vivo and in vitro)

--according to Hayflick we may be dying prematurely, as it is

--make point that gerontologists are working to overcome Hayflick limit

4. Use Walford's U.S. News interview to give list of hot theories about why we age

5. Immunologic Theory

--Introduce/explain theory

--talk about "autoimmunity" (quote Cromie)

--problem for scientists: how to lower autoimmunity without lowering body's ability to fight infection (quote Rosenfeld)

--drugs as anti-autoimmunity possibility--ex. thymosin (quote Kent)

--diet as another anti-autoimmunity possibility (quote Walford and Watkin)

6. DNA Repair Theory

--Introduce/explain theory

--results of DNA damage (quote Schimke and Agniel)

--DNA repair capacity helps us live longer than most animals (quote Kent)

--Problem: DNA damage rate outpaces repair rate (quote Walford)

--paramecia experiment by Sonneborn--maybe DNA repair can be increased

--use "DNA Coils" as another example of scientists working to improve DNA repair

7. Free Radical Theory

--Introduce/explain theory

--damage caused by free radicals (quote Rosenfeld; Harman; Kurtzman and Gordon)

--tell about attempts to counter effects of free radicals

--Harman's experiment with rats; possible helpful effects of vitamins E and C; "SOD" article from Science Digest

8. Thymus Hormone Theory

--Introduce/explain theory

--thymus as "master gland" of immune system (quote Marx)

--what is thymus? where located? (quote Rosenfeld)

--why thymus aids immune system (Marx) T-cells

--explain focus of research on thymus (Marx on hormones)

--Walford and Adler on declining function of thymus

--thymosin related to attempts to use drugs to continue work of
thymus hormone(s)--(quote Kent)

9. Brain Programming Theory

--Introduce/explain theory

--the brain as location of "death clock" (quote Moment)

--tell about attempts to locate "timing element" for aging in
brain and to turn it off before it has too much effect on
immune system

--explain Denckla's theory of "biological clock" for mammals

--bring up Walford's comment about hypothalamus as area of brain
where death clock may well be located

--introduce "neuroendocrinology" (quote Walford)

--use Finch to explain relationship between brain cell change
and neuroendocrine controls--how brain affects glands, which
affect aging process

--Denckla's theory of pituitary gland as gland that starts
aging process at command of the biological clock

--use Walford's comment on Denckla's attempts to isolate "death
hormone" and to make antidote to it

--explain work of scientists experimenting with brain
stimulators to keep information for body's controls from
becoming confused

--use work of Marshall and Berrios as example of experiments
with brain stimulators (apomorphine and L-dopa)

10. Where We Stand

--Make point that theories discussed in this paper may not lead
to success in drive to extend life expectancy

--other theories may arise that may lead to breakthrough

```
--bring up possibility that gerontologists may be engaged in a
  war they cannot win
--refer to Fries, Crapo, Leaf, and Medawar as examples of
  scientists who do not think life expectancy can be extended in
  near future
11. Conclusion
    Return to idea that life expectancy breakthrough will come--if
    at all--through work of dedicated scientists
```

You no doubt noticed that Anita's outline was presented in rather loose form. Subtopics were not always clearly indicated; no real effort was made to distinguish the relative importance of ideas and details; dashes and parentheses were used—but not very systematically—to separate items, rather than the conventional letters and numbers systems of conventional formats; sentences were mixed with phrases to signal points of explanation under subtopics. In short, the overall format showed no consistent organizational approach. And you probably also noticed that some of Anita's entries read more like reminder notes to herself than like clarifying items in a logical pattern of organization.

And yet, despite its breaking the "rules," the outline guided Anita in writing a paper that supported her thesis and related her research findings in an acceptably organized essay.

Anita, a confident writer, explained that she finds it easier to organize her ideas effectively while actually writing an essay than to plan it very precisely before beginning to write. Anita prefers to spend extra time revising a rough draft because she gets a better sense of how to put ideas together after she has tried to organize them into a paragraph. Anita's outlines give her a general sense of direction and remind her of ideas and details she wants to include in her papers. In this sense, then, her outline represents both a plan and a rough, abbreviated first draft. This may explain Anita's frequent use of such directive terms as *explain, make a point of, use, tell about,* and *bring up.*

Other writers use mixes of the traditional outline formats. For example, a writer may use a very precise letter and number system to outline a section that includes many details and then switch to a sentence format to outline theoretical or explanatory sections.

What kind of outlining procedure is best for you? Obviously the one that best guides you in planning an effective essay—the kind of procedure that leads to a logical expression of your ideas and knowledge in essay form. Anita used an unconventional approach. George Pitman and Susanna Andrews used more conventional formats. All three students produced successful research papers. You may have to do some experimenting before you hit upon an outlining approach that best suits your particular talents for planning and writing essays. In general, if you have had problems with writing well-organized essays in the past, then a tighter, more conventional form will probably serve you best. On the other hand, if you are the kind of person who finds that writing comes easily, then you might experiment with unconventional forms that allow you freer range in the planning and writing of your research paper. Your instructor can probably give you some good advice about which way you should go.

Review Questions

1. Why review and arrange all your note cards before beginning to write? What problems might you discover at this stage and how might you deal with them?
2. How do you arrive at a thesis for a paper?
3. What are the usual objectives of an introductory paragraph?
4. What is the function of an outline? What are some problems that you might encounter in constructing an outline?

Exercise

Read the following introductory paragraphs, keeping in mind that such a paragraph should state the thesis, identify the major subtopics for the paper, and describe the general nature of the sources used. Which paragraph best fulfills these objectives? Explain your choice. (Source notes have been left out.)

Topic: *Emily Dickinson's reluctance to publish her poems*

VERSION 1

Emily Dickinson was born in Amherst, Massachusetts, on December 10, 1830. She was the second of three children born to Edward and Emily Dickinson. She had an older brother, Austin, born in 1829, and a sister, Lavinia, who was born in 1833. "The three children were devoted to one another, but their home did not provoke gaiety."

Dickinson went to school at Amherst Academy, and later spent a term at Mount Holyoke College. According to Clark Griffith, in 1858 "she began definitely and noticeably to seclude herself from the outside world." With rare exceptions, she spent the rest of her life in her father's house in Amherst. Emily Dickinson died in 1886, leaving behind over 1700 poems. Only seven of her poems were published while she was alive, and all of these were published anonymously. Today she is considered to be a great poet. During her lifetime, however, she was reluctant to publish, and many people have wondered why.

VERSION 2

Great poets are never appreciated during their lifetimes. Emily Dickinson was a great poet. Yvor Winters, in fact, called her "one of the great lyric poets of all time." Actually, she was so far ahead of her time that she could not be appreciated while she was alive. Only seven of her more than 1700 poems were published during her lifetime, and even these appeared anonymously. Why should any poet try to become famous if fame means that she has to change her poems to conform to the unimaginative poetic standards of her day? To be a great poet requires great confidence in one's artistic ability. Unfortunately, the public is always too tradition-bound to recognize true art when it appears in an unfamiliar form. Emily Dickinson's work is no exception. The question is this: Are there any Emily Dickinsons today whose brilliance remains unappreciated due to our cultural blindness?

VERSION 3

Emily Dickinson, one of America's greatest poets, was all but unknown during her lifetime, for she allowed only a handful of her more than 1700 poems to be published, and these appeared anonymously. Only after her death were her works discovered by her sister and brought forth to a warm public reception. Ever since then, the many persons who have written about this unusual genius have attempted to explain her reluctance to publish. The image created by literary critics and popular historians alike is that of a shy, reclusive,

mystical dreamer--a sensitive soul deeply wrapped up in her personal
joys and sorrows. However, a new picture of the poet has come forth
from scholars working closely with her correspondence and with fresh
biographical evidence. This view reveals an artist who felt so sure
of her own worth that she deliberately kept her creations from a world
she believed was incapable of understanding them and insensitive to
their beauty.

7
Writing the Paper

After you have developed a logical outline and written an introductory paragraph, you are ready to write the paper itself. This task will consume a good deal of time, since you must plan to write at least three versions of your paper: a rough draft, a revised draft, and a polished final manuscript suitable for submission to your instructor. Many writers feel the need for even further revision, but three drafts are the absolute minimum.

Writing the Rough Draft

Writing the rough draft of a research paper can be thought of as "filling in the outline" because the outline provides a structure not just for your own ideas and conclusions but for the many research notes you have taken. If you try to write your rough draft by working only from the note cards, it will be much harder for you to keep in mind the relationships among them. Hardest of all is trying to write the draft from memory, off the top of your head. That approach may work well when writing essays based on personal experience, but if used for a research paper it absolutely guarantees mistakes and omissions.

While writing the rough draft, you may think of a better way to present your case than you had planned. If that happens, stop writing, go back and revise your outline or even construct a new one. Remember that if you change part of your outline, you will probably have to change other parts as well, in order to maintain balance and an orderly and logical presentation of ideas.

Since the first draft is not meant to be seen by anyone but yourself, don't worry if some sentences are weakly written, and some word choices are not as apt as you would like. Concentrate on expressing your ideas clearly. Let your ideas and sentences flow as freely as you can, getting everything down on paper in a form which reflects your thinking, however roughly. When you write the second draft, finding the right words for what you want to say will be considerably easier.

Here are three pieces of advice for the format of the first draft. *First,* leave plenty of space between the lines for later insertions and changes— about two lines of space for every line of writing. *Second,* don't slow yourself down by copying out each quotation, paraphrase, or summary from your cards. When you come to a place where you need to use a note, simply make a memo to yourself that says "copy from card" or "see card." Or, before you start writing, you might take all of your note cards to a copy center or to the copying machine in the library and make photocopies. You can then cut and paste these copies right into the draft. *Finally,* be sure to note briefly in the margin the source of each note you use in the paper, no matter if the note is a direct quotation, a paraphrase, or a summary. You can simply note the author's name or a key word or two from the title, plus the page numbers. If you fail to make a note, you may later forget to add a source note.

INTEGRATING YOUR SOURCES

Though you are by now familiar with your notes, you are for the first time trying to blend them into a coherent whole. As you are writing the first draft, some situations may arise that cause special kinds of problems. The following occur fairly frequently.

No One Source Tells the Whole Story. Often you will have to draw details from different sources in order to deal with a subtopic as fully as you need to. Then you must be careful to keep track of which facts come from which sources. If you simply combine all the details into one account of the situation, with just one source note, your readers may not realize that the picture is a composite, its parts coming from various sources.

Several Sources Disagree over a Question of Fact. Here you have several options. You may simply report the disagreement, especially if you have no basis for trusting one source more than the others. Or you may choose one source if it seems more trustworthy than the others: it may be more fully documented, or merely be the most recent. Or you might try to verify the fact by further research. (The student writing about Emily Dickinson found that various sources said the number of poems published during the poet's lifetime was six, seven, or eight. Since the most exhaustive and best documented source said the number was seven, the student simply used that number in her paper and disregarded the other sources' claims. After all, she was in no position to verify the fact herself, and the exact number was not crucial to her thesis.

Some Sources Disagree in Their Interpretation of a Fact or Facts. Such differences occur all the time; in fact, they are among the things that make research interesting. If the purpose of your paper is not to argue for a particular conclusion but to report the current state of knowledge, you may simply report the disagreement. If, however, your thesis states a definite position regarding your topic, you must not only report the disagreement but also draw your own conclusion as to which interpretation seems more soundly argued or based on more complete or more reliable evidence. In reporting the disagreement, you must be fair to the writers whose interpretations you reject by presenting their views with enough detail for your readers to be able to agree with your preference or not.

As you can see, writing the first draft involves a great deal of thinking about the ideas and information in your notes in order to draw reasonable conclusions about them. It is this thinking, and not the physical act of writing down your thoughts or keeping track of your sources, that makes the first draft a time-consuming and challenging task. This is also why we encourage you not to get bogged down trying to express your thoughts in exactly the right words. You have enough to do without worrying about that.

ENDING IT ALL

When the body of your paper is complete, you must compose a suitable conclusion. As a general rule, the conclusion should not introduce any new ideas or information. Instead, it should restate your thesis in terms that reflect the evidence that you have presented. (If you use the same words that you used to state your thesis in your introduction, your readers may feel that you haven't taken them anywhere.) Above all, your conclusion should bring your paper to a satisfying close with a statement that sums up what you think your research has shown. Don't be afraid to commit yourself in this respect: you ought to be able to stand confidently behind your research.

Now that you have completed a first draft of your paper, set the project aside for at least a few hours and do something else. It would be best if you could take at least a day's vacation. During the time you are not consciously working at the research project, your unconscious mind will be digesting, synthesizing, and generally working with what you have done. Then, as you tackle the second draft, not only will you feel refreshed, but you may also find yourself brimming with new ideas.

Revising the Rough Draft

Once you have brought your outline to life by writing a rough essay, the nature of your job changes significantly. You must now become your own toughest critic. Read what you have written closely, as if for the first time, so that you can find those parts which communicate most effectively as well as those which work poorly or not at all. Then you can become the author again, rewriting and, if necessary, reorganizing the weaker passages so that they become as strong as the best. Finally, you must examine the revised essay very closely in order to correct the spelling, punctuation, and other mechanical details.

Approach your revision in an orderly way, by thinking of the task on four levels of organization: the whole paper, paragraphs, sentences, and individual words and phrases.

First, reconsider the order of the major and minor subtopics as presented in your outline and see if this arrangement still serves your purposes well. Once you are satisfied that these larger elements of the paper have been presented in an effective sequence, reexamine the structure of each paragraph and revise where necessary. Then look for sentences that could use improvement. Long, cumbersome sentences, for example, can be broken down into simpler, more easily digested units, but sometimes your revision will work in the other direction—combining a series of short, choppy sentences into longer, smoothly flowing sentences. Still other sentences must simply be recast to make them clearer. Finally, read through the paper, checking your transitions between paragraphs and the details within each paragraph.

Changes in wording can be made at any stage of your revision, even when you are repairing weak paragraph organization or faulty sentence structure. But you should still give yourself one last chance to improve your choice of words just before writing the final, polished version.

RECONSIDERING THE ORGANIZATION

As you arranged your note cards and constructed your outline, you carefully thought about the best order in which to present the information and ideas that would support your thesis. While writing the first draft, however, you might have felt that your plan was not completely practical. Upon rereading your draft you may be more dissatisfied than ever. What can you do?

Perhaps you decided when constructing the outline to present the evidence supporting your thesis first and the evidence against it afterwards. This strategy is effective if your case is so strong that it will make the opposing arguments seem weak. On rereading your paper, however, you found that the opposing case did not seem weak; instead, it seemed to rebut much of your case point by point. One way to reverse that effect would be to switch the order of those subtopics, stating the opposing case first and rebutting it with your case. At this stage of the revision, you would not need to do any rewriting. You would simply cut the two passages out of the paper and tape or paste them back in the new order. Later you would rewrite them and revise the transitions to make the new order effective.

Rearrangements sometimes require more revision than simple adjustments in paragraph or sentence structure: you might occasionally find it a good idea to rewrite drastically and thereby produce a new ''first'' draft to work with. More often, however, you will find your outline a good guide, and no major reorganization will be necessary. You can then go on to revising the individual paragraphs.

REVISING PARAGRAPHS

Think of a paragraph as a group of sentences that work together to support a controlling idea—the idea expressed in the *topic* (or *main idea*) *sentence*. Ask yourself if a reader would be able to grasp easily the controlling ideas in your paragraphs, either because you have provided clear topic sentences or because you have so carefully constructed your paragraphs that the controlling ideas can be inferred readily from all the sentences taken together. Although you should not feel that you must impose a single rigid concept of paragraph structure on your writing, you should be certain that your paragraphs contribute to a logical progression of ideas in your paper. To the extent that they do not, you must revise.

If you think that one or more of your paragraphs might be confusing to a reader, the first thing to do is to see if the rewriting (or addition) of a topic sentence will clarify your thoughts. If a paragraph remains confusing even after you have improved its topic sentence or created a new topic sentence for it, you must focus on two additional features of paragraph structure:

1. the order in which you have presented the details in support of your topic sentence;

2. the smoothness with which you have moved from one sentence to the next or from one idea to another.

As you review your work, try to read each paragraph as though you were a reader unaware of what the writer intended to say. If you find a paragraph confusing, rearrange the details until you have found the most effective order for them. If the progression from one detail to the next still is not smooth, pick up your composition book or rhetoric and read about achieving coherence, or logical sequence, in paragraphs. Pay special attention to what the book says about using *transitional words and phrases* and other *devices for linking ideas* smoothly and logically. A short review of this kind can enable you to improve the flow of thought within your paragraphs and throughout your paper as a whole.

REVISING SENTENCES

Writing effective sentences is primarily a matter of style, and style develops only through a great deal of practice. Even when you recognize that a sentence calls for improvement, you may have trouble deciding just what changes would make it better. As you revise your paper, you can help yourself by being alert to a few common weaknesses in sentence construction. Pay particular attention to sentences in your rough draft that may be either too complex or too simple and to patterns of construction that may be monotonously repetitive.

First, check the length of your sentences. Some may be too long and complicated for readers to follow comfortably. Usually such sentences can be broken down into more easily digested sentences, as the example illustrates.

too long a sentence   Throughout the war, many Southerners came to think of Lincoln as a power-hungry autocrat, who, in spite of the public speeches in which he advocated peace and reconciliation, was in reality determined to destroy anyone, in the North or South, who stood in the way of his gaining absolute control of the nation he had been elected to govern.

improvement   Throughout the war, many Southerners came to think of Lincoln as a power-hungry autocrat, in spite of the public speeches in which he advocated peace and reconciliation. They believed that he was in

> reality determined to destroy anyone, in the North
> or South, who stood in the way of his gaining
> absolute control of the nation he had been elected
> to govern.

Short sentences are easy to understand, but a series of five or six very short, choppy sentences actually may be more difficult to read than two or three sentences of average length. When you find such a series in your draft, consider combining several of them into longer sentences. Save your short sentences until they can be used most effectively—for example, when emphasizing or summing up a particularly important point.

too many short sentences

Throughout the war, many people detested Lincoln.
They considered him to be power-hungry. His
speeches called for peace and reconciliation. But
these people did not believe him. They included
Northerners as well as Southerners. They believed
that he intended to destroy anyone who opposed
him. They thought he desired to gain absolute
control of the country. They saw his election as
part of his plan to rule as a dictator.

improvement

Throughout the war, many people detested Lincoln,
whom they considered power-hungry. Although his
speeches called for peace and reconciliation,
these people did not believe him. Both Northerners
and Southerners thought that he intended to
destroy anyone who opposed him and sought
dictatorial control of the country he had been
elected to govern.

Also check the patterns of your sentences to see if you have repeated one pattern monotonously. Such repetition may needlessly bore your readers.

repetitive pattern

Hartman says that . . . Anna Freud states that
. . . Mahler claims that . . . And now Kohut
states that . . .

improvement

Hartman says that . . . Further support comes from

```
Anna Freud . . . Mahler agrees, for the most part,
claiming that . . . Recently, Kohut added further
support to this idea when he stated . . .
```

The second example is an improvement over the first not only because it is more varied but also because the writer has taken a set of ideas from different sources and blended them into a smoothly flowing passage that shows how these ideas relate to each other.

REVISING WORD CHOICE

When you revise your word choice, there are three elements you should keep in mind:

1. *variety*—Find appropriate synonyms for words that appear often, except for technical terms which do not allow substitutes
2. *accuracy*—Avoid vague, loose terms that may be misinterpreted
3. *slang*—Avoid words that are not appropriate to the formal context of a research paper

Finding Variety. This example illustrates monotonous repetition of terms:

lacking variety

```
A young, idealistic anthropologist, on first
venturing into a primitive society, is likely to
suffer severe disillusionment. For one thing,
most such societies live under physical
conditions that no one coming from American
society can possibly anticipate. But far more
dispiriting is the fact that these societies often
practice customs radically opposite to the ideal
life in nature that naive students like to
imagine: a society of simple folk, yes, but a
society that knows the true value of love,
kindness, sharing, and mutual respect. The
Yanomamo society provides an example that could
try the soul of any young idealist searching for
simple, natural virtues. Their social practices
include . . .
```

improvement

A young, idealistic anthropologist, on first venturing into a primitive society, is likely to suffer severe disillusionment. For one thing, most such people live under physical conditions that no one coming from America can possibly anticipate. But far more dispiriting is the fact that these communities often practice customs radically opposite to the ideal life in nature that naive students like to imagine: a society of simple folk, yes, but one that knows the true value of love, kindness, sharing, and mutual respect. The Yanomamo tribe provides an example that could try the soul of any young idealist searching for simple, natural virtues. Their social practices include . . .

Avoiding Vagueness. Here are some examples illustrating the emptiness of vague words:

vague

Napoleon was a great man.
Sarah Bernhardt was an outstanding actress.
Einstein was a fantastic thinker.
Oedipus Rex is a first-rate play.

improved

Napoleon was a brilliant military strategist.
Sarah Bernhardt played a wide variety of roles to perfection.
Einstein's theories reshaped the world of modern physics.
The play Oedipus Rex provides meaningful insights into human behavior.

Of course, you cannot entirely avoid vague terms, but you can keep them to a minimum and use them with care. In short, say exactly what you mean, or at least come as close as possible.

Avoiding Slang and Colloquialisms. The following are examples of word choices not appropriate to the formal context of a research paper:

inappropriate

The women in Rubens's paintings are very sexy.

The CIA has been blasted recently for failing to
perform its duties with sufficient
restraint.

The prosecutor called upon a well-known shrink to
testify that the defendant was not really
crazy.

improved

The women in Rubens's paintings are very sensuous.

The CIA has been sharply criticized recently for
failing to perform its duties with
sufficient restraint.

The prosecutor called upon a well-known
psychiatrist to testify that the defendant
was not legally insane.

When revising word choice, be careful if you decide to use a *thesaurus,* or collection of synonyms. Books of synonyms can be valuable in helping you to remember a word whose meaning you know well; they can be dangerous if you use them to select high-sounding words that are unfamiliar to you. The connotations of such words may not be appropriate to the contexts in which you place them. You may find a *dictionary of synonyms* more useful than a thesaurus because the former defines and illustrates the different shades of meaning between synonyms.

SOME SAMPLES OF REVISION

Here is how Anita Barrone moved from rough draft through the various revisions of her opening paragraphs.

Increasing Maximum Life Expectancy:

Myth or Reality?

**opening paragraph
rough draft**

For a long time, people have dreamed of
extending their life spans. In fact Juan Ponce de
Leon discovered Florida in 1513 when he was
searching for the Fountain of Youth. By now we have
pretty much given up hope that there is a fountain

of youth or a marvelous herb that can extend our
life spans. But gerontologists (people who study
aging processes) are working on the problem. They
are carrying out experiments that may or may not
help us to extend our lives. However, many
gerontologists are optimistic that they are on the
right track.

Anita realized that this opening paragraph was not particularly effective as an introduction to her paper. The reference to Ponce de Leon—intended as an "interest grabber"—was left hanging, leaving it to the reader to determine precisely why she had used this reference. She saw the possibility that some readers might interpret "For a long time" as meaning from 1513 to the present, when she had actually intended to suggest that the desire to extend life span has been a dream of human beings for as long as there have been human beings. In addition she saw that the "problem" gerontologists are working on could be interpreted by some readers as the problem of finding a fountain of youth or a marvelous herb. The last two sentences, intended as her thesis statement, were vaguely worded and did not help to pull the paragraph together. All in all—she concluded—a paragraph badly in need of rethinking and rewriting.

After some thought, Anita decided to write a two-paragraph introduction. In the first she would expand upon the Ponce de Leon reference to create a broad introduction to her topic and to generate reader interest. In the second she would introduce her topic more specifically and present a clearer statement of her thesis. This strategy differed somewhat from her original plan for the paper, but Anita saw that the change was necessary to ensure that her paper got off to a good start.

revised opening paragraph

Every American schoolchild learns that Juan
Ponce de Leon discovered Florida in 1513 while
searching for the Fountain of Youth. He believed
the waters of the fountain would make him young
again. But he never found the fountain. Instead he
found death by an Indian arrow. Today we know how
silly Ponce de Leon was for believing in a fountain
of youth provided by a beneficent nature. But his

```
dream of extending his life span was one that many

people have had throughout the ages. It is still

very much with us today.
```

Now Anita felt that she had used her Ponce de Leon example success-fully to present a broad introduction for her paper. She had not been too concerned with her writing style because she was mainly interested in improving the organization and content of the paragraph. Her next step was to take a closer look at her sentences and her word use to see if the writing itself could be improved. Her self-criticism, along with some ad-vice from her instructor, led her to make the following changes.

a bit more accurate—Ponce de Leon did not want to be restored to childhood

sentence combining for variety and to lessen repetition of "fountain"

```
Every American schoolchild learns that Juan Ponce de
Leon discovered Florida in 1513 while searching for the
                        , whose waters, he believed,
Fountain of Youth. He believed the waters of the fountain
        restore him to youthful manhood. Unfortunately,
would make him young again. But he never found the fountain.
                                            Smile
Instead he found death by an Indian arrow. Today we know
at the naivete of
how silly Ponce de Leon was for believing in a fountain of
youth provided by a beneficent nature. But his dream of
extending his life span was one that many people have had
                        , and it is a dream that is
throughout the ages. It is still very much with us today.
```

"unfortunately" works better than "but" to prepare reader for following sentence

"silly" isn't a fair word to describe the explorer's search— in his day, many people believed that nature held the secret to extended life

again, combining for variety and to clarify "it" as referring to "dream"

Satisfied with her first paragraph, Anita turned next to writing the new second paragraph for her paper, using some of the ideas and word-ing that she left out of her revised first paragraph. This second para-graph, with Anita's critical revisions, follows.

more
precise

unnecessary
and wordy

By now we have pretty much given up hope ~~that somewhere~~
~~in nature we may discover~~ a ⌃*of discovering* fountain of youth or a marvelous
herb that can relieve us of the ~~problems~~ *anxieties and debilities* associated with the
process of aging. Instead our hopes of extending life

vague word
in this
context

expectancy are in the hands of scientists. Gerontologists
~~(people~~ *scientists* who study aging processes) are attempting to slow
down--and perhaps even overcome--nature's timetables for
human aging. ~~Not all scientists think that it is possible.~~ *Although not all scientists think that increasing the life span is possible in the near future,*
~~But many do.~~ *Many* gerontologists and knowledgeable
commentators are optimistic about our chances ~~for increasing~~
~~the life span. Gerontological researchers are optimistic~~ *researchers*
because of the promising results ~~they~~ have obtained from
experiments with animals and cell cultures. These
experiments might well lead us to a "fountain" of extended,
healthy life, if not to eternal youth.

rewritten to
improve
clarity and
style of
thesis

wordy
and
repetitious

unclear
pronoun
reference

Writing the Polished, Final Draft

Equipped with a carefully revised draft, you are ready to produce the polished, final version of your research paper. As you write the final version, you may continue to make changes in wording to improve the clarity of your paper. You may also make minor alterations in your paragraphs and sentences in order to improve the flow of thought. However, if at this time you find yourself making major changes in the organization or the content of your paper, then you have embarked upon the final draft without being fully prepared. If this is the case, consider this draft as another revision and work out your problems before again attempting to produce the final draft.

There are two more jobs you must do before you begin to prepare the manuscript of your paper. You must write a complete set of notes acknowledging the source of each quotation or paraphrase in the paper, and you must prepare a final version of your bibliography. The next chapter discusses the form and placement of these source citations.

Review Questions

1. At least how many versions of a research paper must you write? Why?

2. What should you do when your sources disagree?
3. Briefly outline the steps in revising a rough draft.

Exercise

Revise three consecutive paragraphs in your rough draft until you are satisfied with the entire sequence. Show every stage of your revision and explain your reasons for making each change.

8

Documenting Your Sources

After the paper has been written, revised, and polished, one essential step remains: documenting the sources. Documentation consists not only of listing all your sources under Works Cited, but also of inserting notes within the text to tell readers where you found the various ideas and information that form the backbone of your research paper. This final task serves several important purposes.

First of all, notes tell your readers where to find further information about your topic. You may have raised some questions that would send a curious reader back to your source for answers. Or a reader might want to verify your interpretation of what you read. For instance, someone might want to be certain you had not quoted out of context. Another reason for providing notes is to give knowledgeable readers some idea of how authoritative a particular statement is—that is, whether the source's author is an expert in the field or simply a reporter summarizing recent developments for the general public.

Another significant feature of the notes is the date of initial publication. For instance, Sigmund Freud spent more than forty years developing the psychoanalytic theory of personality, and over that period, he revised some of his earlier ideas considerably. Therefore, a well-informed reader might want to know just when Freud made some statement that was quoted in your paper. For this reason, you must be careful to find out the year the source was first published. Don't stop when you learn the year in which the book was *printed*, for many books are printed more than once and by more than one publisher.

Most important, the documentation gives readers an overall sense of how thoroughly you carried out your research. The list of Works Cited reveals at a glance the range of your investigation of the topic; the notes indicate how thoroughly you have read the sources.

The notes themselves can take one of two forms: *parenthetical notes* or *numbered notes*. This book concentrates on the Modern Language Association's 1984 format, which uses parenthetical notes. For an example of this system, see the paper on Emily Dickinson at the beginning of chapter 9. The traditional numbered footnote format, which many history instructors prefer, is briefly explained (see pp. 172–174) and then illustrated in the paper on Jefferson Davis, also found in chapter 9. A third system, devised by the American Psychological Association and used in most of the social sciences is discussed on pages 176–181 and exemplified by the third paper in chapter 9. One further system—the numbered system for scientific research—is briefly explained on pages 181–182.

What to Document

While writing the rough draft, you noted in the margins the sources of all ideas and information that came from your note cards. Now you must add notes to your text, clearly indicating those sources for your reader. Before we discuss how to go about placing these notes in the paper, an important question needs to be answered:

Is it necessary to document the source of every piece of information that goes into your paper?

For instance you might wonder whether it is essential to state where you came across simple facts such as these:

the Battle of Chickamauga was fought on September 19 and 20, 1863;

nitrogen makes up 78 percent of Earth's atmosphere;

the capital of the African nation Chad is Ndjamena.

Depending on the nature of your research topic, identifying the source of every such fact could clutter the paper with distracting and unhelpful notes. To prevent this, it is generally agreed that you do not have to identify the sources for information that is considered ''general knowledge,'' that is, information readily available in the reference section of any library, even a small one. The facts regarding Chickamauga, nitrogen, and Ndjamena clearly fall under the heading of general knowledge.

Naturally, you will sometimes be unsure whether a particular fact is general knowledge. In that case, to be safe, insert a note. The best thing to do before you begin any research paper, however, is to ask your instructor what kinds of information do not call for documentation.

Looking at the problem the other way around, we can say: *Documentation is required for any information that falls into one of these categories:*

1. opinions, judgments, theories, and personal explanations;
2. "facts" that are open to dispute, and virtually all statistics regarding human behavior;
3. factual information gathered by a small number of observers, no matter how expert they may be (for example, the results of a recent scientific test).

OPINIONS, JUDGMENTS, THEORIES, AND PERSONAL EXPLANATIONS

Encyclopedias are filled with facts that are considered general knowledge, but that does not mean that all information found in an encyclopedia can go into your paper without a note. In the following encyclopedia entry, the annotated passages constitute opinions and would therefore require notes if you used them in your paper.

"influenced by her . . . French contemporaries" is an inference; "greatly" indicates a judgment

"refreshing simplicity," "vigorous treatment," and "pleasing color" reflect personal observations and judgments

CASSATT, Mary (1845-1926). American figure painter and etcher, b. Pittsburgh. Most of her life was spent in France, where she was greatly influenced by her great French contemporaries, particularly Manet and Degas, whose friendship and esteem she enjoyed. She allied herself with the impressionists early in her career. Motherhood was Cassatt's most frequent subject. Her pictures are notable for their refreshing simplicity, vigorous treatment, and pleasing color. She excelled also as a pastelist and etcher, and her drypoints and color prints are greatly admired. She is well represented in public and private galleries in the United States. Her best known paintings include several versions of *Mother and Child* (Metropolitan Mus.; Mus. of Fine Arts, Boston; Worcester, Mass., Art Museum); *Lady at the Tea-Table* (Metropolitan Mus.); *Modern Women,* a mural painted for the Women's Building at the Chicago Exposition; and a portrait of the artist's mother. See catalog by A. D. Breeskin (1970); biography by J. M. Carson (1966).

"FACTS" OPEN TO DISPUTE

This category includes commonly accepted "facts" based largely on inference. When new evidence is discovered, new inferences may have to be made. For example, the significance of a particular fossil bone is definitely a matter of judgment, and the astronomical phenomenon known as a "black hole" is by no means as factual as many popular accounts suggest.

Much of the work done by behavioral scientists consists of collecting statistical information (the average number of children in Chinese-American families, the rate of juvenile crime in Boston, and so on). Although the statistics you encounter in your research may seem to be hard facts, these facts can be disputed. Indeed, theories and conclusions based on such facts are continually debated by the experts. Therefore, almost all information in the behavioral sciences must be documented except historical facts about individual persons and events in the field.

FACTUAL INFORMATION GATHERED BY A SMALL NUMBER OF OBSERVERS

Information gathered by observation and experimentation is subject to dispute. The results of similar experiments may vary, or different researchers may interpret identical results differently. Accordingly, such information should be documented so your readers know its source.

For example, you might read in a newspaper or magazine this week that "scientists at the Murphy-Weiss Laboratories in Ipswich, Maine, have shown that cola drinks cause liver cancer in rats and monkeys." The headline might even have read: "Soda Pop Causes Cancer." The experiment may have been honestly and carefully executed, and the information may *eventually* be accepted as fact. But until other scientists have duplicated these scientists' work and arrived at the same results, this information is just a "possible" fact, and therefore, it definitely needs to be documented.

Now for one last question: Is it necessary to provide source notes for ideas and information which you were already aware of before undertaking the research paper?

If the information falls into one of the three categories just discussed, you must take the time to locate a source for it. Readers have a right as well as a need to know of a reliable source for the information in question. Furthermore, finding a source protects you against misremembering what you had previously heard or read. Thus, it is always wise when reading sources to take notes on everything that is relevant to your hypothesis, even when you are familiar with the information.

The MLA System of Parenthetical Notation

Because scholars in various fields have not yet agreed upon a standard system of documentation, for every paper you are assigned be sure to ask your instructor which system is preferred and then consult a guidebook such as this for the proper format. Since most instructors of language and literature follow the system devised in 1984 by the Modern Language Association (MLA), we will describe and illustrate that system in detail.

In general, you will identify the source for any idea or information you discovered through research by placing a brief parenthetical reference within the appropriate sentence, most often directly following the words being cited. Such a note will contain the page number(s) on which the information was found, plus any additional information needed to identify the source, such as the author's name or the title of the work. The amount of information required in a parenthetical note depends on what you have said about the source within the text.

1. If you have mentioned the author's name in your text, the note usually consists of just the page number(s) on which the information was located.

   This fact led the critic Owen Thomas to conclude that Emily Dickinson
   "was well aware of the world outside her little room, that in fact
   she used the language of this outside world to create some of her best
   poetry" (523).

2. If you have not mentioned the author's name, then the note must include that information.

   But an economist who predicted the depression of 1981 a year in
   advance fears the price of gold will decline slowly for at least ten
   years (Goodserve 143).

3. If the author has written more than one of the sources in your Works Cited, your note must include the particular title unless it is mentioned in your text.

   Chomsky claims that all humans inherit the same basic linguistic
   structural framework upon which their community's particular
   language is fitted (Language 29-41).

   The Works Cited in this case also includes Chomsky's *Syntactic Structures*.

4. If the author is unknown, as in many newspaper accounts, the title

must appear in the note, if not mentioned in the text. (Titles may be shortened.)

```
Only Mayor McCarthy expressed the least optimism toward the city's
fate ("Rebirth" 2).
```

The Works Cited for this source shows: "Rebirth of a City." *News-Times* (Danbury, CT) 6 Sept. 1977: 2.

SPACING AND PUNCTUATION

1. Leave one space before the parentheses, and two spaces after whatever punctuation follows them.

```
Morgan believes the whale stands for God (132), whereas Kay claims
it "embodies all that is evil" (19-20). This controversy derives
largely from . . .
```

2. The parentheses are placed *inside* a sentence, directly following the quotation or paraphrase they refer to, and *outside* quotation marks. (See previous example.)
3. When a quotation ends with a ? or a !, the ? or ! goes *inside* the quotation marks. Note: A period is still needed *after* the parentheses.

```
Dickinson's letter to Higginson contained a question: "Are you too
deeply occupied to say if my Verse is alive?" (Letters 2: 403).
```

4. If you quote more than four lines from a source, set the quotation off from the rest of the text by *indenting ten spaces* from the margin. Then, place the parenthetical note *after* the final mark of punctuation, separated by two spaces.

```
Catton also suggests that Davis's attempt to lead his people to
independence was somehow doomed to failure from the start.
            He had done the best he could do in an impossible job, and
            if it is easy to show where he made grievous mistakes, it is
            difficult to show that any other man, given the materials
            available, could have done much better. He had courage,
            integrity, tenacity, devotion to his cause, and like Old
            Testament Sisera, the stars in their courses marched
            against him. (279)
```

NUMBERED NOTES FOR SPECIAL PURPOSES

Once in a while, you will find something that might interest your readers but is not essential to whatever idea you are developing in the paper at that point. If that happens, you may insert a note number directing readers to a footnote or an endnote. Endnotes, if you use them, are placed on a separate page, coming between the end of the paper and the Works Cited.

Insert the note number immediately after the final mark of punctuation for the sentence which led you to think of adding the "comment for interested readers." Raise the number half a line.

Literary critics, serious biographers, and writers of fictionalized accounts of her life created an image of Emily Dickinson as a timid, reclusive, mystical thinker, who was too absorbed in personal sorrows and ecstasies to be concerned with literary recognition. And this image persists, to a great extent, in the public mind today.[1]

Endnote page would show:

[1] For a full discussion of sources leading to the "Emily myth," see Ferlazzo: 13-21.

(This note offers readers more information than they could get from the simple parenthetical note: "Ferlazzo 13-21.")

Variations on the Basic MLA Format

SOURCES HAVING MORE THAN ONE AUTHOR

If the source was written by more than one person, you would need to give the names of all the writers or possibly use "et al." if there were three or more.

Davis took the position that "the President was entrusted with military leadership, and he must exercise it" (Randall and Donald 271).

A recent investigation of iridium levels in the Dolomites revealed traces insufficient to justify Alvarez's hypothesis (Sapperstein et al. 12).

Works Cited would show:

> Randall, J. G., and David Donald. The Divided Union. Boston:
> Little, Brown, 1961.
>
> Sapperstein, M. L., Jonathan Kohn, Natalie Sachs, and R. L.
> Davis. "Iridium Levels in the Dolomites." Astronomy Today Sept.
> 1983: 12-15.

TWO OR MORE SOURCES FOR ONE NOTE

Sometimes a piece of information or an idea will appear in more than one of your sources. Usually, especially with purely factual information, you choose one of the sources and refer only to it. However, occasionally, when each source offers some interesting additional commentary that a curious reader might enjoy investigating, you should mention both of them in your note.

> Many of Davis's personal troubles grew out of his ill health (Catton
> 121-122; Nevins 3: 86-89).

INDIRECT SOURCE: A SOURCE QUOTES ANOTHER WRITER

Frequently, your source will quote another writer's work, and you may want to quote that second writer. When this happens, you must make every reasonable effort to find the original source in order to verify the accuracy of the quotation. For one thing, you should check to be certain it was not "quoted out of context" (see pp. 94–95). When you have seen that source, you can add it to your list of Works Cited and refer directly to it in a parenthetical note.

However, sometimes you will find it very difficult, or even impossible, to locate the original source. In that case, you will be forced to rely on your first source, but your parenthetical reference must indicate that you worked with an indirect source by using the abbreviation "qtd." (for "quoted").

In this example, the author was quoting from an out-of-print book, *Criminal Man*, that was written in Italian.

> Lambroso's racism becomes apparent in his remark that "[criminals']
> physical insensibility well recalls that of savage peoples who can
> bear, in rites of puberty, torture that a white man could never
> endure. All travelers know the indifference of Negroes and American

```
savages to pain: the former cut their hands and laugh in order to
avoid work; the latter, tied to the torture post, gaily sing the
praises of their tribe while they are slowly burnt" (qtd. in
Gould 18).
```

The Works Cited page would show:

```
     Gould, Stephen Jay. "Criminal Man Revived." Natural History
March 1976: 16-18.
```

REFERENCE TO AN ENTIRE WORK

If you refer to an entire source by way of a summary or a paraphrase of its thesis, then you do not need a parenthetical note as long as you mention author and title.

```
Gore Vidal's Lincoln presents a very readable reconstruction of the
President's approach to problems, both personal and political.
```

SUMMARY OF A CHAPTER OR AN ESSAY

Occasionally, you will make a statement that summarizes a major idea from an article or essay or a chapter in a book. For a chapter, you may use the chapter number instead of page numbers.

```
Chomsky claims that all humans inherit the same basic linguistic
structural framework upon which their community's particular
language is fitted (Language ch. 2).
```

For an essay or an article, do not use a note. Just mention the author within your text. A reader can tell from the nature of your statement that it covers a good deal of ground and will expect no note.

```
Gould settled the perplexing question as to whether a Portuguese man-
of-war is an organism or a colony by approaching the problem from a
new point of view, that of overlapping, evolving categories rather
than rigidly fixed definitions.
```

The author's name is enough to lead a reader to the right source in your Works Cited:

```
     Gould, Stephen Jay. "A Most Ingenious Paradox." Natural
History Dec. 1984: 20-29.
```

QUOTATION FROM LITERARY WORKS

When writing on literary topics, you will usually quote from the plays, poems, or prose works under discussion. For novels, short stories, and most poems, indicate the page numbers, as with other sources. But for plays and long poetic works that consist of "books" or "cantos," indicate where you found the quoted material not by page number but by line number. For drama, use act/scene/line notation. For poems like *The Iliad*, give the canto or book number plus the line numbers.

novel

> It would seem that Captain Ahab has forever rejected God as he commences his final soliloquy with, "I turn my body from the sun . . ." (468).

poetry

> Along the same lines, given her deliberate decision to forgo publication rather than compromise her art, the first lines of another poem become significantly clear: "Publication-- is the Auction / Of the Mind of Man" (348). And there can be no doubt that when she wrote the following stanza, Emily Dickinson had accepted the fact that true fame would not be hers in her lifetime.
>
> > Some--Work for Immortality--
> > The Chiefer part, for Time--
> > He--Compensates--immediately
> > The former--Checks--On Fame-- (193)

Note: This student used just one edition of Dickinson's poetry. If she had also quoted from another edition, each note would have to identify which edition was used. For example,

> . . . the first lines of another poem become significantly clear: "Publication is the Auction / Of the Mind of Man" (Complete Poems 348).

drama

(reference to *Othello*)

> Once again, Shakespeare deftly shifts images, this time in Othello's speech over the sleeping Desdemona, from lightness of color (Desdemona as compared to Othello) to light as a symbol of life (5.2.3-13).

(quotation from *Doctor Faustus*)

```
I see there's virtue in my heavenly words;
Who would not be proficient in this art?
How pliant is this Mephistophilis,
Full of obedience and humility!
Such is the force of magic and my spells:
Now, Faustus, thou art conjuror laureate,
That canst command great Mephistophilis.
(1.3.30-36)
```

(Act/scene/line numbers or book/line numbers are always sufficient as long as you use just one edition of the work and you clearly indicate in your text what work you are quoting.)

long poetic work

```
Thus Adam to himself lamented loud
    . . . on the ground
Outstretcht he lay, on the cold ground, and oft
Curs'd his Creation, Death as oft accus'd
Of tardy execution, since denounc't
The day of his offence. Why comes not Death,
```

(quotation from *Paradise Lost*)

```
Said he, with one thrice acceptable stroke
To end me?  (10.845-856)
```

Note the difference between the punctuation of this note and the punctuation for volume and page numbers: *10.845-856* reads "book ten, lines 845-856"; *3:203* reads "volume 3, page 203."

Some Advice About Using Parenthetical Notation

This system of documentation encourages you to name your sources as you refer to them in the essay and to put as little information as possible in the parenthetical notes. Keep in mind that your notes should avoid, as far as possible, breaking a reader's concentration. The example shows how an obtrusive parenthetical note can be made less obtrusive.

obtrusive

```
Certainly then, the woman who has been called
"one of the greatest lyric poets of all time"
(Winters 40) was all but unknown as a poet during
her lifetime.
```

less obtrusive

```
Certainly then, the woman Yvor Winters has called
"one of the greatest lyric poets of all time"
(40) was all but unknown as a poet during her
lifetime.
```

Notice that the parenthetical note was placed directly after the quoted phrase. If it had been put at the end of the sentence (to reduce the inter-ruptive effect), the note would seem to cover the whole idea, not just the part that belonged to Yvor Winters.

When paraphrasing, you will sometimes find it difficult to slip in the source's name, especially when the paraphrase deals with factual matter rather than a judgment, as in this example.

> During her later years, Emily Dickinson had virtually no direct contact with anyone outside her immediate family. While she was still connected to her circle of friends, the poet made at least one tentative attempt to find an audience for her poetry. But only a handful of verses were published anonymously, most of them in a local newspaper, and these were subjected to considerable editing. Upon the poet's death at fifty-six, her sister discovered over one thousand poems and initiated an effort to publish them. Beginning four years later, in 1890, these poems finally appeared in print (Sewall 1: 4-11).

Clearly, you would have had no reason to introduce Sewall's name in the text, since the information is both factual and very general; nothing seems to be particularly the work of a specific biographer.

Both of the next examples are well constructed passages using the same sources; both make good use of the parenthetical note format. The differences are due to a shift of purpose on the author's part. The comments that follow the examples explain the effect of the variation.

1. Recent studies show that anorexia can be successfully treated by psychotherapy (Kline; Evans et al.; Yaster and Korman). These studies dealt mostly with young persons who came to therapy voluntarily and continued treatment for at least six weeks. The authors of the studies concluded that anorexia is a "socially induced disorder" (Kline 214) and not a biologically caused illness.

2. Recent studies show that anorexia can be treated successfully by psychotherapy. Kline achieved an 85 percent cure for twenty cases in adolescent women. A group of Illinois therapists found that "most victims underwent marked improvement following four sessions" (Evans et al. 35). In California, Oscar Yaster and T. G. Korman, working with a population of males and females ages

16-30, produced "significant remission rates" among those
completing five sessions or more of group and individual
treatment (17-18).

Notice that in (1) the writer did not intend to make a specific statement about each of the sources. Therefore, she cited all three of them after the introductory sentence of the paragraph. However, when she decided to quote a phrase from one of the three sources, which she felt spoke for all three, she then cited that one study.

If, on the other hand, the writer had wanted to say something about each source, she might have constructed the second paragraph. In that case, she would delay citing the sources until she got to each one individually. No special note was needed for Kline because the writer was summarizing the full study. But with Evans et al., she introduced a quotation, and that called for a note indicating the page number. Although the last of the three sources was quoted very briefly, a note was still needed to show where the phrase could be found. (Putting that note directly after the quoted phrase would have created an unnecessary interruption.)

General Guidelines for Listing Sources in Works Cited

A list of all your sources must appear at the end of your paper, in a section titled *Works Cited*. Arrange the items alphabetically according to the authors' last names. If a source has no known author, list it alphabetically according to the first word of its title (ignoring **A**, **An**, or **The**). See the Works Cited list for the paper on Emily Dickinson, on page 207.

Do not inflate your list of Works Cited by including items that were not direct sources of the information in your paper. This means that, as a rule, no item should appear among your Works Cited unless at least one note in the paper refers to it.

To be useful to your reader, a bibliography or list of Works Cited must answer several basic questions about each source.

What is its full title?

Who wrote or created it?

Where and when was it published? And by what publisher?

And for articles in periodicals and for essays in books, on what pages can it be found?

Occasionally other kinds of information will have to be added. For books, there may be translators and editors, or volume numbers; for periodicals, the handling of dates and of volume and issue numbers varies according to the type of periodical (annual, monthly, weekly, daily); and for non-print sources, such as films, recordings, television programs, yet other kinds of information must be included.

Our list of sample entries in this section covers the most common variations, dividing them into three categories: *books, periodicals,* and *other kinds of source materials.* Later in your college career, advanced research may lead you to rarer kinds of publications. At such times you may need to check the *MLA Style Manual* for the correct format. But of course you will often discover these unusual sources through specialized indexes or in bibliographies attached to other sources, in which case, you would see the correct entry form before you picked up the source.

Group One: Sample Entries for Books

BASIC FORMAT

Pay close attention to spacing and punctuation in each case. In general, however,

1. Periods separate main parts of an entry—author. title. publisher & date.
2. Each period is followed by TWO spaces.
3. Titles of books are underlined.
4. Quotation marks are used to indicate titles of essays and other short works contained within books or periodicals. (Exception: See ''Critical Review'' below.)

A SINGLE AUTHOR

Author of a Book

note punctuation and indentation; *Viking* is a press owned by Random House, so note both

Thomas, Lewis. <u>The Lives of a Cell</u>. New York: Viking, Random House, 1974.

Author of an Essay in a Collection

"Eds." stands for "editors," the compilers of the book's essays or other

Frake, Charles O. ''How to Ask for a Drink in Subanum.'' In <u>Directions in Sociolinguistics</u>. Eds. John J. Gumperz

writings; pages on which full essay appears are shown, even if only a page or two are used as sources	and D. Hymes. New York: Holt, Rinehart and Winston, 1972. 127-32.

Note: If all the essays in a collection are by the same author, you do not need to include the individual essay title in the Works Cited entry. But if the collection contains essays by various authors—as in the second example here—the essay title should be cited.

TWO OR MORE AUTHORS

authors' names in the order in which they appear on title page of source	Bar-Adon, Aaron, and Werner F. Leopold. Child Language. Englewood Cliffs, NJ: Prentice-Hall, 1971. Dugan, James, Robert C. Cowen, Bill Barada, and Richard M. Crum. World Beneath the Sea. Washington: National Geographic Soc., 1967.

TWO OR MORE SOURCES HAVING SAME AUTHOR

line of three hyphens is used in place of author's name for all entries after the first works listed alphabetically by title	Thomas, Lewis. The Lives of a Cell. New York: Viking, Random House, 1974. ---. The Medusa and the Snail. New York: Viking, Random House, 1979.

AUTHOR OF SEVERAL SOURCES HAVING DIFFERENT COAUTHORS

	Chomsky, Noam. Syntactic Structures. The Hague: Mouton, 1957.
coauthored books follow singly authored books alphabetically by coauthor	Chomsky, Noam, and Morris Halle. The Sound Pattern of English. New York: Harper and Row, 1968. Chomsky, Noam, and George A. Miller. Analyse formelle des langues naturelles. No. 8 of Mathematiques et sciences de l'homme. The Hague: Mouton, 1971.

Special Cases

AFTERWORD

A commentary coming at end of some books: see "Preface," p. 166.

ANONYMOUS AUTHOR

Classical Literature

> The Song of Roland. Trans. Frederick B. Luquines.
> New York: Macmillan, 1960.

Unsigned Pamphlet

both writer and
publisher unknown

> Push for Pot. Ann Arbor: n. pub., 1969.

THE BIBLE AS A SOURCE

No need to list this work in Works Cited unless you use a version other than the King James. Just provide the book, chapter, and verse numbers in your parenthetical note (Gen. 3:14–20).

CORPORATION AS AN AUTHOR

could also be entered
by title; choice is yours

> Phillips Petroleum. 66 Ways to Save Energy.
> Bartlesville, OK: 1978.

EDITOR

Editor's Ideas Were Cited

> Gardner, Martin, ed. The Annotated Alice. Alice's
> Adventures in Wonderland and Through the
> Looking Glass. By Lewis Carroll. New York:
> Clarkson Potter, 1960.

The Work Itself Was Cited

> Carroll, Lewis. The Annotated Alice. Alice's
> Adventures in Wonderland and Through the
> Looking Glass. Ed. Martin Gardner. New
> York: Clarkson Potter, 1960.

ENCYCLOPEDIA ARTICLE

although article's title
is "Isaac Newton,"
it is entered under
"Newton," under which
a reader would look it
up; second example
shows form for signed
article; publisher's
name is not necessary

> "Newton, Isaac." The New Columbia Encyclopedia,
> 1975.
> Kaufmann, Walter. "Friedrich Nietzsche."
> Encyclopaedia Britannica, 1969.

ENLARGED EDITION

See "Revised edition," below.

FOREWORD

A commentary at the beginning of some books: see "Preface," below.

GOVERNMENT AS AUTHOR

could also be entered by title; choice is yours

Federal Council for Science and Technology. First Annual Report of Ad Hoc Committee on Geodynamics. USIGP-F476, Washington, 1978.

PREFACE, FOREWORD, INTRODUCTION, OR AFTERWORD

reference here is to Edel's rather than Wilson's writing; had Wilson's text also been cited, book would be entered twice, once under each author's name

Edel, Leon. Foreword. The Thirties. By Edmund Wilson. New York: Farrar, Straus & Giroux, 1980.

REPRINT

note distinction between reprint and revised edition; revision means that changes were made, and date given is that of the changes; reprint leaves everything as in the original; important date is that of the first writing

Boys, C. V. Soap Bubbles and the Forces Which Mould Them. 1916; rpt. New York: Doubleday, 1959.

REVISED OR ENLARGED EDITION

editions other than first must be identified

Chomsky, Noam. Language and Mind. Enl. ed. New York: Harcourt Brace, 1972.

TITLE WITHIN A TITLE

Especially in the field of literary criticism, titles of books and essays often contain titles of other works.

When a book's title includes the title of another *book*, do not underline the interior title.

The Theological Underpinning of Moby Dick.

When a book's title includes the title of a *poem* or *essay*, do not underline the interior title, but place it within quotation marks.

The Anthropological Background of "The Wasteland" of T. S. Eliot.

TRANSLATOR

Translator's Ideas Are Cited

Fitzgerald, Robert, trans. Iliad. By Homer. Garden City, NY: Anchor, 1974.

Only the Work Is Cited

Homer. Iliad. Trans. Robert Fitzgerald. Garden City, NY: Anchor, 1974.

VOLUME NUMBERS

For works that are published in more than one volume, you must indicate which volume(s) you used in your paper.

More Than One of the Volumes Was Cited

bibliographic entry indicates that all three volumes have been used

Dickinson, Emily. The Poems of Emily Dickinson. Ed. Thomas H. Johnson. 3 vols. Cambridge, MA: The Belknap Press, Harvard Univ. Press, 1955.

Just One Volume Was Cited

Wellek, René. A History of Modern Criticism: 1750-1950. Vol. 2. New Haven: Yale Univ. Press, 1955.

a volume will often have its own title; if that title is prominent in its own right, it is cited first

Nevins, Allan. The Organized War, 1863-64. Vol. 3 of The War for the Union. New York: Scribner, 1971.

Group Two: Sample Entries for Periodicals

A periodical entry contains two titles: that of the article (within quotation marks) and that of the periodical (underlined, like the title of a book).

Volume numbers are needed for periodicals that do not carry specific dates—month, or day and month. Academic journals are especially likely to go by volume and issue rather than a date.

Page numbers of the full article are placed at the end of the entry.

BASIC FORMAT

Pay close attention to spacing and punctuation for each case. In general, however,

1. Periods separate main parts of an entry—author. article title. periodical title & date & pages.
2. Each period is followed by TWO spaces.
3. Names of periodicals are underlined.
4. Quotation marks are used to indicate titles of articles.

A SINGLE AUTHOR

> Bethell, Tom. ''Agnostic Evolutionists.'' Harper's Feb. 1985: 49-61.

ARTICLE IN AN ANNUAL, SEMIANNUAL, OR QUARTERLY PERIODICAL

when author's name is not given, source is listed by title

> Moore, John B. ''The Role of Gulliver.'' Modern Philological Quarterly 25 (1928): 169-80.
> ''Do Cities Change the Weather?'' Mosaic 5 (Summer 1974): 29-34.

ARTICLE IN A MONTHLY PERIODICAL

volume number is generally unnecessary; " + " indicates article continues at end of magazine

> Premack, Anne James, and David Premack. ''Teaching Language to an Ape.'' Scientific American Oct. 1972: 92-99.
> Sahgal, Pavan. ''Idiot Geniuses.'' Science Digest May 1981: 12-13+.

ARTICLE IN A WEEKLY PERIODICAL

issue is identified by date, month, and year

> Dorschner, John. ''Look Out! Here Comes the Sahara!'' Tropic 29 Dec. 1974: 34-45.

"Women's Bank: A Modest Profit." Newsweek 20
April 1981: 16.

ARTICLE IN A DAILY NEWSPAPER

when only writer's initials are known, they follow normal order (not "K., J."); note quotation marks within quotation marks in the third example; section number or letter, if there is one, is included; when the paper's title does not include the name of the city, that information is shown in parentheses (the *Daily Worker* was a *national* newspaper)

Roughton, Roger. "Barber's Bust with Loaf on
Head." Daily Worker 8 April 1936: 7.
J. K. "Explodes an Illusion." Daily Worker 30
Dec. 1936: 7-8.
"Presidential Panel Holds Hearings on 'Right to
Die.' " New York Times 12 April 1981, late
ed., sec. 1: 24.
"Rebirth of a City." News-Times (Danbury, CT) 6
Sep. 1977: 2.

Special Cases

CRITICAL REVIEW OF ANOTHER WORK

Chomsky, Noam. Review of Verbal Behavior by B. F.
Skinner. Language 35 (1959): 26-58.

(Note that the title is neither underlined nor enclosed within quotation marks.)

ISSUE NUMBERS

Some journals do not publish in "volumes"; they assign issue numbers only. Treat the issue number exactly as you would a volume number. In this example, 94 is the issue number.

Pritchard, Allan. "West of the Great Divide: A
View of the Literature of British Columbia."
Canadian Literature 94 (1982): 96-112.

REPRINT OF A JOURNAL ARTICLE

Mazzeo, Joseph A. "A Critique of Some Modern
Theories of Metaphysical Poetry." Modern
Philology 50 (1952): 88-96. Rpt. in
Seventeenth-Century English Poetry. Ed.

```
William R. Keast. New York: Oxford Univ.
Press, 1962. 63-74.
```

TITLE WITHIN A TITLE

Underline the titles of books, plays, and long poems (Iliad).

```
''Hawthorne's Reaction to Moby-Dick.''
```

Place single quotation marks around the title of an essay, short story, or short poem.

```
''A Psychoanalytic Interpretation of 'The Emperor
of Ice Cream.' ''
```

Group Three: Sample Entries for Other Material

COMPUTERIZED INFORMATION, FROM DATABASE SOURCE

```
''Thomas Jefferson.'' Academic American
Encyclopedia, 1981; rpt. Columbus, OH:
CompuServe, 1983. Record No. 1823.
```

COMPUTER SOFTWARE

```
Connections. Computer software, Krell Software,
1982.
```

FILM

can be entered either by title or director, depending on how used as a source: when studying director's work, name is given first; when studying film itself (as art form or as adaptation of a novel) title is used

```
A Clockwork Orange. Dir. Stanley Kubrick. Based
on Clockwork Orange by Anthony Burgess.
1971.
Kubrick, Stanley, dir. 2001: A Space Odyssey.
1969.
```

INFORMATION SERVICE MATERIAL

Use the format for a book, adding the code numbers used by the service (e.g., ERIC ED 187 864) at the end. (ERIC stands for Educational Resources Information Center.)

INTERVIEW

Moynihan, Patrick, Sen. Personal interview, 17
March 1983.

LECTURE

Thomas, Lewis. "Notes of a Biology Watcher."
Lecture at the Princeton Club of New York, 21
Feb. 1978.

LETTER

Entwhistle, Jacob, M.D. Personal letter to this
writer, 28 May 1980.

MICROFILM OR MICROFICHE

Just be sure to add in parentheses at the end of the entry the word
"microfilm" or "microfiche."

RECORDING

again purpose
dictates order in
which information is
presented: when topic
is music, second form
is used; when artist is
topic, his/her name is
entered; when artist or
author is identified
by nickname or
pseudonym, supply
the true name in
parenthesis

Leadbelly (Huddie Ledbetter). Rock Island Line.
    Notes by Frederick Ramsey, Jr. Folkways, FA
    2014, 1956.

"Black Girl." Rock Island Line. Sung by
    Leadbelly (Huddie Ledbetter). Folkways, FA
    2014, 1956.

TELEVISION PROGRAM

Marshall was
program's narrator

"Gorilla." National Geographic Society. Narr.
    E. G. Marshall. WNET-PBS, 15 April 1981.

TESTIMONY, OFFICIAL

note absence of
underlining or
quotation marks

Bell, Mark. Testimony before the Subcommittee on
    the Environment and the Atmosphere.
    Committee on Science and Technology, House of
    Representatives, 22 May 1975.

Documentation of Illustrative Materials

A final matter regarding documentation concerns the layout and labeling of graphs, tables, and other illustrative materials.

Tables are referred to as "tables," but graphs, pictures, diagrams, and other kinds of illustration are all referred to as "figures." Each kind of item is numbered consecutively throughout the paper with arabic numerals (Table 1, Table 2; Figure 1, Figure 2, Figure 3).

TABLE 1

U.S.-JAPAN MERCHANDISE TRADE: 1975-1978

Year	U.S. domestic exports to Japan	U.S. general imports from Japan
1975	$ 9,421,000,000	$11,268,000,000
1976	10,027,000,000	15,504,000,000
1977	10,422,000,000	18,550,000,000
1978	12,689,000,000	24,458,000,000

Source: U.S. Bureau of the Census, Statistical Abstract of the United States: 1979. (Washington, DC: GPO, 1979) 920.

FIGURE 1

U.S.-JAPAN MERCHANDISE TRADE: 1975-1978

figure shows same
information as
preceding table;
captions below the
figure are sometimes
used instead of titles
above

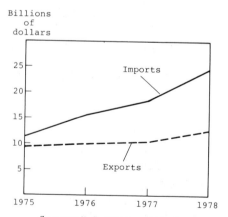

Source: U.S. Bureau of the Census, Statistical Abstract of the United States: 1979. (Washington, DC: GPO, 1979) 920.

The Endnote/Footnote System of Documentation

Some instructors, particularly those in the fields of history, philosophy, political science, and religion, may prefer that you document your

sources by inserting numbers in your text to refer to notations on a separate page of endnotes or at the foot of each page. These guidelines
should prove helpful for such situations.

Insert a single number slightly above the line at all points where you
would have used a parenthetical note. These numbers must run in sequence throughout the paper: 1, 2, 3, etc. If you find you have left out a
note after inserting all the numbers within the text, you must change all
the succeeding numbers. Do not create "5a," for instance, when inserting an entry between 5 and 6.

After all the numbers have been placed within the text, make a list of
"endnotes." Next to each number enter the bibliographic information
that precisely identifies the source of the quotation, paraphrase, or summary. On rare occasions, an instructor may ask you to place footnotes at
the bottom of each page, rather than compile a list of endnotes. The rules
for punctuating and spacing footnotes are the same as those for endnotes.

INSERTION OF NUMBERS WITHIN THE TEXT

1. Each number is typed *half a space* above the line, and directly (no
   space) after the final punctuation of the sentence it refers to.
2. For quotations that end in the middle of a sentence, place the number directly after the final quotation mark.
3. Always skip TWO spaces after each number.

Here are examples in which numbers replaced parenthetical notes in
the paper on Emily Dickinson.

```
Dickinson sent Higginson four poems, along with a

letter containing this question: "Are you too

deeply occupied to say if my Verse is alive?"8

This . . .

Certainly then, the poet Yvor Winters called "one

of the greatest lyric poets of all time"2 was all

but unknown as a poet during her lifetime.

Paul Ferlazzo, for example, infers that

Higginson's response to her first letter must have

included some recommendations for altering, or

"regularizing," her poems, along with a request

for more of her work.9
```

> The general reading public that asked for meter
> that is smooth, rhythm that is easy, and words that
> are limited to only one obvious meaning interested
> her not at all. She was willing to wait.[15]

When you quote from a literary work, simply insert the pages or, as in the following quotation from *Paradise Lost*, the "book" and line numbers, rather than send readers to an endnote.

> Evil into the mind of God or Man
> May come and go, so unapprov'd, and leave
> No spot or blame behind: Which gives me hope
> That what in sleep thou didst abhor to dream,
> Waking thou never wilt consent to do. (5.117-21)

BASIC ENDNOTE FORMAT

This format differs from that of the Works Cited, although the same basic questions are answered—Who? What? Where? When?

Works Cited   Bernstein, Jeremy. Einstein. New York: Vintage,
                    Random House, 1973.

Endnote   [1] Jeremy Bernstein, Einstein (New York:
                    Vintage, Random House, 1973) 79.

Here is the basic endnote format:

1. Author's name is given in normal order.
2. Commas and spaces replace the periods used in Works Cited.
3. Parentheses surround publishing information.
4. Page number(s) are added at the very end. Do not use **p.** or **pp.** No colon or comma comes between parentheses and page number(s).

A few samples of the most common situations should give you an idea of how to handle this system.

EDITOR AND TRANSLATOR

> [1] Martin Gardner, ed., The Annotated Alice.
> Alice's Adventures in Wonderland and Through the
> Looking Glass, by Lewis Carroll (New York:
> Clarkson Potter, 1960) iv-vi.

2 Feodor Dostoevsky, Crime and Punishment, trans. Jessie Coulson, ed. George Gibian (New York: Norton, 1964) 142.

ESSAY IN A BOOK OF ESSAYS

3 Charles O. Frake, "How to Ask for a Drink in Subanum," in Directions in Sociolinguistics, eds. John J. Gumperz and D. Hymes (New York: Holt, Rinehart, and Winston, 1972) 129-30.

INTRODUCTION, FOREWORD, AFTERWORD, PREFACE

4 Leon Edel, foreword, The Thirties, by Edmund Wilson (New York: Farrar, Straus & Giroux, 1980) vii.

PERIODICALS

5 Stephen Jay Gould, "A Most Ingenious Paradox," Natural History Dec. 1984: 20.

(Note the colon between date and page number, unlike the format for books.)

6 William Howard, "Emily Dickinson's Poetic Vocabulary," PMLA 72 (1957): 227.

(Note use of parentheses around the date *when volume number is given.*)

7 John Dorschner, "Look Out! Here Comes the Sahara!" Tropic 29 Dec. 1974: 38.

(No comma after title that ends with ? or !)

8 "Presidential Panel Holds Hearings on 'Right to Die,'" New York Times 12 April 1981, late ed., sec. 1: 24.

SHORTENED FORM FOR SECOND AND FURTHER REFERENCES TO SAME SOURCE

After you have produced one complete note for a particular source, you can use a shorter form for all subsequent references to the same source.

¹⁰ Bernstein 231.

(No comma between author and page.)

DO NOT use "ibid." or "loc. cit." or other Latin abbreviations you may see in out-of-date journals or books.

If the author wrote more than one of your sources, you have to put the title (in a shortened form) in the note. In the next example, earlier notes would have given the complete bibliographic information for Freud's *The Interpretation of Dreams* and his *Moses and Monotheism*.

¹⁶ Freud, Dreams 303.
¹⁷ Freud, Moses 68.

(Comma goes between author and title only.)

In this system, as in the 1984 MLA system, mentioning the source or the author in the text affects the amount of information that appears in the note.

Jehovah was originally the god of a local volcano, according to Freud.¹⁹

¹⁹ Moses 23.

Don't carry this too far, however. Always mention either the author or the title in the shortened notes. Never give just the page number(s).

For a full example of this system of documentation, see the sample paper by George Pitman in chapter 9.

The APA (Author/Year) System of Documentation

Many behavioral science instructors will ask you to follow the system devised by the American Psychological Association (APA), which is similar in form to the 1984 MLA system. The major difference lies in the basic contents of the parenthetical notes.

- In the APA system, you generally give the year of publication in the note, whereas in MLA, you never put the date in the note.
- In the APA system, you give the page numbers only for a quotation, not for paraphrases or summaries, as in MLA.

These differences are not trivial. The APA believes the most important information is the time the idea was presented to the world; the MLA is primarily concerned with precisely locating the information within the source.

The APA system is a variant on a general approach called the author/year system. (Some disciplines within the behavioral sciences have arrived at their own slightly different versions of author/year. Several of these are briefly illustrated at the end of this section.)

PUNCTUATION OF NOTES

1. As in MLA, parenthetical notes are included within the sentences to which they refer.
2. Commas separate name from date when both appear inside a note.
3. An ampersand (&) is used instead of "and" between authors' names, when more than one name appears in a note.
4. The abbreviations **p.** and **pp.** are used to indicate "page" and "pages," except after volume numbers.

BASIC FORMAT

Insert the parenthetical note immediately after the name of the author. You are strongly encouraged to mention the author's name in your text rather than in the parenthetical note. The note contains just the year of publication.

```
Robinson (1980) asserted that child abuse in
upper middle class homes manifests itself in
subtler ways.
```

If a source has two authors, mention them both.

```
Martin and Elder (1969) demonstrated that abusive
parents were usually themselves abused.
```

If, for stylistic reasons, you do not mention the authors' names in your text, then place them inside the note.

```
It was shown in the late sixties (Martin & Elder,
1969) that abusive parents were usually
themselves abused.
```

You can avoid using a note by mentioning both author and date in your text.

```
In 1969, Martin and Elder demonstrated that
abusive parents were usually themselves abused.
```

When you quote a source directly, use a note to indicate the page number as well as the date and author if they are not already clear in the text.

> Rogers (1979) believes that "virtually all female abusers suffered from primary splitting" (p. 67).
>
> One theorist believes that "virtually all female abusers suffered from primary splitting" (Rogers, 1979, p. 67).

When a source has several authors, use "et al." after the first full citation. But watch out for the situation when two of your sources have several authors with the same person heading both series of names.

> Gold, Bache, Cohen, and Arnach (1978) found that . . .
>
> Gold et al. (1978) were not so sure that . . .
>
> Marx, Walcott, Blau, and Johanssen (1975) said . . .
>
> Marx, Martin, and Schuster (1980) were convinced that . . .
>
> A study completed ten years ago (Marx, Walcott, et al. 1975) concluded that . . .

If two authors have the same last name, use initials to distinguish them, both in notes and within the text.

> J. Prescott (1983) tried testing infants . . .
>
> A later study (D. Prescott, 1985) could find no . . .

If the "author" is a corporation or government agency, place the full name in the first note and the abbreviation in brackets; abbreviate thereafter.

> The government (National Institute of Mental Health [NIMH], 1981) took a strong interest in . . .

```
A hotly contested government survey (NIMH, 1981)
came to the conclusion that . . .
```

If an author contributed more than one source to your list, and two of them were published in the same year, small letters are added to the year numbers.

```
Freud (1923a) first announced . . .

In a now famous essay (Freud, 1923b), the idea

of . . .
```

When a source has no author, use a short form of the title in the parenthetical note.

```
One source ("Study finds," 1982) predicted

that . . .
```

The Reference page listed this article as follows:

```
Study finds free care used more. (1982, April).

APA Monitor, p. 14.
```

If one of your sources mentioned the work of another author, and you want to refer to that other work, use this form:

```
Ashkenazi's work (cited in Beatty, 1982)

showed . . .
```

Note: Be sure to list Beatty's work, not Ashkenazi's, under "References," for that is where you found the information.

LISTING SOURCES UNDER REFERENCES

Punctuation

1. Underline book titles and names of periodicals.
2. Do not use quotation marks around titles of essays and periodical articles. (And do not underline them.)
3. Capitalize only the first word and proper nouns in essay and article titles. But capitalize all main words in names of periodicals.
4. Use an ampersand (&) to join authors' names.

Format

1. Sources are listed alphabetically by their authors' names, or when author is not known, by the first word of the title, excluding **A, An, The**.
2. No first names given for authors, just initials (unless two persons have same last names and initials).
3. When a source has multiple authors, all authors' names are entered by last name, followed by initials.
4. The year of publication (inside parentheses) follows the author's name. When two or more sources have the same author, list the sources chronologically. If two or more articles appeared in the same year, use letters (a, b, c) to distinguish them and list them alphabetically. Repeat the author's name in each case; do not use –––––––.

(In this sample list, only authors and titles are shown, so you can concentrate on the above points.)

```
Freud, A. (1951). An experiment in group
     upbringing. . . .
Freud, S. (1905). Three essays on the theory of
     sexuality. . . .
Freud, S. (1910a). Five lectures on psychoanal-
     ysis. . . .
Freud, S. (1910b). Leonardo da Vinci and a memory
     of his childhood. . . .
Freud, S. (1931). Female sexuality. . . .
Goldstein, J., Freud, A., & Solnit, A. J. (1979).
     Before the best interests of the child. . . .
Klein, M. (1961). Narrative of a child anal-
     ysis. . . .
```

Note also the following list of standard abbreviations for common bibliographical terms.

chap.	ed. (edition)	
Vol. 4	Ed. (editor)	Trans. (translator)
4 vols.	rev. ed.	rpt. (reprint)
No. (number)	2nd ed.	

AN ANNOTATED SAMPLE LIST OF REFERENCES

```
Arlow, J.A. (1981). Theories of pathogenesis.
Psychoanalytic Quarterly, 50, 488-514.
```

Arlow, J.A., & Brenner, C. (1964). Psychoanalytic
concepts and the structural theory. New
York: International Univ. Press.

Becker, L.J., & Seligman, G. (1983). Welcome to
the energy crisis. Journal of Social
Issues, 37(2), 12-19.

Ferenczi, S. (1911). On obscene words. In Sex in
psychoanalysis. New York: Basic Books, pp.
132-153.

Gardner, H. (1981, December). Do babies sing a
universal song? Psychology Today, pp. 70-76.

Lublin, J.S. (1980, December 5). On idle: the
unemployed shun much mundane work, at least
for a while. The Wall Street Journal, pp.
1, 25.

Luria, A.R. (1969). The mind of a mnemonist (L.
Soltaroff, Trans.). New York: Avon Books.
(Original work published 1965)

Oremland, E.K., & Oremland, J.D. (Eds.) (1973).
The effects of hospitalization on children.
Springfield, IL: Thomas.

Paivio, A. (1975). Perceptual comparisons
through the mind's eye. Memory & Cognition,
3, 635-647.

Study finds free care used more. (1982, April).
APA Monitor, p. 14.

FORMATS FOR OTHER KINDS OF SOURCES

Maas, J.B. (Producer), & Gluck, D.H. (Director).
(1979). Deeper into hypnosis (Film).
Englewood Cliffs, NJ: Prentice-Hall.

Bowers, K.S. (1982). Deeper into "Deeper into
hypnosis" [Review of Deeper into hypnosis].
Contemporary Psychology, 27, 223-224.

Newman, P. (1985, January). [Interview with
William Epstein, editor of JEP: Human
Perception and Performance].
APA Monitor, pp. 7, 39.

See also the sample paper by Anita Barrone in chapter 9.

The Numbered System of Documentation

A fourth system, the so-called *numbered* system, is employed primarily
in chemistry, physics, and engineering. It, too, uses parenthetical notes,

but the sources are assigned numbers in the list of References, and these numbers are what readers see within the parentheses, instead of page numbers or years.

```
Widlow (1) discovered that cells injected

    with . . .

Breitenstein and Forester (2) attempted to con-

    vert . . .

Morgan (3) and Stanley (4) both argued that

    stress . . .
```

If you prefer not to mention the author within your text, then the name may be placed in the note.

```
The latest evidence from Switzerland (Kreut-

    zer, 5) . . .
```

If you refer to three or more sources at a time, you can omit the names.

```
Recent experimentation (6, 7, 8) seems to indi-

    cate . . .
```

In these sciences, writers rarely quote their sources directly; however, if you quote, the page number must be included in the note.

```
As Elsasser stated (6, p. 18), "The outcome

    depended on . . .
```

Listing Sources under References

Some disciplines ask for alphabetical listing by author, with each item assigned a number. Other disciplines want the sources listed in the order in which they are cited in the paper. Check for your instructor's preference. The above set of examples followed the "order cited" format, as you can see.

Format Preferences for Various Academic Disciplines

Be sure to look for the differences in these areas:

- placing of publication date;

* use of underlining and quotation marks and capitalization for titles;
* abbreviation of periodical names.

SCIENCES

Biology uses the numbered system and lists references in alphabetical order.

first words in titles and proper nouns are capitalized; when article appears on just one page, page number is repeated; date follows all other information

1. Bernal, J. D., and I. Frankuchen. X-ray and crystallographic studies of plant virus preparations. J. Gen. Physio. 25:111-165; 1941.
2. Crick, F. H. C. Is α-keratin a coiled coil? Nature. 170:882-882; 1952.
3. Judson, H. F. The eighth day of creation. Simon & Schuster, New York: 1979.

Botany and *Zoology* use the author/year system and list references in alphabetical order.

first words in titles and proper nouns are capitalized; volume numbers are underlined; the number of pages is noted for books

Hairston, N. G., F. E. Smith, and L. B. Slobodkin. 1960. Community, structure, population, control, and competition. American Naturalist 94: 421-425.
Muller, W. H. 1974. Botany: a functional approach. Macmillan, New York. 601 p.

Chemistry uses the numbered system and lists references in the order in which they are cited in the paper.

note omission of titles for periodical articles and use of quotation marks for book titles

(1) T. Raptolinsky, "Chemists and the New Technology," Mills Ltd., Manchester, 1976, pp. 102-109.
(2) R. Johnstone, J. Am. Chem. Soc., 89, 405-412 (1978).
(3) L. Pauling, R. B. Corey, and H. R. Branson, Proc. N. A. S., 37, 205-211 (1951).

Engineering uses numbered system and lists references in the order in which they are cited in the paper.

normal capitalization

1. Keenan, J. H., and Keyes, F. G. Thermodynamic Properties of Steam, Wiley, New York, 1936.
2. Cook, E. G. "Stress Patterns in Danbury Bridge," ACBL 42, August 1979.

Geology uses the author/year system and lists references in alphabetical order.

follows same format as botany and zoology, except that order of publisher and city is reversed	Purrett, L. A. 1972. Before Pangaea—what? Science News 102: 220-222. Sullivan, W. 1974. Continents in motion. New York, McGraw-Hill. 399 p.

Mathematics uses the numbered system and lists references in alphabetical order.

note that all titles are underlined	1. Petr Beckmann, A History of Pi, New York, St. Martin's, 1976. 2. Paul Bennacerraf, God, the Devil, and Goedel, Monist 51 (1967), 9. 3. J. R. Lucas, Minds, Machines, and Goedel, in Minds and Machines, ed. A. R. Anderson, Englewood Cliffs, NJ, Prentice-Hall, 1964.

Physics uses the numbered system and lists references in the order in which they are cited.

page numbers for books tell which pages are relevant to paper	[1]A. Baker, Modern Physics and Anti-physics (Addison-Wesley, Reading, MA, 1970), pp. 45-49, 102-10.
titles of articles are not given; titles of periodicals are not underlined	[2]J. M. Jauch, Are Quanta Real? A Galilean Dialogue (Indiana University Press, Bloomington, 1973), pp. 72-77. [3]D. R. Hofstadter, Physical Review B, 14, no. 6, 45-64 (1976).

SOCIAL SCIENCES

Economics uses the author/year system and lists references in alphabetical order.

note that last item, although numbered like a periodical, is a pamphlet or small book and no page numbers are given	R. Easterlin, "Does Money Buy Happiness?" The Public Interest, Winter 1973, 30, 1-17. E. E. Lawler II, Pay and Organizational Effectiveness: A Psychological View, New York, 1971. United States Department of Commerce, Survey of Current Business, July 1979, 59, no. 7.

Education uses either the MLA format or the author/year system and lists references in alphabetical order.

preferred form

Bruner, Jerome S., "The Growth of Mind," <u>Amer.</u>
<u>Psychol.</u> 20: 1007-17; Oct. 1977.
Jones, Richard M., <u>Fantasy and Feeling in</u>
<u>Education</u>. New York: New York Univ. Press,
1968. 276 p.

History follows the MLA format or the numbered footnote system.

Political Science usually follows the MLA format.

Psychology commonly uses the author/year system, but some journals use the numbered system. Both systems follow alphabetical order when listing references. Ask your instructor which to use.

preferred form

Blos, P. (1962), <u>On adolescence</u>. New York: Free
Press.
Erikson, E. H. (1956), The problem of ego
identity. <u>J. Amer. Psychoanal. Assn.</u>,
<u>4</u>: 56-121.
Mahler, M. S., Pine, F., & Bergman, A. (1975). <u>The</u>
<u>psychological birth of the human infant</u>.
New York: Basic Books.

Sociology uses the author/year system and lists references in alphabetical order. Book and journal titles are not underlined and article titles are not capitalized (after the first word) or enclosed in quotation marks. Your instructor's preferences may vary this somewhat.

preferred form

Gumperz, John J. (1971). Language in social
groups. Stanford, CA: Stanford Univ. Press.
Maranda, Elli (1971). Theory and practice of
riddle analysis. Jour. Amer. Folklore 84
(July): 51-61.

Review Questions

1. Why do research papers include parenthetical notes? Is the answer the same for all disciplines?
2. When might you use a traditional footnote number while working with the MLA system of documentation?

3. Explain why you would or would not cite a source for each of the following pieces of information.

* the definition of "palindrome"
* the names of Emily Dickinson's father and mother
* the latest census data about the size of the average American household
* the poet T. S. Eliot's interpretation of the river in *Huckleberry Finn*
* Dr. Elizabeth Kübler-Ross's concept of the appropriate attitudes toward dying patients
* author Willa Cather's date and place of birth
* results of a recent study of caffeine's effect on sleep
* the population of Saigon, Vietnam, before and after the Vietnam War
* American patriot Nathan Hale's last words, "I regret that I have but one life to give for my country."

Exercise

Construct a Works Cited page for the following sources, putting all of the information in the correct order according to the MLA format.

If you need help getting started, the first five of the following items appear in the bibliography for the Dickinson paper in chapter 9.

1. Your research led you to a book titled Emily Dickinson: A Collection of Critical Essays, in which you found an essay called Emily Dickinson and the Limits of Judgment. The book was edited by Richard B. Sewall, and the essay was the work of Yvor Winters. The essay began on page 38 and ended on page 56. The book was published in 1963 by Prentice-Hall, located in Englewood Cliffs, New Jersey.

2. Your research uncovered an essay, Father and Daughter: Edward and Emily Dickinson, which was published in a journal, American Literature, in January 1960. This was volume 40, and the essay covered pages 510 to 523. The writer was Owen Thomas.

3. When quoting Emily Dickinson's poetry, you used a collection called The Complete Poems of Emily Dickinson, which was published in 1960 by Little, Brown and Company, located in Boston, Massachusetts. The person who edited the poems was Thomas H. Johnson.

4. When quoting the poet's letters, you used a three-volume collection called The Letters of Emily Dickinson, which was published in Cambridge, Massachusetts, by the Harvard University Press in 1958. The editors were Thomas H. Johnson and Theodora Ward.

5. You read a book written by the critic Paul J. Ferlazzo in 1976. The book was titled Emily Dickinson and was published by Twayne Publishers, which is located in Boston, Massachusetts.

6. You read a tribute to the poet, called The First Lady of Mt. Holyoke, which appeared in the South Hadley (Massachusetts) Gazette on December 10, 1980. This unsigned essay appeared on the second and third pages of the second section of the newspaper.

7. You also wrote a letter to a professor at Mt. Holyoke College, Joanna Caldwell, who is an authority on the poet and her works. You quoted a remark from her reply to you, which was written on November 4, 1980.

8. You read an article in the magazine Psychology Today, written by John Forsyte, Joanna Caldwell, and Edgar Polishook. The article, titled Emily Dickinson: Inhibited Genius?, appeared in the July 1979 issue on pages 68 to 80.

9. You read a review of Ferlazzo's book (see item 5), written by Joanna Caldwell, which was published in PMLA, volume 65, pages 343 to 345. This issue was published in May 1980.

9
Preparing the Final Manuscript

As you no doubt already know, appearances count. After investing so much time and energy in the research assignment, you would be foolish to hand in a paper containing numerous typographical errors, insertions, and corrections. A messy manuscript could easily mislead your reader to think you had done the whole job in haste. Be sure, therefore, to leave enough time for preparing a clean, attractively designed manuscript.

First and foremost, type the paper, at all costs. Most instructors will insist that you type research papers, but even if you find one who accepts handwritten papers, you would be wise to get the paper typed, even if you believe your script is exceptionally neat and easy to read.

Follow precisely whatever format your instructor specifies. If none is recommended, however, the advice given here will meet most instructors' standards.

The Mechanics of Manuscript Preparation

MATERIALS

1. Use 8½- by 11-inch white paper, 20-pound bond.
2. Do not use erasable paper—it smudges easily. Do not use onionskin paper, either, except for your own carbon copy if you choose to

make one. (You must always keep a copy when you hand in a manuscript.)

3. Type on just one side of each page.
4. Use a *new* ribbon, black only.

SPACING AND MARGINS

1. In general, leave a one-inch margin at the top and bottom of each page and on the left-hand side. Of course, you cannot know where lines will end on the right-hand side, but you should try to leave a one-inch margin there, as well. Break up long words with hyphens before they extend into the margin.
   Exception: The top of the first page looks a bit different. Type the title two inches from the top; then double-space twice before the first line of your text.

2. Double-space lines throughout the paper, including pages listing Endnotes, Works Cited, or References.
   Exception: Long quotations indented from the margin may be single-spaced.

3. Indent each paragraph five spaces. Long quotations—more than four lines long—should be indented ten spaces and single-spaced, unless your instructor says to double-space. When indenting a long quotation, do not enclose the quotation in quotation marks. (See page 199ff.)

PAGE NUMBERING

Starting with the second page, type the page number in the upper right-hand corner. The Works Cited and any endnote pages are usually given numbers. It is a good idea to type your name below each page number and on the unnumbered pages to prevent confusion if your paper should become mixed up with someone else's.

TITLE PAGE

The following information appears on the title page: the title, your name, your instructor's name, the course and section numbers, and the date on which the paper is submitted.

BINDING

In order to keep the pages of your paper together, use an extra large paperclip or a lightweight, clear plastic folder. Do not staple your pages together.

CORRECTIONS

Proofread the final draft with extreme care. If the paper contains a few errors, these may be corrected neatly *in ink*. Make your changes above the lines in which they occur. Do not use the margins for this purpose. Insert a word or phrase neatly above a caret, as in this sentence.

Most historians today conclude that Jefferson

Davis, despite his personal shortcomings,

insertion   was the most capable president the South could

have chosen.

Three Sample Research Papers

Here are three sample student research papers. These papers were selected as samples not only because they demonstrate competence in the research techniques described in this book, but also because the students were writing for different academic disciplines and therefore used slightly different approaches to their projects. The first paper, "Emily Dickinson's Reluctance to Publish," illustrates the new (1984) MLA documentation style and procedures; the second paper, "Jefferson Davis as President: A Confederate Asset," illustrates the traditional numbered endnote (footnote) method of documentation; the third paper, "Increasing Maximum Life Expectancy: Myth or Reality?," illustrates the author/year system of the American Psychological Association (APA), a system used by researchers in various scientific and social science disciplines.

Emily Dickinson's Reluctance to Publish

Submitted by Susanna Andrews
to Professor Ann Leigh

English 102 American Literature
Section 3c
June 2, 19--

```
                        OUTLINE
         Emily Dickinson's Reluctance to Publish


   Introductory paragraph, including thesis statement
    I. Background of the "myth of tragic Emily"
       A. Life in brief
          1. Retreat from social life
          2. Tentative effort to find an audience
          3. Eventual publication of her work
       B. After death
          1. The myth's genesis
          2. Its revision in recent years
       C. Refutation of "unworldly" image through
          analysis of poems
          1. The vocabulary (Thomas; Howard)
          2. The content (Griffith)
   II. The correspondence between Dickinson and
       Higginson
       A. The beginnings of their dialogue
          1. Higginson's article
          2. Dickinson's approach
       B. Higginson's first letter to the poet
          1. "Surgery" advised
          2. Request to see more poems
```

C. Higginson's second letter

   1. Further revision advised

   2. Dickinson's response--disavowal of
      ambition

D. Interpretations of Dickinson's reaction

   1. Disavowal questioned

   2. Higginson's blindness apparent

III. Dickinson's view of herself as an artist

A. Her state of mind

   1. Self-confidence

   2. Realization that the world was not ready

   3. Refusal to compromise

B. Dickinson's real reason for approaching
   Higginson

   1. Need for special kind of advice

   2. The painful first publications

C. Higginson's effect on Emily Dickinson

   1. His limitations recognized

   2. His confusion in face of genius

   3. Her rejection of his advice

IV. Evidence from Dickinson's poetry

A. Choice between fame and popular recognition

   1. Kher's interpretation of poem

   2. Poem's suggestion of her choice

B. Choice between publication and artistic
   integrity
   1. Dickinson's decision to forgo publication
   2. Opposition of immortality and time

   Conclusion

Emily Dickinson's Reluctance to Publish

    At her death in 1886, Emily Dickinson left behind
over 1,700 poems, of which only seven were published--
anonymously--while she was alive (Johnson, Poems 1:
1x). Certainly then, the woman Yvor Winters called
"one of the greatest lyric poets of all time" (40) was
all but unknown as a poet during her lifetime. For many
years after her poems first appeared in 1890, her
reluctance to publish was attributed to a supposed
unconcern for worldly matters, including literary
fame. Literary critics, serious biographers, and
writers of fictionalized accounts of her life created
an image of Emily Dickinson as a timid, reclusive,
mystical thinker, who was too absorbed in personal
sorrows and ecstasies to be concerned with literary
recognition. And this image persists, to a great
extent, in the public mind today.[1] Since the late
1950s, however, a new view of the poet has been
emerging. This view, based on close studies of
Dickinson's life, letters, and poetry, reveals an
artist well aware of her worth, who deliberately chose
to withhold her poems from the world until they could be

Introductory
paragraph

Note includes title
because Johnson
authored several
Works Cited

Question behind
this research

The traditional view

Readers offered
extra information in
a footnote

Nature of sources

Thesis statement

2

valued as unique artistic creations, even if this meant postponing fame until after her death.

Beginning in her mid-twenties, Emily Dickinson gradually retreated from the many stimulating personal relationships that had filled her early life. By her late thirties, her retirement was complete; she passed the rest of her days living with her parents and her younger sister, who managed the household. During her later years, Emily Dickinson had virtually no direct contact with anyone outside her immediate family. While she was still connected to her circle of friends, Dickinson made at least one tentative attempt to find an audience for her poetry but only a handful of verses were published anonymously, most of them in a local newspaper, and these were subjected to considerable editing. Upon the poet's death at fifty-six, her sister discovered over one thousand poems and initiated an effort to publish them. Beginning four years later, in 1890, these poems finally appeared in print (Sewall 1: 4-11).

Over the years, as her following grew, Emily Dickinson became the subject of a number of highly romanticized biographies. Her admirers were trying to establish a connection between her cloistered

Subtopic: background of the myth

Note refers to the entire paragraph, summarizing source

3

existence and the powerful passions that course through
much of her finest poetry. Only after scholarly
editions of her letters and poetry appeared in the
1950s were literary critics in a good position to
produce an accurate picture of the poet's life and her
attitude toward her art. Even so, a good deal of the
mystery remains with us.

The idea that Emily Dickinson knew very little of
the real world has been disputed by recent studies of
her life and works. One biographer and critic, Owen
Thomas, finds a remarkable number of legal, political,
and financial words and expressions in her poetry. This
fact leads him to conclude that Dickinson ''was well
aware of the world outside her little room, that in fact
she used the language of this outside world to create
some of her best poetry'' (523). In the same vein,
William Howard points out that the largest group of
specialized words in Dickinson's poems reflects the
scientific and technological discussions of her day
(230). Further disagreement with the image of the poet
as a shy, unworldly creature comes from Clark Griffith,
who sees her as a person whose sensibility was
''responsive to the brutalities which life imposes on
the individual, and acutely aware of the nothingness

**Subtopic: refutation
of myth**

**Note clearly refers
to Thomas's work**

**New source,
identified in text**

4

with which existence seems surrounded" (5-6). If we

Connection of subtopic with thesis

reject the image of Emily Dickinson as a mystical recluse who had little interest in the real world, we must also question the theory that she did not publish her poems out of the same lack of interest.

Subtopic: correspondence with Higginson

Perhaps the most substantial evidence regarding Dickinson's reluctance to publish can be found in her letters to a professional writer and social reformer named Thomas Wentworth Higginson. This correspondence began in 1862, after Higginson published an article in the April issue of the Atlantic Monthly, entitled "Letter to a Young Contributor," which offered some practical advice for beginning writers seeking to publish. As a result of reading this article, Dickinson sent Higginson four poems, along with a letter containing this question: "Are you too deeply

Reference to primary source; Letters are clearly Dickinson's

occupied to say if my Verse is alive?" (Letters 2: 403). This and other early letters in their correspondence reveal the poet's interest in gaining recognition. Later correspondence with Higginson seems, however, to have dampened her hope of achieving critical praise.

Unfortunately, almost all of Higginson's letters to Emily Dickinson have been lost. Nevertheless, the main points of his answers to her early letters have

5

been inferred by numerous critics, using the poet's
replies to Higginson as the basis for these
conclusions. Paul Ferlazzo, for example, infers that
Higginson's response to her first letter must have
included some recommendations for altering, or
"regularizing," her poems, along with a request for
more of her work (136). Ferlazzo bases this judgment on
Dickinson's second letter to Higginson, which says, in
part, "Thank you for the surgery--it was not so painful
as I supposed. I bring you others--as you ask--though
they might not differ--" (Letters 2: 404). The
"surgery" surely refers to some changes recommended
by Higginson, and Ferlazzo thinks it is significant
that the poet admits that she was sending him more of
the same kind, for this indicates that she did not
intend to follow his advice (137).

    In a second letter to Dickinson, Higginson must
have recommended that she not try to publish for the
present time, perhaps suggesting that she rewrite her
poems along the lines he had prescribed. This can be
inferred from her reply to this letter, which reads, in
part:

> I smile when you suggest that I delay "to
> publish"--that being foreign to my thought,
> as Firmament to Fin--If Fame belonged to me,
> I could not escape her--if she did not, the

Quotation from
Letters interrupts
reference to
Ferlazzo; otherwise,
one note at end of
paragraph [(136-37)]
would be sufficient

Support for thesis

6

Note referring to long, indented quote comes *after* concluding punctuation and is preceded by two spaces

longest day would pass me on the chase--
. . . My Barefoot--Rank is better. (<u>Letters</u>
2: 408)

Those critics who believe that Dickinson's reluctance to publish was a deliberate choice on her part do not take at face value her avowal to Higginson that publishing was ''foreign'' to her. Instead, they see Higginson's inability to recognize the genius in her work as a major factor in her decision to renounce her desire to publish. As Richard Sewall says it, Dickinson's

Extended quotation; student felt it was necessary to identify "him" in brackets

. . . disavowal about publishing can hardly be taken literally. After all, she had sent him [Higginson] the poems in response to his article on how young writers could get their work published. . . . What she said . . . about publishing could perhaps mean that, in view of Higginson's hesitance, she was renouncing her ambition to be a public poet . . . perhaps in the hope that some far-off Tribunal would render different and unequivocal judgment. . . . (2: 555)

Subtopic: Dickinson's view of herself as an artist

In suggesting that Dickinson chose obscurity after Higginson's ''hesitance,'' Sewall does not mean to imply that she was unsure of herself as a poet because of his criticism. On the contrary, Sewall states that ''in her exalted conception of herself as a poet and in her confidence in her powers, she had no

7

. . . reason to be deferential to Higginson . . . and
she knew it" (2: 555). Thus, it was not a sense of
inferiority that moved the poet to her decision.
Rather it was the realization that her poems would not
be accepted in the forms she had created for them and
that public recognition would require her to alter them
to meet public expectations. Robert Spiller, in
finding that Dickinson "failed to publish" because
she would not accept compromise as a path to
recognition, makes much the same point as Sewall:

> The general reading public that asked for
> meter that is smooth, rhythm that is easy,
> and words that are limited to only one
> obvious meaning interested her not at all.
> She was willing to wait. (Spiller 127)

In this same regard, Johnson remarks that,
although Dickinson's early letters to Higginson do
indicate an interest in publication, she is also asking
for a special kind of advice. "At the time she wrote
Higginson," Johnson explains in his biography of the
poet, "she does not seem to be trying to avoid
publication as such; she is inquiring how one can
publish and at the same time preserve the integrity of
one's art" (11). This inquiry, Johnson continues, was
a real concern for Dickinson because prior to her

Support for thesis

Two sources
connected

Reader could be
confused because
Sewall's name
precedes quotation,
so Spiller's name is
added to the note

Mixture of
paraphrase and
quotation

8

writing to Higginson, two of her poems had been
published anonymously in the <u>Springfield Daily
Republican</u>, an influential newspaper of that time, and
both poems had been altered radically by editors to
suit their sense of regularity.

Modern critics and biographers are in almost
universal agreement that she was disappointed in
Higginson's response to her poetry. They also agree
that, as Ferlazzo puts it, the man ''lacked discernment
as to her purpose as an artist'' (139). Thomas Johnson,
in his appraisal of their correspondence, concludes
that Higginson, though somewhat impressed by the
wording and thoughts in Dickinson's poems, ''literally
did not understand what he was reading'' (<u>Biography</u>
111). By this, Johnson means that Higginson was
confronted with the work of an ''original genius'' and
was bewildered as to what to make of it. Throughout his
correspondence with her, Higginson was apparently
attempting to get her to write more traditional poetry,
or as Johnson observes: ''He was trying to measure a
cube by the rules of plane geometry'' (<u>Biography</u> 107).
There is no evidence, however, that she ever followed
any of Higginson's suggestions, despite the fact that
she maintained a friendly correspondence with him for
many years.

Here and below it would be difficult to work "biography" into the text smoothly

9

For Emily Dickinson, then, the idea of revising
her creations for the sake of achieving quick--and
probably fleeting--recognition was what was ''foreign''
to her, not recognition based on acceptance of her poems
as unique works of art. This conviction comes through
clearly in several of her poems; for example:

> Fame is the one that does not stay--
> Its occupant must die
> Or out of sight of estimate
> Ascend incessantly--
> Or be that most insolvent thing
> A Lightning in the Germ--
> Electrical the embryo
> But we demand the Flame.
> (Complete Poems 623-24)

In commenting on this poem, Inder Nath Kher says
that it does not mean that Dickinson is ''averse to
genuine fame.'' It means, he continues, ''that she does
not wish to be considered as writing simply for the sake
of some cheap glory'' (128). Reinforced by this poem--
assuming ''we'' in the last line refers to the poet--is
the conclusion that Dickinson would rather have had
''the Flame'' of her artistic integrity than the
''insolvent thing'' called popular recognition.

Along the same lines, given the deliberate
decision to forego publication rather than compromise
her art, the first lines of another poem become

Subtopic: evidence from poetry

Reference to primary source

Support for thesis

10

significantly clear: "Publication--is the Auction/Of
the Mind of Man" (Complete Poems 348-49). And there
can be no doubt that when she wrote the following
stanza, Emily Dickinson had accepted the fact that true
fame would not be hers in her lifetime.

> Some--Work for Immortality--
> The Chiefer part, for Time--
> He--Compensates--immediately
> The former--Checks--on Fame--
> (Complete Poems 193)

She chose to maintain her artistic integrity and await
that immortality.

The personality of Emily Dickinson will continue
to fascinate those who enjoy speculating about
brilliant artists whose lives were cloaked in privacy.
Since she said so little about herself outside of her
somewhat enigmatic poetry and her letters, the popular
image of a mystical, romantic Emily is likely to co-
exist for many years with scholarly appraisals of her
life and work. Her poetry, however, does more than
create an aura of mystery about its author; it reveals a
dedicated genius moved by deep, religious reverence for
her craft. Yet Emily Dickinson, gifted with the power
to create extraordinary works of art, also felt
compelled to preserve the uniqueness of her creations

11

by refusing to compromise in order to attain public
recognition. She was willing to trust that future
generations of readers would award her the fame her
work deserved.

12

Note

[1]For a discussion of the sources of the "Emily myth,"
see Ferlazzo 13-21.

13

Works Cited

Dickinson, Emily. The Complete Poems of Emily
    Dickinson. Ed. Thomas H. Johnson. Boston: Little,
    Brown, 1960.
---. The Letters of Emily Dickinson. Eds. Thomas H.
    Johnson and Theodora Ward. 3 vols. Cambridge,
    MA: Harvard Univ. Press, 1958.
---. The Poems of Emily Dickinson. Ed. Thomas H.
    Johnson. 3 vols. Cambridge, MA: The Belknap
    Press, Harvard Univ. Press, 1955.
Ferlazzo, Paul J. Emily Dickinson. Boston: Twayne,
    1976.
Griffith, Clark. The Long Shadow: Emily Dickinson's
    Tragic Poetry. Princeton: Princeton Univ. Press,
    1964.
Howard, William. "Emily Dickinson's Poetic
    Vocabulary." PMLA 72 (1957): 225-48.
Johnson, Thomas H. Emily Dickinson: An Interpretive
    Biography. Cambridge, MA: Harvard Univ. Press,
    1955.
---, ed. The Poems of Emily Dickinson. 3 vols.
    Cambridge, MA: The Belknap Press, Harvard Univ.
    Press, 1955.
Kher, Inder Nath. The Landscape of Absence: Emily
    Dickinson's Poetry. New Haven: Yale Univ. Press,
    1974.
Sewall, Richard B. The Life of Emily Dickinson. 2
    vols. New York: Farrar, Straus and Giroux, 1974.

14

Spiller, Robert E. The Cycle of American Literature: An
    Essay in Historical Criticism. 2nd ed. New York:
    Free Press, 1967.
Thomas, Owen. "Father and Daughter: Edward and Emily
    Dickinson." American Literature 40 (1960):
    510-23.
Winters, Yvor. "Emily Dickinson and the Limits of
    Judgment." In Emily Dickinson: A Collection of
    Critical Essays. Ed. Richard B. Sewall.
    Englewood Cliffs, NJ: Prentice-Hall, 1963.

Jefferson Davis as President: A Confederate Asset

Submitted by George C. Pitman, III
to Professor David Mason

History 121 United States History
Section 7C
November 10, 19--

OUTLINE

Jefferson Davis as President: A Confederate Asset

Introductory paragraph, including the thesis statement

I. Extreme views of Davis's leadership

   A. Negative (Pollard)

      1. Responsibility for loss of the war

         a. Squandering of South's resources

         b. An "imbecile and barren" administration

         c. Personal vanity

      2. Pollard's bias

         a. Personal dislike of Davis

         b. Need for a scapegoat (Patrick)

   B. Positive (Strode)

      1. Davis's strengths

         a. Unselfishness and integrity

         b. Minor nature of his flaws

         c. Refusal to play politics at expense of civil liberties

      2. Superiority to Lincoln in regard to civil liberties

         a. Implied comparison

         b. Direct comparison (Dodd)

3. Nobility of Davis in a doomed cause

II. Moderate views of Davis's leadership

  A. One view (Nevins)

    1. Davis's failings

      a. Obsession with details and military matters

      b. "Inability to labor amicably" with other leaders

    2. Davis's strengths

      a. "Vision" of South's potential greatness

      b. "Unshakable integrity"

      c. Experience in government

      d. Personal dignity

    3. Support for Nevins's view (Randall and Donald)

      a. Weaknesses in administrative and military areas

      b. Accomplishments in light of problems faced

  B. Another view (Catton)

    1. Odds against Davis and the South

      a. North's enormous advantages

      b. Dissension within the South (Dodd, too)

    2. A tragic view of Davis

III. Analysis of two major charges against Davis

   A. Reputed weakness as a military leader (Barney)

      1. The charge of "meddling"

         a. The tendency to make scapegoats of losing captains (Patrick)

         b. Comparison to Lincoln, another "meddler"

      2. Both sides' ignorance of modern warfare

         a. The nature of war at that time

         b. North's discovery of "war of attrition"

         c. Defense of Davis in this light

   B. Supposed weakness as political leader (Rabun)

      1. Refusal to surrender to special interests

      2. Bitter quarrel between Davis and Stephens

         a. Davis's loyalty to South as a whole

         b. Davis's concern for liberty

         Conclusion

Jefferson Davis as President: A Confederate Asset

For many years after Robert E. Lee surrendered at

Introductory paragraph

Appomattox, historians tended to lay much of the blame
for the South's crushing defeat upon the president of
the Confederacy, Jefferson Davis. One writer, however,
in comparing Davis to Lincoln, claims that Davis's
reputation would have been quite different if he had
been on the winning side. When a leader fails to
achieve victory, even if his cause is doomed from the
start, his "errors and defects and limitations of

character . . . stand out as do a few spots of ink on a

Ellipsis

white sheet of paper."[1] This does not mean that Davis
had no faults. Almost all historians agree that the man
suffered from character flaws. He spent far too much
time on administrative details; he often interfered in
purely military matters; and he allowed himself to be
drawn into bitter controversies with other political

leaders. The question all Civil War analysts must

Question behind this research

answer is this: To what extent did Davis's failings

contribute to the defeat of the Confederacy? A survey

Nature of sources

of modern studies of Davis and the Civil War reveals a
softening in the historical judgment of Davis as a

2

leader. Most historians today conclude that Jefferson
Davis, despite his personal shortcomings, was probably
the most capable president the South could have chosen.

Thesis statement

Indeed, given the enormous problems the Confederacy
faced, Davis was a definite asset in the struggle to
secede from the Union.

Subtopic: negative view of Davis

The most extreme negative criticism of Jefferson
Davis places the full weight of the Southern defeat on
his head. Edward A. Pollard, in 1869, took the view
that the South, for the greater part of the war, had the
necessary resources, morale, manpower, and military
talent to defeat the North. Thus, for Pollard, the
cause of the South's defeat "must come down by logical
reduction to one man--he the ruler who permitted these
advantages to be conquered through an imbecile and

Mixture of paraphrase and quotation

barren administration."[2] Pollard admitted that Davis
served the Southern cause with "distinguished
personal devotion," but he also claimed that Davis
destroyed this cause primarily through "his jealous
repulsion of advisers and assistants, and his descent
to rivalry in popularity with his subordinates and
lieutenants." In all, Pollard's picture of Davis is of
a man who combined strong devotion to a cause with
vanity and self-serving ambition: a man who displayed a

3

consistently "puerile eagerness to appropriate all the
honors of the Confederate cause and to wear them
conspicuously in the sight of the world."[3]

  One note covering several quotes

  Pollard was a Southerner, a contemporary of Davis,
and a persistent critic of Davis throughout the war.[4]
His rather harsh evaluation of Davis, written shortly
after the war, may therefore reflect not only his
longstanding dislike of Davis as a leader but also his
dejection over the South's defeat. The need to find
someone to blame for such a loss may have influenced
other writers to accept, at least in part, Pollard's
views. Rembert W. Patrick points out that the
Confederate defeat "dimmed Davis's reputation for
leadership." According to Patrick, the world often
"fails to appreciate the quality of leadership that
falls short of attaining the goal."[5]

  One note covering two quotes

  A relatively modern evaluation of Davis presents a
completely different view of the Confederate president
than that of Pollard. "After years of investigation,"
Hudson Strode states, "I have concluded that one of
Davis's most outstanding characteristics was his
unselfishness, and it supported his integrity."[6]
Strode prefers to attribute common human "flaws" to
Davis rather than any special weaknesses of character

  Subtopic: positive view of Davis

4

or ability. He admits that, on occasion, Davis's
"consciousness of intellectual superiority" made him
appear to be "imperious." Further, because of his
"genius" for getting to the heart of complex issues,
"it was sometimes hard for Davis to delegate
responsibility." In addition, Davis "was sensitive
and somewhat thin-skinned, and he often made the
mistake of answering his critics and wasting his

One note covering several quotes

time."[7]

Perhaps Strode's most significant point may be his
conclusion that Davis lacked the gift for playing
practical politics.

Extended quotation

> He was not always conciliatory, and he made
> enemies by letting his petitioners know his
> opinion or decision at once, not permitting
> them to go away still hoping and maneuvering.
> . . . Davis was not formed of elements that
> would make of him a revolutionary dictator.
> He could not be ruthless. . . . Therein, in
> the view of some critics, he failed. Others
> believe that he should have muzzled inimical
> newspapers and jailed the editors, because
> of the dissension and distrust they created
> in the camps and on the home front. But to
> Davis, the right of free speech was
> fundamental.[8]

Student's interpretation

Implied in this discussion of Davis's political
flaw is a comparison with Abraham Lincoln's evident

5

disregard for civil liberties. In the North, some
''inimical newspapers'' were ''muzzled'' and some
editors jailed in the name of eliminating unpatriotic
dissension. William E. Dodd, among others, makes this
comparison directly: ''Davis was not indifferent to the
personal liberty of his people nor forgetful of the
rights of individuals. . . . In this respect the   **Support**
contrast with President Lincoln is all in favor of the
Southern leader.''[9]

What emerges from Strode's discussion of Davis is
the picture of a noble leader who would not compromise
his integrity or treat civil liberties lightly under
the guise of emergency war powers. Strode clearly
favors a historical interpretation of Davis's
presidency that views him not as the architect of the
South's defeat, but as the devoted leader whose
''personal ability and determined exercise of will
. . . kept defeat off so long.''[10]

Several other modern writers take a less generous   **Subtopic: one**
view of Davis's failings, but they agree that he was an   **moderate view of**
Davis
excellent choice for the presidency and that the South
stood no chance of winning the war. Allan Nevins's
evaluation of Davis's presidency is less flattering
than Strode's. He faults Davis's performance as a

6

leader on several grounds. Davis, he argues,
"overburdened himself with details and overemphasized
his military responsibilities at the expense of his
civil functions." A still more damaging shortcoming
was Davis's "inability to labor amicably with other
men." His quarrels with some of his generals and
cabinet members could have been avoided, Nevins claims,
if the Confederate president had not possessed "a
natural disposition to quarrel" and had been, instead,
as "selfless, patient, and generous as Abraham
Lincoln."11

Nevins goes on to state, however, that in spite of
these shortcomings "Davis was unquestionably the best
man who could have been chosen to guide the
Confederacy." He bases this judgment upon Davis's
"vision," his "unshakable integrity," his "large
experience" in government, and his "dignity in
bearing and speech." These strong points
"constituted a greater body of assets than any rival
leader of the South could have offered."12

J. G. Randall and David Donald agree with Nevins
that Jefferson Davis spent too much of his time dealing
with trivial matters and with strictly military
affairs. These historians find that Davis took his

One note covering several quotes

Direct support of the thesis statement

One note covering several quotes

Support for first moderate view

7

constitutional duties as commander-in-chief too
seriously, causing him to become involved with tactical
considerations that were best left to the military
commanders in the field. Davis took the position that
"the President was entrusted with military leadership,
and he must exercise it."[13] In their overview of his
performance, however, Randall and Donald balance their
negative criticism of Davis with a number of positive
characteristics, similar to those ascribed to him by
Nevins. As a final evaluation, they conclude that it
was not any individual flaw or combination of flaws
that caused Davis's failure but rather the enormity of
the task he confronted. "Much of the criticism of the
Confederate President fails to take into account the
insuperable difficulties of his position and to realize
that no other Southern political leader even approached
Davis in stature."[14]

Another historian who has devoted many years and
many volumes to the Civil War, Bruce Catton, agrees that
Davis's problems as president were overwhelming. For
one thing, he was faced at the outset of his
administration with the job of preparing a new nation
for war against an enemy that possessed enormous
advantages "in respect to manpower, riches, and the

A secondary aspect
of thesis statement

Subtopic: another
moderate view

Support of thesis

8

commercial and industrial strength that supports
armies."[15] For another, Davis was opposed continually
by prominent Southerners who were unable to share his
vision of a united Confederacy. "The administration
had to have broad wartime powers, but when Davis tried
to get and use them he was bitterly criticized."[16] On
this last point, Catton would seem to be expressing
agreement with the view that Davis was a leader who, in
order to do what was best for the whole South, had to
fight with those Southerners who wanted only what they
thought was best for themselves or for their respective
states. The disastrous effects that this internal
dissension had on Davis's ability to lead are also
emphasized by Dodd. In writing of the objections to
Davis's policies voiced by men like Stephens and Joseph
E. Brown, the governor of Georgia during the war, Dodd
states that their opposition "must be pronounced as a
most important, if not the greatest, cause of the final
collapse of the Confederacy."[17]

His appreciation of the problems Davis had to
confront leads Catton to a final evaluation of Davis's
presidency that is close to that expressed by Randall
and Donald. Catton, however, also suggests that Davis's
attempt to lead his people to independence was somehow
doomed to failure from the start.

Two sources connected

9

> He had done the best he could do in an
> impossible job, and if it is easy to show
> where he made grievous mistakes, it is
> difficult to show that any other man, given
> the materials available, could have done
> much better. He had great courage,
> integrity, tenacity, devotion to his cause,
> and like Old Testament Sisera, the stars in
> their courses marched against him.[18]

Perhaps no defense of Jefferson Davis's

presidency can be concluded without some reference to

the most persistent criticism of his leadership. This

criticism, mentioned by Randall and Donald as well as

by Nevins, asserts that Davis was a "meddler" in

military affairs, a frustrated former field commander

whose interference in military tactics prevented the

South from winning those major battles that might have

discouraged the more powerful North from continuing the

war. This criticism, however, may support Rembert

Patrick's observation that history tends to underrate

the positive qualities of a leader who fails to achieve

a desired goal: the world also tends to exaggerate that

leader's weaknesses. Certainly, there is ample

evidence that Lincoln was just as much a meddler in

strictly military affairs and equally prone to making

errors in military judgment. William L. Barney, for

example, points out that Lincoln was constantly urging

his generals to attack, despite the fact that the Union

Subtopic: Davis's
involvement in
military affairs

Moderate view
reaffirmed

10

armies were often unprepared for bold advances and
therefore suffered heavy casualties and gained no
tactical advantages in doing so. "Slow to perceive the
military realities of the war, Lincoln often made
unreasonable demands."[19]

It is Barney's contention that neither Lincoln nor
Davis nor, for that matter, the leading generals on
either side, really understood the nature of a war that
was being fought with thousands of men in the field,
using weapons of an advanced technology. "In fact,
very few Civil War battles ever resulted in a decisive
victory for either side. . . . The cost of battle was
almost as high for the victor as for the defeated."[20]
What finally brought victory to the North were not
battlefield tactics. Victory came when the North used
its superior resources and manpower to wage against the
general population a war of attrition which ultimately
destroyed the structure of Southern society. "To win
its war of conquest, the Union turned to a theory of war
that made civilians as well as armies its target."[21]
In the light of Barney's analysis, therefore, it seems
unfair to accuse Davis alone of being seriously flawed

Student's judgment   as a military leader. Apparently, the inability to
direct armies to stunning battlefield victories was a

11

"flaw" shared by the leadership on both sides in the
Civil War.

 As for the frequently expressed opinion that Davis
had a "natural disposition to quarrel," there is
evidence that the Confederate president's reputation
for obstinacy was derived in large measure from his
refusal to surrender his presidential prerogatives to
men who believed states' rights and private interests
ranked higher than the overall Confederate cause. One
such man was the Confederacy's vice-president,
Alexander H. Stephens. After about a year of active
service to the Confederacy, Stephens withdrew to his
native Georgia where he advocated a strong states'
rights position and became an increasingly outspoken
critic of Davis's policies. In tracing Davis's
relationship with Stephens, James Z. Rabun leaves
little doubt that the president's actions were almost
always motivated by a genuine concern for the Southern
cause, while Stephens's actions were almost always
motivated by "self-righteousness" and narrow
political concerns. As president, Davis "had given
his loyalty to the South as a whole, and he was ready to
sacrifice the supposed interests of any part to the
attainment of the independence of the whole."[22] Rabun

Quotation
documented earlier

Further support for
moderate view of
Davis

Subtopic: Davis as
a political leader

Summary of a
source

Note referring to a
periodical article

12

makes clear that much of the virulent criticism of
Davis as a "dictator" and "tyrant" sprang from
privileged Southerners who, like Stephens, were blind
to the need to unite with Davis in the South's struggle
for independence. Thus, Rabun's analysis of the
quarrels between Stephens and Davis leads him to the
conclusion that, far from being a dictator, "Davis gave
ample evidence of loving liberty more dearly . . . than
Stephens did."[23]

Conclusion: summary of the paper and restatement of the thesis

The results of this research into Jefferson
Davis's presidency point strongly to the conclusion
that Davis's major "error" consisted of accepting the
leadership of a confederacy that was intent upon
fighting a war that it had very little chance of
winning. As a result, his name has become associated
with the South's defeat, and his shortcomings as a
leader have been emphasized in the light of that
defeat. Undoubtedly, Davis had his fair share of
weaknesses as a leader, but those weaknesses cannot
reasonably explain the Confederacy's failure to
achieve independence. Along with his weaknesses, Davis
had many strengths as a leader, and these strengths were
essential ingredients in the South's ability to hold
out for so long against an enemy so superior in manpower

13

and resources. The Confederacy's only president was,
on balance, a devoted and able leader who, faced with an
impossible task, failed to perform a miracle.

14

Notes

[1] Rembert W. Patrick, Jefferson Davis and His Cabinet (Baton Rouge: Louisiana State University Press, 1944), pp. 44-45.

[2] Edward A. Pollard, Life of Jefferson Davis, With a Secret History of the Southern Confederacy (1869; rpt. Freeport, NY: Books for Libraries Press, 1969), p. 167.

[3] Pollard, p. 102.

[4] For a brief summary of Pollard vs. Davis, see Charles P. Roland, The Confederacy (Chicago: University of Chicago Press, 1960), pp. 55-56.

[5] Patrick, p. 44

[6] Hudson Strode, Jefferson Davis: Tragic Hero (New York: Harcourt, Brace and World, 1964), p. xvi.

[7] Strode, p. xviii.

[8] Strode, pp. xviii-xix.

[9] William E. Dodd, Jefferson Davis (1907; rpt. New York: Russell and Russell, 1966), p. 291.

[10] Strode, pp. xvi-xvii.

[11] Allan Nevins, The Organized War 1863-1864, vol. III of The War for the Union (New York: Scribner's, 1971), p. 37.

[12] Nevins, p. 39.

[13] J. G. Randall and David Donald, The Divided Union (Boston: Little, Brown, 1961), p. 271.

[14] Randall and Donald, p. 273.

[15] Bruce Catton, The Civil War (New York: American Heritage Press, 1971), p. 28.

15

[16] Catton, p. 220.
[17] Dodd, p. 268.
[18] Catton, p. 279.
[19] William L. Barney, Flawed Victory: A New Perspective on the Civil War (New York: Praeger, 1975), p. 9.
[20] Barney, pp. 7-8.
[21] Barney, p. 41.
[22] James Z. Rabun, "Alexander H. Stephens and Jefferson Davis," American Historical Review, 58 (1953), 301.
[23] Rabun, p. 321.

228 PREPARING THE FINAL MANUSCRIPT

16

Bibliography

Barney, William L. Flawed Victory: A New Perspective on
    the Civil War. New York: Praeger, 1975.
Catton, Bruce. The Civil War. New York: American
    Heritage Press, 1971.
Dodd, William E. Jefferson Davis. 1907; rpt. New
    York: Russell and Russell, 1966.
Nevins, Allan. The Organized War 1863-64. Vol. III of
    The War for the Union. New York: Scribner's, 1971.
Patrick, Rembert W. Jefferson Davis and His Cabinet.
    Baton Rouge: Louisiana State University Press,
    1944.
Pollard, Edward A. Life of Jefferson Davis, With a
    Secret History of the Southern Confederacy,
    Gathered Behind the Scenes in Richmond. 1869;
    rpt. Freeport, NY: Books for Libraries Press,
    1969.
Rabun, James Z. "Alexander H. Stephens and Jefferson
    Davis." American Historical Review, 58 (1953),
    301-24.
Randall, J. G., and David Donald. The Divided Union.
    Boston: Little, Brown, 1961.

17

Roland, Charles P. *The Confederacy*. Chicago:
    University of Chicago Press, 1960.
Strode, Hudson. *Jefferson Davis: Tragic Hero*. New
    York: Harcourt, Brace and World, 1964.

Increasing Maximum Life Expectancy: Myth or Reality?

Submitted by Anita Barrone
to Professor Alvin Frascall

Contemporary Issues in Science
Section 1F
December 9, 19--

Note: See pp. 129–132 for Anita Barrone's outline.

Increasing Maximum Life Expectancy: Myth or Reality?

Every American schoolchild learns that Juan Ponce
de Leon discovered Florida in 1513 while searching for
the Fountain of Youth, whose water, he believed, would
restore him to youthful manhood. Unfortunately he
never found the Fountain. Instead he found death by an
Indian arrow. Today we smile at the naivete of Ponce de
Leon for believing in a fountain of youth provided by a
beneficent nature. But his dream of extending his life
span was one that many people have had throughout the
ages,[1] and it is a dream that is still very much with us
today.

By now we have pretty much given up hope of
discovering a fountain of youth or a marvelous herb that
can relieve us of the anxieties and debilities
associated with the process of aging. Instead our
hopes are in the hands of scientists. Gerontologists
(scientists who study aging processes) are attempting
to slow down--and perhaps even overcome--nature's
timetable for human aging. Although not all scientists
think that increasing the life span is possible in the
near future, many gerontologists and knowledgeable

(margin annotations)

Introductory
paragraph

Note refers to
source offering
information for
further research,
rather than merely
citing a source

Thesis statement

2

commentators are optimistic about our chances because
of the promising results researchers have obtained from
experiments with animals and cell cultures. These
experiments might well lead us to a "fountain" of
extended, healthy life, if not to eternal youth.

Before undertaking a brief survey of some of the
theories behind research into the causes of aging and
of some of the experiments that have inspired

**Indicates
organizational
approach of the
paper**

confidence in researchers, we should be clear about
just what gerontologists mean when they speak of
"increasing maximum life expectancy."

To begin with, the question might be asked:
"Aren't people already living longer than they did in
the past?" And the answer is yes and no. If by living
longer we mean that more people are achieving the
biblical three score years and ten, then the answer is
yes. If, on the other hand, by living longer we mean
that people are exceeding the maximum life span that
some human beings have always been able to achieve, then

**Date of Rosenfeld's
work, which can be
found in Works
Cited**

the answer is no. Rosenfeld (1976) explains this point
in reference to ancient Greece, where "the average
life expectancy was something like twenty-two years.
But individuals did live to ripe old ages in those days
too." True, Rosenfeld continues, not many people in

3

ancient Greece reached seventy, but those who did "had
just as many years to live . . . as does the seventy
year old of today . . ." (p. 9). Diseases, poor

**Page on which
quotation appears**

sanitation, deaths related to child birth, and the
generally low state of medical science all played their
part in holding down the average life expectancy of
ancient Greeks. Average life expectancy has improved
as we have become more knowledgeable about how to combat
diseases and as technology has provided better tools
for the medical and health sciences. Despite these
advantages, the utmost limit of life expectancy has
remained the same throughout the ages. More people are
living longer, but no one is living any longer today
than a few of us have lived in previous ages.

In addition, for gerontologists, extending human
life span must also mean extending the number of years
that human beings live useful, healthy, and productive
lives. Walford writes in <u>Maximum Life Span</u> (1983b) of a
future in which " 'functional' or 'physiologic' age
will no longer equal 'chronologic' age" (p. 188). If
gerontologists succeed, we will have to change the way
we think about getting old. The years we consider as
old age today will be more like middle age in the
future. As Walford explains: "With life span extended

4

to 130 years a person chronologically 75 years old will have the same vigor and appearance as a 50 year-old today'' (p. 189).

There is another line of questioning, based on a concept of the ''good life,'' that has gained a certain amount of popularity. But this popularity is based upon misinformation. The line of questioning goes as such: ''Aren't there places in the world, far from the tensions and pollutions of advanced societies, where many of the people live to ages of 100 or more? Don't these people prove that the secret of extended life consists of living the simple life, which includes hard work and a simple, healthy diet?''

Alexander Leaf, a professor of medicine, has investigated areas of the world where, presumably, more people than average were living lives of extraordinary longevity. Leaf (1982) examined records and people in a mountainous region of the Soviet Union known as the Caucasus. He also visited the mountains of West Pakistan and the village of Vilcabamba, located in the Andes Mountains of Ecuador. These investigations led Leaf to doubt strongly that people in these areas live any longer on average than people anywhere else in the

5

world. In Vilcabamba, for example, he found that birth
records were highly inaccurate. In one case Leaf
discovered that a woman reputed to be 106 years old had
been mistakenly assigned the birth certificate of
another woman with the same name who had died thirty or
forty years earlier. Further, Leaf discovered that the
elders of Vilcabamba were prone to exaggerate the ages
of their people and the life-enhancing environment of
their area in hopes of turning Vilcabamba into a
thriving resort area for tourists seeking a few weeks'
exposure to the conditions that might add years to
their lives. In West Pakistan and in the Soviet
Caucasus, Leaf found much the same kind of confusion in
regard to accurate birth records. Wars and political
upheavals have made the validation of reputed old ages
virtually impossible. And because old age is highly
respected in these areas, old people often exaggerate
the length of time they have been alive, especially
since their word is all the proof that exists as to when
they were born. In the end Leaf found no reason to
believe that these areas produced unusually high
percentages of people who lived extraordinarily long
lives. "There has been no extension of the limit of

6

the lifespan; only the proportion of the population reaching the apparent biologic limit of about 85+/− [plus or minus] 10 years is increasing" (pp. 486-487).

What we seem to be left with so far is the proposition that human beings are somehow fated by nature to live within certain time limits. Some people die at young ages; a very few reach 100 years or a bit more; but most of us, if present trends continue, will die between the ages of 75 and 95. From this "programmed" point of view there is little we can do to extend maximum life expectancy, unless scientists can somehow alter the processes that control aging.

We can gain some insight into serious scientific attempts to retard the aging process by referring to the work of Leonard Hayflick and Paul Moorhead, whose research brought to light a major obstacle to increased life expectancy. These two scientists carried out experiments that led them to conclude that there were built-in limits to the number of times normal human cells could divide and reproduce themselves, even under ideal laboratory conditions. According to Hayflick (1977), normal cells "undergo approximately 50 population doublings . . . before losing proliferative powers . . ." (p. 161). This finding has come to be

Brackets indicate student's explanation of symbols used in source, not part of actual quotation

known (in the literature of gerontology) as the
"Hayflick limit," and overcoming this limit is the
task that many scientists have taken on. But before
gerontologists can overcome the Hayflick limit, they
must first come to grips with another observation by
Hayflick, that "the maximum proliferative capacity
. . . is rarely, if ever, reached by cells in vivo
. . ." (p. 168). In other words, human cells undergo
more divisions when they are isolated from the body and
kept alive in chemical solutions under ideal laboratory
conditions (in vitro) than they do when part of a living
human body (in vivo). What this adds up to is the
strong possibility that--even as things now stand--
human beings may be dying prematurely as a result of
cellular malfunctioning or genetic programming that
inhibits our cells from achieving their full
reproductive capacity. Why this should be so, and what
to do about it, are questions that researchers are
attempting to answer.

Scientists have developed a number of theories and
have undertaken many experiments to discover the
cause(s) of biological disintegration. It is not
necessary to discuss all of these theories to
demonstrate the seriousness of gerontological

8

research, and, besides, such a survey would be
impossible within the scope of this paper. But a
sampling of some of the current theories should serve
to indicate the general direction researchers are
taking in the battle against aging.

In an interview in U.S. News and World Report, July

Only first word of source title capitalized when using APA documentation guide, except when proper name is part of the title

1983, entitled "How people will live to be 100 or
more," Roy Walford mentions a number of theories that
scientists are currently following for exploration and
experimentation purposes. Those theories are

No need for a note—all bibliographic information provided in the text

1. the immunologic theory;

2. the DNA repair theory;

3. the free radical theory;

4. the thymus hormone theory;

5. the brain programming theory.

The Immunologic Theory

The immunologic theory is based upon the concept
that as a person grows older his immune system does not
function as efficiently to protect his body against

9

diseases as it did when he was younger. In fact one sign
of aging is the decreasing ability of the body to
protect itself against such dangers as infections and
cancers. Even worse, there are strong indications that
in its later stages of dysfunction the immune system
operates more and more out of control so that, as Cromie
(1981) explains, the body's defense system
malfunctions and attacks healthy tissue. Obviously,
then, an immune system that destroys beneficial
elements in the body is a system that is working against
extended longevity.

Much research based upon the immunologic theory
is aimed at finding ways to maintain the efficiency of
the immune system so that it does not degenerate into
"autoimmunity"--the condition in which the immune
system goes out of control and attacks beneficial
elements in the body. The problem, Rosenfeld (1976)
tells us, is to decrease autoimmunity without reducing
the aging body's ability to fight against disease.
Scientists working on this problem have had some
success in building up the immune systems of laboratory
animals with the use of various drugs. One method, for
example, consists of injecting mice with thymosin--a
hormone extract from the human thymus gland, but also

10

obtainable from cows. In summarizing research on thymosin, a science writer and life-extension consultant, Kent (1980), sees a good possibility that thymosin may prove useful in combating diseases associated with the weakening of the immune system.

In addition to manipulating the immune system with the use of drugs, some researchers are studying the relationship between diet and longevity. Success in extending the life spans of laboratory animals by maintaining them on low calorie but adequately nourishing diets has been the catalyst for much of this research.[2] Just why stringent, low-calorie diets seem to have a positive effect on longevity has not been determined by researchers. Walford (1983) offers the proposition that "dietary restriction" helps the immune system to ward off autoimmunity by slowing "the age-related decline in response to foreign materials" (p. 106). In this sense, the immune system stays healthier simply because it is called on less often to combat the undesirable by-products that enter our bodies as a result of the food we eat. But whatever the relationship between diet and aging, one leading nutrition expert (Watkin, 1983) sees progress in the fact that evidence is growing to strengthen the link

Author's name appears in note— name not mentioned in text

11

between "appropriate nutrition" and extended
longevity, and he points to studies on laboratory
animals as sustaining "the hope that nutritional
manipulations decelerate the rate of aging by some
mechanism as yet unknown" (p. 19).

The DNA Repair Theory

Because DNA[3] contains the genetic information our
cells need to repair and replicate themselves,
researchers are studying the relationship between DNA
damage and aging. "DNA damage can result in altered
cell growth, division and transcription, and also in
cell death, mutation, and malignant transformation.
All of these phenomena are characteristic of the aging
process" (Schimke and Agniel, 1983, p. 42). Actually,
DNA is always undergoing damage and is always in the
process of repairing itself. Kent (1980) explains that
research shows "an increase in the rate of DNA repair
of about tenfold from the shortest-lived animal to the
longest-lived animal, which indicates that the
increased capacity to repair DNA may be necessary to

12

achieve a longer life span" (p. 19). Human beings live
longer than most animals because our DNA repair rate is
better than that of most animals. The problem, however,
is that DNA damage takes place at a greater rate than
DNA repair (Walford, 1983). Thus, unless ways can be
found to increase the ability of DNA to repair itself,
the damage rate will continue to outstrip the repair
rate and contribute to the aging process.

Seeking knowledge about DNA repair capabilities,
Sonneborn (1979) discovered how to boost the repair
rate of the one-celled organisms, Paramecia. She
exposed Paramecia to ultraviolet light, a procedure
that brought on "ultraviolet-induced DNA damage," in
order to study the repair capacity of DNA when the
damaged Paramecia were exposed to "photoreactive"
light. Sonneborn found that "ultraviolet plus PR
[photoreactive] favored a repair process beneficial to
survival" (pp. 1116-1117). It is, of course, a long
way from manipulating the DNA repair system of a
Paramecium to manipulating the same system in a human
being. But optimists like to think that what can be
accomplished with one-cell organisms might one day be
accomplished with human beings. "If," as Sonneborn
puts it, "higher organisms have maintained a DNA

13

reserve repair capacity, activation should lead to
reduction in mutagenesis and degenerative diseases in
higher organisms'' (p. 1117).

Another example of experimentation motivated by
the DNA repair theory can be seen in Omnimax, a
scientific research company in Philadelphia. There,
researchers have discovered that the ''packaging'' of
DNA in extremely tight ''supercoils'' in our system
''induces stress in the DNA double helix, which the
helix can relieve by becoming undone, or opening up at
certain spots'' (DNA coils, 1983, p. 85). Omnimax
researchers are working at finding ways to counteract
this stress-induced damage. According to Phil Lepitz,
the president of Omnimax and a biophysicist, ''Using
supercoiling as a marker for physiological age, we may
have a way to identify potential antiaging drugs in a
relatively short time'' (cited in DNA coils, p. 85).

Title, in shortened
form, in the note
because source did
not provide author's
name

                    The Free Radical Theory

    We know that food exposed to the atmosphere for too
long becomes spoiled, primarily because of oxidation,

14

the same chemical reaction that causes metal to rust.
In oxidation, certain molecules come into being that
attack other molecules, causing cellular damage.
These molecules that inflict damage on other molecules
are known in gerontology as free radicals. Rosenfeld
(1976) tells us that free radicals can do considerable
damage to molecules, accelerate the production of
lipofuscin, and interfere with cellular information.

Denham Harman, a professor of medicine and
biochemistry, theorized as early as 1956 on the
possibility that free radicals were detrimentally
involved in the aging process. Given the fact that free
radicals can also be produced in our bodies through the
effects of "environmental pollutants such as lead"
(Kurzman and Gordon, 1977, pp. 168-169), we can
understand that our bodies are continually producing
free radicals that bring on and sustain aging
processes.

To counter free radicals, researchers are
following Harman's opinion that the free radical theory
suggests chemical procedures for extending healthy
life (1956). In other words, if free radicals are at
least partly responsible for our inability to increase
maximum life span, then scientists may be able to

Student chose to
put all information
in a note rather than
in text

15

discover chemicals that we can take to combat free
radical damage. For example, Harman, following his own
hunch, was able to show that certain chemicals,
including BHT--commonly used as a food preservative--
"had a beneficial effect on the mortality rate of male
LAF_1 mice when added to the daily diet" (1968, p. 481).
In addition, scientists are following up experiments
which indicate that vitamin E and vitamin C, singularly
and in combination, may prove to be effective anti-free
radical agents.[4] And recently, as reported in <u>Science</u>
<u>Digest</u> (1982), researchers have discovered a "gene
cluster" that produces an enzyme known as "superoxide
dismutase," shortened to "SOD," which combats free
radicals. Knowing this, scientists are seeking ways to
stimulate SOD artificially so as to add to the body's
protective mechanism against free radicals.

The Thymus Hormone Theory

The thymus hormone theory is related to the
immunologic theory because both theories follow the
premise that aging can be retarded by manipulating the

immune system. Thymus hormone theorists, however, are
primarily interested in trying to zero in on a major
cause of immune system deterioration. By doing so,
they hope to simplify the measures that have to be taken
to keep the immune system working efficiently. Thus,
rather than work to boost immunology with a number of
individual booster strategies, the thymus hormone
theory promotes the idea that we may be able to keep the
immune system working to our benefit by finding and
then learning to control the mechanism that may be the
prime regulator of the system. As its name points out,
promoters of the thymus hormone theory think that the
"thymus gland, once thought to be as useful as the
human appendix, may well be the master gland of the
immune system" (Marx, 1975, p. 1217).

   The thymus gland, which Rosenfeld describes as
"the pinkish-gray mass located just behind the
breastbone and just below the neck" (1976, p. 82), has
become a focus of gerontological research because of
the increasing knowledge accumulating over the years
about how certain cells function to aid--and also
damage--human immunological processes. As Marx (1975)
explains, "The thymus is necessary for the normal
differentiation and maturation of T (for thymus-

17

derived) cells'' (p. 1183). If we understand that T
cells, like other white blood cells, protect us against
infections, then we see why a gland that programs such
cells and helps them to mature might well be the center
of investigation by gerontologists.

In general, research into the thymus gland has
focused on trying to discover the hormone(s) that this
gland produces because, as Marx (1975) tells us,
research has shown that T cell growth depends a great
deal upon the secretion of one or more hormones by the
thymus gland. If the thymus secreted its beneficial
hormones at the same rate as we get older as it does
when we are very young, then, the theory implies, we
would probably live longer. But Walford (1983) informs
us that this gland shrinks early in life and becomes
markedly smaller by the time a person reaches puberty.
Hormone secretion becomes less as the thymus shrinks,
and this decline in hormone output continues with age
until its influence probably becomes negligible (Adler,
1975). The attempt to isolate and to study the thymus
hormones, therefore, is being carried on with the hopes
of someday producing a drug or combination of drugs
that we can take to compensate for the decreasing
activity of our shrinking thymus glands.

18

Thymosin, discussed under the "Immunologic Theory" section of this paper, is one of the first thymus hormones to be identified and extracted. Since then, according to Kent (1980), researchers have reported on "more than two dozen . . . thymus extracts that influence the immune system" (p. 202). These reports would seem to indicate that attempts to manipulate the immune system through externally produced and administered thymus hormones may be extremely complicated, especially if researchers continue to find increasing numbers of hormone possibilities. However, Kent also points out that these thymus hormones may, with further research, turn out to be just a few basic types with a number of variations.

The Brain Programming Theory

As the title of this section indicates, there are scientists who are investigating the possibility that aging may be the result of a programmed mechanism in the brain that dictates just when degenerative aging will begin in a human being. Or, as Moment (1975) stated:

19

"For those favoring a more specific program for aging,
the brain has become the favorite site for a death
clock" (p. 626). As with the thymus hormone theory,
interest in the "death clock," or brain programming
theory, stems from the attempt to locate the activator,
or timing element, of the aging process and to turn it
off or divert its effects before widespread
disintegration of the immune system takes place.

Specific research into the brain programming
concept of aging grew, in part, out of the work of W. D.
Denckla, who was one of the first scientists to
"suggest that the lifespan of mammals is regulated by a
biological clock which, in turn, acts on the endocrines
to produce failure of the . . . immune and circulatory
systems" (1975, p. 31). Denckla derived this theory
from research on dead mammals which indicated that they
had all died as a result of diseases related to immune
and circulatory failure. This similarity of mammalian
death led Denckla and others to speculate on the
possibility that there exists a similar process of
aging for all mammals and, by extension, a common
programmed element for activating this process,
located somewhere within mammals. Subsequent
research, Walford (1983) informs us, has led some

20

scientists to conclude ''that the 'clock' of aging
lurks in the hypothalamus, a pea-sized area of brain a
bit posterior to a spot midway between your ears''
(1983, p. 89).

What has come about as a result of research into
the brain programming theory is an area of
gerontological concern called ''neuroendocrinology.''
This term refers to the relationship between ''the
hypothalamus in the brain and the various endocrine
glands, particularly the pituitary, adrenal, thymus,
and thyroid glands'' (Walford, 1983, p. 170). In
general, neuroendocrinology holds that some change
occurs in the brain, and this change signals the onset
of dysfunction in one or more endocrine glands. As
Finch (1975) explains: ''Changes in a limited, critical
population of cells in the brain (e.g. the
hypothalamus) could have many consequences throughout
the body.'' And because the endocrines are known as
producers of hormones, Finch sees a possible link
between brain cell change and ''multifaceted changes in
aging throughout the body.'' In short, ''in some
neuroendocrine controls, a change of only one hormone
could generate a cascade of events'' (pp. 647-648).

In line with neuroendocrine concepts, Denckla
(1975) suspects that the hormone that starts the

21

degenerative aging process at the command of the
biological clock is produced by the pituitary, a gland
that rests very close to the brain. He reports "a
considerable restoration of immune competence in older
rats" after their pituitaries have been removed
surgically (p. 41). This scientist, however, is also
apparently trying to outwit the death clock through
another approach. Walford informs us that Denckla "is
presently trying to isolate his theoretical 'death
hormone' and, if successful, to make an antidote or
antiserum to it, thereby avoiding complications
arising from removing the pituitary gland itself"
(1983, p. 179).

Other scientists are experimenting with brain
stimulators, working on the concept that certain brain
cells run down with aging, thereby reducing the
competency of the brain to process the information it
needs to control efficiently the functioning of the
body's control systems. Marshall and Berrios (1979),
for example, were able to improve dramatically the
swimming ability and endurance of aged rats by
stimulating their brains with "apomorphine or L-
dopa"--drugs that revived brain neurons and, thus, the
"neurotransmission" ability of the brain. If brain
stimulators can be developed that will help to revive

22

human brain cells safely and effectively, then we may be able to "rewind" the death clock that forms the basis for the brain programming theory.

Whether or not the theories briefly touched upon in this paper motivate research that will result in substantial life extension remains to be seen. Perhaps other theories now being tested, or a theory not yet formulated will provide the breakthrough sought by gerontologists in the war against aging. And we must also consider the possibility that life-extension believers are involved in a war they may never win. Some scientists take this point of view. Fries and Crapo (1981), for example, are not particularly optimistic about the chances of increasing life span any time in the near future because they think that science is still far from having the necessary knowledge to do so. These doctors see little chance that the maximum life span will be any longer in the near future than it has been in the past. Leaf (1982) is equally unimpressed by the experimental results of life-extension researchers, seeing in their work no significant proof that gerontologists will be able to "stop or retard" the aging process. He concedes, however, that from time to time, scientists will make discoveries that will "fire the imagination" of those

Student introduces opposing views to ensure objectivity

23

who strive to change the length of our life span. In like manner, Sir Peter Medawar (1984), while acknowledging the potential of scientific attempts to extend human life, especially in regard to the free radical theory, is not confident that such attempts will succeed. He doubts that the side effects of aging, such as infections and cancers, can be controlled, even if life is extended with the use of drugs to counteract the damage inflicted by free radicals. But this Nobel scientist also strongly believes that gerontologists should continue their attempts to conquer aging, despite the objections of those who see life-extension research as some kind of "crime against nature." He states that his "personal sympathies are with the daredevils who want to try out these new procedures" (pp. 19-20).

The scientific world, then, is far from united in the belief that human life span can be significantly extended in the near future through research into the causes of aging. But those who share the age-old dream of all the Ponce de Leons who have ever lived should keep their eyes on the gerontological research laboratories of the world. For it will be through the efforts of dedicated and daring scientists that the "secret" of extended life will be discovered--if it is to be discovered at all.

Conclusion: recalls introduction and restates thesis

24

Notes

[1] For a broad historical view of the struggle between those who have championed the cause of life-extension throughout the ages versus those who have accepted the inevitability of aging and death, see Walford, 1983, chap. 2.

[2] See, for example: McCay, C. M., et al. (1939). Retarded growth, life span, ultimate body size and age changes in the albino rat after feeding diets restricted in calories. Journal of Nutrition, 18, 1-13. This is considered a "classic study" in the literature of gerontology.

[3] DNA, short for: deoxyribonucleic acid. Described as "a long, twisted double chain of atoms found in the nucleus of each cell. It controls all the characteristics of living things, including metabolism in cells and body structure" (Kurtzman & Gordon, 1977, p. 241).

[4] See, for example, Walford's discussion of the possible relationship of Vitamins C and E in retarding the aging process (1983, pp. 145-147).

25

References

Adler, W. H. (1975). Aging and immunal function.
    BioScience, 25, 652-656.
Cromie, W. J. (1981, January). Genetic trade-offs:
    the hidden cost of survival. SciQuest, pp. 10-14.
Denckla, W. D. (1975, August). A time to die. Life
    Sciences, pp. 31-44.
DNA coils: link to aging. (1983, April). Science
    Digest, p. 85.
Finch, C. E. (1975). Neuroendocrinology of aging: a
    view of an emerging area. BioScience,
    25, 645-649.
Fries, J. F., & Crapo, L. M. (1981). Vitality and
    aging. San Francisco: W. H. Freeman.
Harman, D. (1956). Aging: a theory based on free
    radical and radiation chemistry. Journal of
    Gerontology, 11, 298-300.
Harman, D. (1968). Free radical theory of aging:
    effect of free radical reaction inhibitors on the
    mortality rate of male LAF_1 mice. Journal of
    Gerontology, 23, 476-481.
Hayflick, L. (1977). The cellular basis for
    biological aging. In Handbook of the biology of
    aging (Eds. Finch, C. E., & Hayflick, L.). New
    York: Van Nostrand Reinhold, pp. 159-181.
Kent, S. (1980). The life extension revolution. New
    York: William Morrow.
Kurtzman, J., & Gordon, P. (1977). No more dying. New
    York: Laurel-Dell.

26

Leaf, A. (1982). Long-lived populations: extreme old age. Journal of American Geriatrics Society, 30, 485-487.

Marshall, J. F., & Berrios, N. (1979). Movement disorders of aged rats: reversal by dopamine receptor stimulation. Science, 206, 477-479.

Marx, J. L. (1975). Thymic hormones: inducers of T cell maturation. Science, 188, 1183-1217.

Medawar, P. (1984, March). When we are old. Atlantic Monthly, pp. 16-21.

Moment, G. B. (1975). The Ponce de Leon trail today. BioScience, 25, 623-627.

Rosenfeld, A. (1976). Prolongevity. New York: Knopf.

Schimke, R. T., & Agniel, M. (1983). Biologic mechanisms in aging: summary of conference proceedings. Journal of American Geriatrics Society, 31, 40-44.

Sonneborn, J. (1979). DNA repair and longevity assurance in Paramecium tetraurelia. Science, 203, 1115-1117.

Supergene cluster fights aging. (1982, August). Science Digest, p. 91.

Walford, R. L. (1983, July). How people will live to be 100 or more. U.S. News and World Report, pp. 73-74.

Walford, R. L. (1983). Maximum life span. New York: Norton.

Watkin, D. M. (1983). Handbook of nutrition health, and aging. Park Ridge, IL: Noyes.

Index